A Confused and Confusing Affair

Other books written or edited by Mark K. Christ:

Rugged and Sublime:
The Civil War in Arkansas (1994)

"Getting Used to Being Shot At":
The Spence Family Civil War Letters (2002)

"All Cut to Pieces and Gone to Hell":
The Civil War, Race Relations, and the Battle of Poison Spring (2003)

"The Earth Reeled and Trees Trembled":
Civil War Arkansas 1863–1864 (2007)

"Ready, Booted, and Spurred":
Arkansas in the U.S.–Mexican War (2009)

The Die Is Cast:
Arkansas Goes to War, 1861 (2010)

Civil War Arkansas, 1863:
The Battle for a State (2010)

"This Day We Marched Again":
A Union Soldier's Account of War
in Arkansas and the Trans-Mississippi (2014)

I Do Wish This Cruel War Was Over:
First-Person Accounts of Civil War Arkansas
from the Arkansas Historical Quarterly (2014)

Competing Memories:
The Legacy of Arkansas's Civil War (2016)

A Confused and Confusing Affair

Arkansas and Reconstruction

Edited by
Mark K. Christ

BUTLER CENTER BOOKS
LITTLE ROCK, ARKANSAS

Contributors:

Kenneth C. Barnes

Jay Barth

Thomas A. DeBlack

Rodney Harris

Carl H. Moneyhon

Blake Wintory

BUTLER CENTER BOOKS

The Butler Center for Arkansas Studies
Central Arkansas Library System
100 Rock Street
Little Rock, Arkansas 72201
www.butlercenter.org

April 2018

ISBN 978-1-945624-15-5 paperback
ISBN 978-1-945624-16-2 hardcover

Manager: Rod Lorenzen
Book and cover design: H. K. Stewart
Copyeditor: Ali Welky

This book was published in part with the generous assistance of the Old State House Museum, a museum of the Department of Arkansas Heritage

Cataloging-in-Publication data

Names: Christ, Mark K., editor.
Title: A confused and confusing affair : Arkansas and Reconstruction / edited by Mark K. Christ ; contributors: Kenneth C. Barnes, Jay Barth, Thomas A. DeBlack, Rodney Harris, Carl H. Moneyhon, Blake Wintory.
Description: Little Rock, Arkansas : Butler Center Books, a division of the Butler Center for Arkansas Studies at the Central Arkansas Library System, 2018. | Includes bibliographical references and index.
Identifiers: LCCN 2018006325| ISBN 9781945624155 (pbk. : alk. paper) | ISBN 9781945624162 (hardcover : alk. paper)
Subjects: LCSH: Reconstruction (U.S. history, 1865-1877)--Arkansas. | Arkansas--History--1865-
Classification: LCC F411 .C75 2018 | DDC 976.7/05--dc23 LC record available at https://lccn.loc.gov/2018006325

Butler Center Books, the publishing division of the Butler Center for Arkansas Studies, was made possible by the generosity of Dora Johnson Ragsdale and John G. Ragsdale Jr.

Table of Contents

Contributors....7

Introduction and Acknowledgements....11

Chapter 1: The Complex Character of Post–Civil War Reconstruction, 1863–1877....15
By Carl H. Moneyhon

Chapter 2: An (Un)Exceptional Moment: The Politics of Reconstruction-Era Arkansas....63
By Jay Barth

Chapter 3: African American Legislators in the Arkansas General Assembly, 1868–1893: Another Look....87
By Blake Wintory

Chapter 4: Brindletails, Minstrels, Hercules, and Lady Baxter: The Brooks-Baxter War and the End of Reconstruction in Arkansas....147
By Thomas A. DeBlack

Chapter 5: "It Ain't Over Till It's Over": Political Violence in Reconstruction Arkansas, 1865–1892 171
By Kenneth C. Barnes

Chapter 6: Redeeming Arkansas: The Constitution of 1874 and Post-War Politics 207
By Rodney Harris

Notes 239

For Further Reading 267

Index 273

Contributors

Kenneth C. Barnes received his bachelor's degree from the University of Central Arkansas (UCA) and then studied for a master's degree in European history at the University of East Anglia (England) and a PhD in history at Duke University. He taught at Concordia University–Chicago and the University of Southern Mississippi before returning to UCA as a faculty member in 1992. He teaches German history and the intellectual, cultural, and religious history of modern Europe, and he has published a book and several articles on German religious history. Since returning to Arkansas, he has produced scholarship on Arkansas and Southern history including *Who Killed John Clayton?: Political Violence and the Emergence of the New South* (Duke University Press, 1998); *Journey of Hope: The Back-to-Africa Movement in Arkansas* (University of North Carolina Press, 2004), and *Anti-Catholicism in Arkansas: How Politicians, Religious Leaders, the Press, and the Klan Imagined an Enemy* (University of Arkansas Press, 2016).

Jay Barth is the M.E. and Ima Graves Peace professor, director of the Odyssey Program, and director of civic engagement projects at Hendrix College, where has served on the faculty since 1994. He co-authored the second edition of *Arkansas Politics and Government: Do the People Rule?*, was named Arkansas Professor of the Year by the Carnegie Foundation for the Advancement of Teaching, and received the Steiger Congressional Fellowship from the American Political Science Association. He previously served on the staff of U.S. Senator Paul Wellstone, D-Minn. Barth is chair of the Arkansas State Board of Education and has served as chair of the board of directors of the National Association of State Boards of Education. A native of Saline County, Barth earned a bachelor's degree from Hendrix and master's and doctorate degrees from the University of North Carolina at Chapel Hill.

Mark K. Christ (editor) is community outreach director for the Arkansas Historic Preservation Program. A 1982 graduate of the University of Arkansas at Little Rock, he received his master's degree in 2000 from the University of Oklahoma. The Arkansas Historical Association presented him with a Lifetime Achievement Award in 2015, and the Civil War Trust awarded him the 2013 State Preservation Leadership Award. He is president of the board of trustees of the Arkansas Historical Association, is a member of the Arkansas World War I Centennial Commemoration Committee, and previously served on the Arkansas Civil War Sesquicentennial Commission and as chairman of the board of directors of the Arkansas Humanities Council. He has written and edited several books and articles on Arkansas history, particularly on the Civil War in the state.

Thomas A. DeBlack is a professor of history at Arkansas Tech University in Russellville. He holds a BA from Southern

Methodist University in Dallas, Texas (1973), an MSE from Ouachita Baptist University (1979), and a PhD from the University of Arkansas (1995). DeBlack taught in the public schools in Arkansas for twelve years. He is a past president of the Arkansas Historical Association and the Arkansas Association of College History Teachers, and he serves on the board of the Arkansas Humanities Council. He is co-author of *Arkansas: A Narrative History* (University of Arkansas Press, 2002; 2nd edition, 2013) and author of *With Fire and Sword: Arkansas 1861–1874* (University of Arkansas Press, 2003). In 2003, *Arkansas: A Narrative History* was named the winner of the Arkansas Library Association's Arkansiana Prize, and *With Fire and Sword* was named the first winner of the Butler-Remmel Arkansas History Literary Prize.

Rodney Harris is an assistant professor of history at Williams Baptist College in Walnut Ridge. He holds a BA in political science from Arkansas State University and earned an MA in history at the University of Central Arkansas. He received his PhD from the University of Arkansas in Fayetteville in 2017; his dissertation was titled "Arkansas's Divided Democracy: The Making of the Constitution of 1874." He previously spent ten years as a real estate broker, ran for Arkansas state representative in 2004, and was named one of the 25 Outstanding Young Executives in Northeast Arkansas.

Carl H. Moneyhon is a professor in the History Department at the University of Arkansas at Little Rock and a specialist in the history of the American South, the Civil War, and Reconstruction. He holds BA and MA degrees from the University of Texas at Austin and a PhD from the University of Chicago. He is faculty liaison with the University History Institute, an organization that develops closer ties between the department and the community, and he serves on the editorial boards of the *Arkansas Historical Quarterly* and the *Encyclopedia of Arkansas History & Culture*. He has won the UA Little Rock Faculty Excellence Award for Research and the UA Little Rock Faculty Excellence Award for Teaching. Among his works on Arkansas are *The Impact of the Civil War and Reconstruction in Arkansas: Persistence in the Midst of Ruin* (1994), *Arkansas and the New South* (1997), and *Portraits of Conflict: A Photographic History of the Civil War in Arkansas* (1987). He has also authored numerous articles and book chapters on the Civil War in Arkansas.

Blake Wintory, a native of Fort Smith, received his PhD from the University of Arkansas in 2005. Since August 2008, he has been the on-site director at the 1859 Lakeport Plantation, an Arkansas State University Heritage Site near Lake Village. He is on the boards of Preserve Arkansas and the Friends of the Arkansas History Commission. He is the author of *Chicot County* (2015) in the Images of America series published by Arcadia. Wintory edits the newsletter for the Arkansas Historical Association and has published articles on Arkansas history in the *Arkansas Historical Quarterly*, the *Arkansas Review*, the *Encyclopedia of Arkansas History & Culture*, and the *African American National Biography*. Previously he was director of research and interpretation at the Mosaic Templars Cultural Center, a museum of the Department of Arkansas Heritage. Wintory is currently researching different topics on the history of Lakeport and the surrounding region.

Introduction and Acknowledgements

Reconstruction has been called one of the most tumultuous and controversial periods of Arkansas's history, an era in which African Americans sought to secure the benefits of their hard-won freedom, the former leaders of the state pursued restoration of their pre-war economic and political status, and the U.S. Army and the Freedmen's Bureau sought to maintain a balance between the two. By the time Reconstruction ended in 1874, Arkansas had been wracked by brutal political violence, black legislators had had their first opportunities for service, and the Republican Party was sundered amid the tragi-comedy of the Brooks-Baxter War, setting the stage for the rise of the Democratic "Redeemers."

While tens of thousands of books have been written about the American Civil War, the tense period that followed has received relatively little attention. The Old State House Museum in Little Rock brought a distinguished group of experts together in 2017 to discuss Reconstruction and its effects on Arkansas in a day-long seminar. Speakers discussed the greater issue of Reconstruction across the South, the political situation in

Arkansas during the period, the activities of African American legislators in the state, political and military violence during Reconstruction, the long-lasting effects of the 1874 state constitution, and the bizarre affair in which two governors fought over control of the State Capitol.

In the essays collected here, Carl H. Moneyhon provides an overview of Reconstruction in the United States, Jay Barth explores post–Civil War politics, Blake Wintory enumerates and discusses the African Americans who served in the Arkansas General Assembly, Kenneth C. Barnes gives insights into the political violence that convulsed the state, Thomas A. DeBlack unravels the Brooks-Baxter War, and Rodney Harris visits the 1874 Constitution and its effects on Arkansas's future. The essays brought together in this volume offer valuable insights into Reconstruction in Arkansas and show how its effects still resonate today.

Many people have assisted in the development of this publication. In addition to the talents of our scholarly speakers and authors—Carl Moneyhon, Jay Barth, Ken Barnes, Blake Wintory, Tom DeBlack, and Rodney Harris—the members of the staff of the Old State House Museum were the gracious hosts of our Reconstruction seminar, with special thanks to Georganne Sisco, Daniel Cockrell, and Leah Lambert. Bill Gatewood, Gail Stephens, and JoEllen Maack of the museum were also instrumental in the preparation of this publication. Carolyn Newbern helped in ways big and small, and David Newbern shared some interesting artifacts from his family papers. Many thanks are due to Julienne Crawford and Bridget Wood of the Arkansas State Archives, Brian Robertson of the Butler Center for Arkansas Studies, David Trulock and Ernestine Wallace of Pine Bluff, David Ware of the Arkansas Secretary of State's Office, Shannon Marie Lausch and Jared Craig of the UA Little Rock

Center for Arkansas History and Culture, Sarah Wells of the Department of Arkansas Heritage, and William Darrow, a descendant of the martyred James Hinds. The preternatural patience of Butler Center Books publisher Rod Lorenzen is greatly appreciated, as are the consummate editing skills of Ali Welky and design skills of H. K. Stewart. Others helped in other ways, and I apologize for any omissions.

I, along with all the contributors, hope you enjoy this collection, and we trust it will guide readers into further exploration of this "confused and confusing" period of Arkansas history.

— Mark K. Christ
2018

Chapter 1: The Complex Character of Post–Civil War Reconstruction, 1863–1877

By Carl H. Moneyhon

The Reconstruction era is the term applied to the fourteen-year period when the United States government attempted to restore the former Confederate states to the Union. In those states, former slaves struggled to assert their freedom, tried to integrate themselves into the economy as free workers, and attempted to establish their place in society as men and women with equal rights. For whites, the era was one in which families adjusted to life without slavery, faced the results of military defeat, and tried to rebuild what had been lost economically and socially as a result of the war. From the national perspective, however, Reconstruction was largely a political matter and reflected the efforts at reintegrating the former Confederate states into the Union. For Arkansans, national politics and policies—plus the response of other former Confederate states—established the framework within which they attempted to reconstruct themselves. While events at a local level were significant as well, understanding the Reconstruction era in Arkansas ultimately requires some awareness of the broader national context.

Efforts at restoring the Union began in December 1863 with President Abraham Lincoln's Proclamation of Pardon and Amnesty and ended in 1877 when President Rutherford B. Hayes ordered Federal troops laying siege to the statehouses in South Carolina and Louisiana back to their barracks. Federal efforts actually went through three distinct stages—Presidential Reconstruction, Congressional Reconstruction, and, finally, the variously designated period of Radical or Black Reconstruction. While the Federal government imposed plans of restoration on these Southern states, these plans always involved some degree of self-determination on the part of the people of the South. The problem the government faced was the Constitution of the United States and its requirement that government ultimately be based on the voluntary adherence of the people to the government. To understand the course of the Reconstruction era, it is critical to appreciate the difficulty of securing that voluntary adherence from a people who had just fought four years of war to sunder the Union, and, at the same time, obtain their agreement to re-join the Union in a way that accepted the basic results of the war—acknowledging Union victory and the emancipation of the enslaved.

The end of the year 1862 saw Federal armies push deep into the South, creating a need for some sort of governments to be created there. Initially, President Lincoln attempted to begin the reconstruction process by appointing military governors over four areas with a significant Federal presence: Tennessee, North Carolina, Louisiana, and Arkansas. In Arkansas, he appointed John S. Phelps, a Democratic congressman from Missouri. Military government, however, was not Lincoln's view of a long-term solution. His ultimate plan for restoring the Southern states was based on two assumptions about the war that he had made from its outbreak. The first was that the majority of Southerners had remained loyal to the Union. The second was that the states had never legally seceded, so were in fact still in the Union. On that basis, in his view, all that was needed to restore normal relations within the Union was to have loyal citizens, those individuals willing to take an oath of allegiance, regain control of their state governments.

As a result, on December 8, 1863, he issued his Proclamation of Pardon and Amnesty, providing the basis for this restoration. Lincoln offered all Southerners still in rebellion the opportunity to resume their allegiance to the United States and to reinaugurate loyal state governments by taking an oath of loyalty to the Union and accepting the acts of Congress and proclamations of the president concerning slavery. The only exceptions to this proffered pardon were officers of the Confederate government, officers of the Confederate military above the rank of colonel in the army or lieutenant in the navy, all who had previously taken an oath of allegiance to the United States and subsequently aided the rebellion, and, finally, war criminals. When a number of residents of each state equal to one-tenth of the number who had cast their vote in the 1860 presidential election had taken this oath, reestablishment of a state government that "shall be republican" was allowed. This requirement became the basis for Lincoln's program, one that became known as the Ten Percent Plan. He further encouraged the men who created these new governments to make provisions for the freedpeople—recognizing their permanent freedom, providing for their education, and taking what other measures were necessary for the transformation of this landless and homeless laboring class into free laborers. In this proclamation, Lincoln set out the basic goals of reconstruction that remained central to the government's effort for the next fourteen years.

Reconstruction demanded loyalty from the people of the South and recognition of the results of the war, particularly acknowledging that the former slaves were truly free.[1]

President Lincoln's Ten Percent Plan became the basis for what is known as Presidential Reconstruction, the period extending from 1863 to 1867. Arkansas made its first attempt to reconstruct itself under this plan. Arkansas had been a divided state in 1861, with many of its citizens opposed to secession. In fact, in the course of the war, almost nine thousand white Arkansans joined the Union army. Nearly six thousand African Americans from Arkansas served in the army. Political Unionism was revived in Arkansas in 1863 when Federal troops occupied Fort Smith on September 1 and a Union army under General Frederick Steele captured Little Rock on September 11. Unionists returned to both places at this time and held mass meetings during which they expressed their loyalty and their desire for Arkansas to be restored to its normal relationship in the Union. When the president issued his December 8 proclamation, a group of Unionists headed by William M. Fishback, a prewar politician who had recruited for the Third Arkansas Infantry (US) and Fourth Arkansas Cavalry (US), prepared to take advantage of the offer and in mid-December called on Unionists throughout the state to send delegates to a constitutional convention to be held in Little Rock on January 8, 1864.[2]

General Steele, a Democrat politically, was skeptical of the convention movement, but many of the more radical members of the army supported it. On January 10, 1864, General Christopher C. Andrews, a political enemy of Steele, wrote to the president and informed him that the delegates had assembled in Little Rock and that he thought they would move quickly to carry out the president's programs, especially abolishing slavery. Andrews noted that they represented more than half of the counties in the state, and he characterized the delegates as "men of intelligence and weight of character."

The Little Rock convention proved everything predicted by General Andrews and acted quickly to adopt the state's 1836 constitution as its basis, dispensing with the revisions of 1861. They declared secession null and void. They repudiated all debts incurred by the government in support of the war. The delegates abolished slavery and limited the use of indentures, although it was clear that they had not fully grappled with the issue of emancipation. Only free white men, for example, were assured the right to keep and bear arms. Further, no explicit provisions were included guaranteeing rights to all men, regardless of color. The convention elected Isaac Murphy as provisional governor, then provided for an election to ratify the constitution and elect state and congressional officers on March 14, 15, and 16. General Steele remained reluctant to accept the work of the Fishback convention, but on January 30, 1864, President Lincoln telegraphed him to say that, having received accounts of the convention, he believed that they seemed to be doing well. He encouraged Steele to help them "on their own plans," although he left it up to Steele to determine the best course.[3]

There was relatively little campaigning for the March election, and Steele remained skeptical of the results. He was surprised, however, when a total of 12,405 men voted for governor, members of the General Assembly, and congressmen despite guerrilla efforts at disrupting the election in some counties. The vast majority cast their votes in favor of the new constitution. On April 14, 1864, the newly elected General Assembly gathered and elected two of its more radical members to Congress: William Fishback and Elisha Baxter. On April 18, Isaac Murphy, who had been chosen as governor, took office amidst a celebration that included large numbers of white Unionists and newly freed slaves. General Nathan Kimball informed Lincoln of the inauguration of the loyal government on April 25, 1864. In what surely must have been hyperbole, he reported that ten thousand people, including white citizens, Union troops, and freedpeople, had joined the process, creating a parade three miles in length. "God has granted us a magnificent triumph," he wrote, "& Arkansas is once more an organized state with National Union free from slavery."[4]

Reconstruction under the Ten Percent Plan proved only partially successful in Arkansas and Louisiana. Critically, Congress refused to recognize the results of the election and would not seat the congressmen chosen in the state elections. The so-called Radical faction of the Republican Party had looked for much more and did not believe that the ten percent prescribed by the president could assure loyal government. Members like Congressman Thaddeus Stevens, for example, wanted a reconstruction that revolutionized the South, redistributed land, and destroyed the power of the antebellum political and economic elites. The moderates within the Republican Party did not advocate such revolutionary goals, but they did want the freedmen to be protected in their new status. Neither group was particularly pleased with what they saw as foot dragging on the part of Unionists organizing their new governments in Louisiana and Arkansas. They, thus, used their power to exclude the representatives of these states from their seats in Congress, delaying the reconstruction process.

Lincoln, indicating that the representatives who had gone from Arkansas to Washington to be seated feared that the action of Congress meant that General Steele would not support the newly elected state government, wrote to Steele at the end of

June instructing him to "give the same support and protection that you would if the members had been admitted, because in no event, nor in any view of the case, can this do any harm, while it will be the best you can do towards suppressing the rebellion." Murphy's government could accomplish little, despite the president's advice. It proved unable to collect enough taxes to actually govern. In addition, General Steele provided little support for the governor and particularly his desire to create an armed militia to deal with guerrillas.[5]

Reflective of this growing opposition to the president's plan was a bill proposed by Congressman Henry Winter Davis of Maryland and Senator Benjamin Wade of Ohio that offered an alternative plan to that of the president. The Wade-Davis Bill passed through Congress on July 2, 1864, and further articulated the evolving demands of many Northerners. The bill required a number equal to over fifty percent of the number who had voted in 1860 to swear an oath of allegiance prior to the reformation of the government. This oath, sometimes known as the Iron Clad Oath, had been passed by Congress on July 2, 1862. This oath required a declaration that the person taking the oath had never voluntarily borne arms against the United States, thus disfranchising many of the adult white males of the Southern states. In addition, it required the new governments to recognize the end of slavery and even provided for punishment of any individuals who attempted to retain people in any form of involuntary servitude. President Lincoln recognized the bill as one possible means of reconstruction, but in the end he killed the bill, submitted on the last day of the session, with a pocket veto. He simply did not sign it. The fact that the bill passed through Congress with a majority vote, however, was a clear indication that the members of Congress had reservations about any policy that proved too lenient toward the South. Congressmen Wade and Davis responded to the veto with a statement asserting that Congress should have paramount authority over the reconstruction process; hence, the president should confine himself to his constitutional duties and leave reconstruction to Congress.[6]

Lincoln indicated in a proclamation that he issued after his veto of the Wade-Davis Bill that he remained flexible as to the best way forward in reconstructing the South, although still maintaining that he had the power to proceed. In the spring of 1865, he considered the possibility of making black suffrage a necessary requirement for a state's return to the Union. Lincoln's course in the future must remain speculative, however, for on April 14, 1865, John Wilkes Booth assassinated him, and Vice President Andrew Johnson took over. Johnson faced the same dilemma as Lincoln: resolving the differences between the executive and legislative branches over how to proceed in reuniting the former Confederate states with the Union.

In his action, however, he failed to recognize the level of tension that had existed and decided not to call a special Congress to consider the reconstruction process. Instead, he decided to continue along Lincoln's path and use his executive powers. As historian Eric McKitrick noted, he faced little initial opposition because most Republicans assumed that "his purposes and those of Congress would prove, in their course, to have been more or less in harmony throughout." Johnson actually embraced Lincoln's plan as his own, determined to bring as quick an end to the process as possible. He established the basic program for all the Southern states in his Proclamation of Amnesty and Pardon and Proclamation Reorganizing a Constitutional Government in North Carolina, both issued on May 29, 1865.

In the first, he prescribed an oath for former Confederates similar to that of Lincoln's, simply requiring a statement of future loyalty to the U.S. government. He excepted the same groups as Lincoln, with the addition of all persons who had participated in the war with taxable property in 1860 in excess of $20,000, but he provided that even these could make a special application to the president for pardon. In the second proclamation, he named provisional governors to each of the states, asked them to facilitate the calling of a constitutional convention to revise constitutions to put them in line with that of the national government, and required them to ratify the elections. He gave none of the governors specific instructions, however, concerning the steps that should be taken. The closest he came to providing a list of "indispensable" actions came in an interview with the newly appointed governor of South Carolina. He told the governor that the state convention should abolish slavery, ratify the proposed Thirteenth Amendment, and renounce the doctrine of secession. With little other guidance, each of the Southern states proceeded in this way, holding their constitutional conventions and electing new governments. On April 2, 1866, the president issued a declaration announcing the insurrection in the South to be at an end. Another proclamation on August 20, 1866, declared that peace, order, tranquility, and civil order existed throughout the United States.[7]

At this point the president may have believed the reconstruction process was at an end, but none of the congressmen that the new governments had elected had been seated in Congress. The South had been allowed to reconstruct itself, but the results did not appear to reflect the loyalty that not only the Radical Republicans but the Moderate Republicans and the majority of Northerners expected the South to have exhibited. Arkansas had already rewritten its constitution, but the other former Confederate states began holding elections for delegates and holding constitutional conventions, beginning with Mississippi in mid-August 1865.

The results of these elections should have given the president pause in the pursuit of his policy, as the antebellum Democratic elites were absent among the candidates in most of the states. Although a majority of delegates to the convention actually had been opposed to secession or reluctant secessionists, almost all of them had gone with their states after the war began and actively supported the new Confederacy. Many of them were actually ineligible to hold office under the president's own policies. This fact alone raised concerns in the North, but the presence of active secessionists who often were vocal in their demands may have created even greater apprehension. In Texas, for example, one of the candidates who ran for that state's convention told voters that, as far as the freedmen were concerned, he would "concede them nothing but the station of 'hewers of wood and drawers of water.'...I desire the perpetuation of a white man's government." The Texans subsequently elected James W. Throckmorton as president of the convention, a man who had voted against secession but who had served as an officer in the Confederate army and should have been ineligible under the president's amnesty proclamation. Texans created an even greater affront and public relations disaster when they elected the man who had been president of the state's secession convention to the new convention.[8]

The debates in the convention and the resulting constitutions also indicated a failure to recognize fully the results of the war. The Mississippi convention, the first to meet, spent a considerable amount of time addressing the question of whether or not to repeal the secession ordinance or to declare it null and void from the beginning. The difference between the two positions was significant, for to declare secession to be null and void from the beginning would be to say that secession was illegal and label Confederates as traitors. Only three of the former Confederate state conventions approved a null and void measure. When the conventions considered state war debts, South Carolina and Mississippi both failed to repudiate their debts. Only when President Johnson indicated that repudiation was indispensable to readmission to the Union did the other states, and then only grudgingly, repudiate their debts. As to slavery, only North Carolina passed measures that took responsibility for emancipation. In all the others, the conventions passed carefully crafted provisions that indicated the federal government had emancipated the slaves. As historian Dan Carter pointed out, this was done in some cases in the hope that there might be some sort of compensation for the freed slaves and in other cases to avoid admitting their state's responsibility for what they considered a catastrophic action. Carter quoted T. N. Dawkins of South Carolina, who attempted to have a clause inserted in that state's constitution that would have read that "immediate emancipation, with all its travail for both races, has come to us against our will, and better judgement." In the end, all the states besides North Carolina adopted phrasing such as that in the Texas constitution, which stated that, "African slavery having been terminated by the United States government by force of arms and its reestablishment prohibited by an amendment to the Constitution of the United States" no longer existed. Northern observers saw these grudging steps as indicating that the South's leadership at this point was neither truly willing to accept the results of the war nor loyal.[9]

The general elections held in those states that had completed the reconstruction process in the fall of 1865 and 1866 raised further suspicions in the minds of Northerners. As historian Eric Foner wrote, in the lower South, "service to the Confederacy emerged as a virtual perquisite for victory." While many of the men elected to state legislatures in 1865 and 1866 had opposed secession in 1861, most of them had gone with their states following secession and actively participated in the Confederate war effort. Reconstruction scholar John Hope Franklin pointed out in his study of the era that when Southerners went to the polls, they elected Vice President of the Confederacy Alexander Stephens, four Confederate generals, five Confederate colonels, six Confederate cabinet officers, and fifty-eight Confederate congressmen to the Thirty-ninth Congress.

At the level of state government, the results also indicated that Southerners appeared unwilling to address the Northerners' suspicions about the loyalty of their governments, as candidates who had been wartime Unionists suffered widespread defeat. In the Arkansas congressional election, Unionist George H. Kyle won in the First District, but in the Second District, Lorenzo Gibson, a man who was unable to take the congressional oath, defeated the Unionist candidate. In the Third District, no official returns were ever received. Mississippians elected Confederate general Benjamin G. Humphreys governor. South Carolinians chose as their governor James L. Orr, their Confederate senator. Of the Southern governors elected in 1865, only one could even take the Iron Clad Oath. State legislatures displayed equally large numbers of former Confederates, and Arkansas joined them in this choice of men who had supported the Confederacy. In the state's 1866 legislative election, Arkansans sent three former members of the Confederate state legislature, three Confederate brigadier generals, and three Confederate colonels to the twenty-five-seat state Senate.[10]

In addition, these state legislatures pursued legislative programs that rewarded former Confederates and placed controls on the freedmen that many considered similar to the Black Codes of slave days. Rewards to former Confederates came in the form of new state jobs that often were given to these ex-Rebels. As to the freedmen, these new Black Codes placed serious restrictions on their labor. Almost every state passed labor laws that required workers to have written contracts for the next year's labor at the beginning of each year. If they did not have contracts, they were considered vagrants. Under new vagrant laws, they could be

Many state legislatures during Reconstruction pursued legislative programs that rewarded former Confederates and placed controls on freedmen that many considered similar to the Black Codes of slave days, placing serious restrictions on their labor. These African American men are gathered in front of a store in Augusta. Copy negative of a tintype: "Blacks in front of store building in Augusta, Arkansas, about 1870," ASA_Photo_G5653, Arkansas State Archives, Little Rock, Arkansas.

arrested and then put out to labor to pay off onerous fines that frequently amounted to as much as they might make in a year. Most states passed laws that forbade blacks from holding office, serving on juries, voting, or testifying in cases against whites. Miscegenation was banned in most states as well. In Texas, blacks were segregated on public transportation and the railroads were required to run separate cars for black passengers.[11]

Arkansas came into line with its sister Confederate states following its state elections in August 1866. The subsequent legislative session indicated even more clearly what had happened, as the legislators dedicated ten percent of the state's revenues to a fund to support wounded and disabled Confederate soldiers. They went on to grant pardon and amnesty to Confederate soldiers and to elected officials who had done anything in the line of duty liable to prosecution, such as the seizure of the property of Unionists or the execution of men who offered resistance to conscription. Another bill exempted taxpayers from having to pay any of the taxes levied prior to 1865, thus providing relief for men who had been unable to pay their taxes during the war, especially Confederate soldiers. The one area in which Arkansas did not follow its sister states was in the passage of Black Codes, although it did place all disputes between landlords and workers in the hands of local justice courts, courts usually controlled by landowners.[12]

Provoking further concern in the North was the actual treatment of the freedmen. Historian Dan Carter described the underlying assumption held by whites about blacks as being the "all-pervasive belief in the fixed and immutable racial inferiority of blacks." As a result, whites' and blacks' dealings in labor disputes or in such simple interactions as passing each other on the street could lead to violence. Even though the majority of freedmen had either gone back to work as farm laborers on the land of their former masters or some other white landowner, their employers complained that they did not work as hard as they had in slavery. Officials of the Freedmen's Bureau, sent to protect the freedmen, reported that some employers, as a result of this perception, treated their workers as slaves, even whipping them for not working as hard as the landowner desired. In addition, bureau agents found that the whites readily exploited the lack of basic education among the freedmen, readily violating the contractual relationship they had with their laborers. Bureau records also contained accounts of whites murdering blacks for failing to behave in a subservient manner. A South Carolina planter, for example, admitted to shooting one of his former slaves simply for wanting a bureau official to examine his labor contract.[13]

General John Sprague, head of the Freedmen's Bureau in Arkansas, cited a disturbing number of murders of African Americans and widespread defrauding of former slaves in the state in his call for government protection for Arkansas's black population. Courtesy of the Library of Congress Prints and Photographs Division.

The records of the Freedmen's Bureau present the fullest picture of events across the South, and those for Arkansas indicated that the treatment of freedmen in the state took the same path as it did in the other former Confederate states. General John W. Sprague, commissioner of the Freedmen's Bureau in Arkansas, stated in his first report in 1865 that murderous attacks on the freedmen were widespread, with twenty-nine murders having taken place in the previous July and August alone. He believed these were only half of the actual cases that had occurred and concluded that the freedmen could not obtain justice in the civil courts. He saw that the biggest problem came at the end of the first season that the ex-slaves had worked as freedmen, with their landlords taking advantage of their condition and defrauding them of their wages. He estimated that they stood to lose as much as a third of their wages as a result of such swindles. Sprague insisted that, in the end, the national government had to protect these workers or they would be treated by the people of the South as "beasts of burden." His report in January 1866 indicated that conditions had deteriorated further. One Unionist informed him that he feared that, without protection, blacks would be "starved, murdered, or forced into a condition more horrible than the worst stages of slavery."[14]

Congress stepped into the reconstruction process in the winter of 1865, convinced that President Johnson's policy was not working but seeking some sort of moderate solution to the dilemma presented by events in the South. Congressional efforts to establish some sort of oversight of reconstruction began with the creation of the Joint Committee on Reconstruction. This was followed in early 1866 when Senator Lyman Trumbull of Illinois introduced two bills designed to protect the former slaves in their new freedom. Trumbull's sponsorship of the bills was particularly critical since it reflected the perspective of the moderate Republicans as to the bare minimum of action that should be taken.

The first bill extended the life of the Bureau of Refugees, Freedmen, and Abandoned Lands. The bureau, usually referred to simply as the Freedmen's Bureau, had been created in 1865 to handle the various problems associated with "refugees, freedmen, and abandoned lands." Its focus by 1866, however, had to a large degree been reduced to assisting the freedmen in their relationships as laborers and in the protection of their bodies and lives. The bureau had agents across the South who helped freedmen when they signed labor contracts and who also acted as judges in contract disputes between the workers and their employers when the civil courts failed to help.

The second bill was the Civil Rights Act of 1866. This legislation was revolutionary in its scope, for it created for the first time national citizenship, granting American citizenship to all persons born in the United States, excluding Native Americans. In the granting of citizenship, the law gave all citizens, regardless of color, the same rights as white citizens and equal protection in the law. It further gave the United States government the authority to protect these rights, including the use of the militia or the army, and prohibited any state from depriving a citizen of these rights. Both bills

The Leake-Ingham Building in Camden served as the office of the Freedmen's Bureau in the turbulent years following the Civil War. The signature of the Freedmen's Bureau agent can still be seen etched into the glass of a window. Courtesy of the Arkansas Historic Preservation Program, Little Rock, Arkansas.

received almost unanimous support among Republicans in Congress, indicating the degree to which the Radical and Moderate Republicans had achieved agreement on that basic issue.[15]

The extension of the life of the Freedmen's Bureau and the creation of national citizenship may have created a basis for an end to the reconstruction process. The latter simply created a set of rights that had to be respected at the state level, regardless of whether or not the former Confederates had returned to power. They could control their states, but they would have to assure the rights of their citizens. This simple resolution was not to be, however, because President Andrew Johnson vetoed the Freedmen's Bureau bill on February 19, 1866. He declared the bill to be unconstitutional, insisting that the Constitution had never promised that the nation would create a system to support indigent citizens. Further, since he believed civil government had been established in most of the former Confederate states, the military courts that were part of the bureau were an unconstitutional usurpation of the powers of the civil courts. Finally, touching on the question of the exact place of the state governments legally, he contended that since they were not represented in Congress at this time, the laws could not be applied to them. This raised serious questions about the application of all laws since 1861 to the Southern states. On March 27, he vetoed the Civil Rights Bill on the grounds that since the former Confederate states were not yet represented in Congress, that body could not pass legislation that applied to those states. Rather than resolving the problem, President Johnson's actions only pushed the Republican majority in Congress to further action.[16]

Congress responded to Johnson's action by passing the civil rights and Freedmen's Bureau bills over the vetoes. The body acted on the bureau bill on April 9 and the civil rights bill on

July 16. In addition, the congressional majority moved to translate the measures of the civil rights bill into a proposed constitutional amendment that would assure the protections guaranteed by the bill against future legislative repeal. The Joint Committee on Reconstruction submitted the proposal, the future Fourteenth Amendment to the U.S. Constitution, on April 30. The measure, along with the civil rights act, defined national citizenship and the rights that accrued to it, although simplifying this statement to an assurance that no state would abridge the "privileges or immunities of citizens." The proposals also ensured that the states could not "deprive any person of life, liberty, or property" without due process of law. Further, the state could not deny any person the "equal protection of the laws." In addition, the proposal overturned the amnesty and pardons that had been granted by President Johnson and disqualified from holding public office all individuals who had previously sworn an oath of allegiance to the U.S. government and then voluntarily supported the Confederacy. It did, however, provide that Congress could remove this disability with a two-thirds vote. In addition, in response to the elusiveness by the state conventions on the Confederate debt, the proposed amendment guaranteed the national debt and repudiated the Confederate debt. In a particularly revolutionary step, the proposal indicated that suffrage was a right of male American citizens. It did not do so in a direct way, a failure with future consequences, but rather threatened a proportional reduction in congressional representation for any state that withheld suffrage to American citizens. The measure received the necessary approval in Congress, and the proposed amendment was sent to the state legislatures for ratification.[17]

Even as the belief within Congress that even more radical action was demanded to assure the successful outcome of the war continued to grow, conditions in the South worsened for African Americans. Two events, more than any individual acts of violence, may have convinced even the most reluctant Republican that action was needed. In May 1866, a relatively mild argument between whites and demobilized black soldiers

Frank Leslie's Illustrated Newspaper *lampooned U.S. president Andrew Johnson's efforts at Reconstruction in this June 16, 1866, cartoon. Johnson holds a leaking kettle, labeled "The Reconstructed South," toward a woman representing Liberty carrying a baby representing the just-approved Fourteenth Amendment.* Courtesy of the Library of Congress Prints and Photographs Division.

broke out into a riot in Memphis. The riot quickly turned into a massacre of African Americans, with mobs that included the city's policemen rampaging through black neighborhoods, burning and murdering. When it was over, some forty-six blacks had been killed and the mob had burned ninety-one homes, four churches, and eight schools. The second event was a July 30 confrontation in New Orleans that started as a political affair but quickly turned into a racial massacre. A mob of whites, again including the city police, attempted to break up an effort to reconstitute the state's constitutional convention. The mayor of the city, a former Rebel pardoned by President Johnson, ordered the police to prevent the gathering of the convention. When a party of black former soldiers marched to support the convention, the mob met it with bricks. Another riot-turned-massacre broke out in which at least thirty-seven blacks and three of their white allies were killed. One of the latter, a prominent New England minister, was shot down while waving a white flag in hopes of surrendering, an act that received an illustration on the front page of illustrated magazines in the North. Historian James Hollandsworth Jr. observed that these riots and the general violence against blacks across the South undoubtedly

Thomas Nast characterized President Andrew Johnson as a would-be king in this cartoon depicting the New Orleans Massacre, a July 30, 1866, riot in which whites attacked and killed at least thirty-seven black and three white men outside the building where the Radical Republican constitutional convention was being held. Courtesy of the Library of Congress Prints and Photographs Division.

"increased the perception in the North that white southerners were determined to unleash a reign of terror on the recently emancipated slaves," discredited President Johnson's policy, and convinced many in Congress that it would have to step in to save the reconstruction process.[18]

The Northern congressional elections in 1866 became a mandate on the question of reconstruction, largely caused by President Johnson, who campaigned nationwide in hopes of securing support for candidates who supported his policies. His notorious campaigning effort was unprecedented in presidential history for its insults against his opponents. In August, he began what came to be known as his "Swing Around the Circle." He boarded a train and carried out a campaign that took him from Washington DC to New York City, then across the Midwest to Chicago, south to St. Louis, and then back to Washington. At every stop he made essentially the same speech, contending that he was like Jesus Christ, willing to pardon repentant sinners and move on. Southerners were not holding up the reconstruction process. Instead, he blamed this failure on the radicals in Congress who he contended were trying to keep the Union broken up. He was a man who was known for being goaded into fiery speeches, and the crowd egged him on to the point that he actually called for the hanging of Congressman Thaddeus Stevens and the prominent abolitionist Wendell Phillips. The Republican coalition of radicals and moderates, however, campaigned simply on moving forward with reconstruction and advancing the Fourteenth Amendment. The result was an election disaster for the president's supporters. Northern voters sent an even more radical Republican majority to Congress, a majority determined to force the South to reconstruct itself in a way long advocated by Northern politicians after its failure to do so voluntarily.[19]

At this point, once again, reconstruction may have come to an end if the leaders of the Southern states had accepted that they had to assent to black equality as citizens and perhaps even extend qualified suffrage to them. The South simply refused. James McPherson quotes the governors of North and South Carolina as saying on the matter, "If we are to be degraded we will retain some self-esteem by not making it self-abasement....Worse terms may be imposed by Congress, but they will be *imposed* and not *voluntarily accepted.*" To make matters worse, when the legislatures in Alabama and Virginia indicated that they might ratify the proposed amendment, President Johnson encouraged them not to do so. In the end, all of the Southern legislatures considered the proposed amendment. All of them except for Tennessee refused to ratify it. Subsequently, Congress seated the representatives from Tennessee. For the rest, the governors of the Carolinas could have been prophets, for in their obstinacy they provoked worse terms.[20]

In the spring of 1867, the Reconstruction era entered a new stage. At this point Congress began considering alternative approaches to the problem. The Thirty-ninth Congress remained in session at this point, but the Republicans in Congress were aware of the results of the election and moved forward with their own plan of reconstruction. Southerners would look back at Congress's ultimate plan as radical, but it in fact represented a moderate solution in their efforts at securing blacks in their freedom when compared with the range of plans considered. The most radical proposal considered by Congress was territorializing the South and placing it under a territorial government. The House of Representatives actually passed a bill in February 1867 that would have done this. Other Republicans, unwilling to go that far, looked at disfranchising all ex-Confederates. Some believed that a redistribution of land might destroy the power of the old elites and make possible a reconstruction on a different basis. Additional proposals considered the creation of a permanent federal presence in the South, particularly in terms of federally funded public schools. None of this came to pass, since many of the Republicans in Congress considered them to be too radical.[21]

Moderate Republicans in Congress ultimately managed to put together legislation that the radicals could vote for even if it was not completely satisfactory. The bill, approved first by the Senate and then the House of Representatives, came to be known as the First Reconstruction Act. It declared that no legal state governments existed in these states, nor was there protection of life and property. As a result, it divided the states remaining unrepresented in Congress into five military districts. Arkansas was put, along with Mississippi, into the Fourth District. The president was to assign a military commander to each district and provide a military force sufficient for that officer to protect the people of the states, restore order, and supervise the registration of voters in preparation for new constitutional conventions. These commanders could use the existing governments and courts, considered now to be provisional, to effect these ends, but they also had the power to establish military courts in the event that the civil officials failed.

The first unique aspect of this new reconstruction was that black citizens would be allowed to register to vote for the new convention. This fit nicely within the framework of the moderates' view of constitutional government. In addition, the bill disfranchised men who had previously sworn an oath of allegiance to the United States and then supported the Confederacy, a policy somewhat vague in its application. Government would be based on the people. "The people" was redefined. Only after the conventions had written a constitution in conformity with the

Constitution of the United States and elected a legislature that ratified the proposed Fourteenth Amendment, the first real demand imposed on the South, would the state be entitled to representation in Congress.[22]

President Johnson vetoed the bill, and his veto message pointed directly to the entire purpose of the new reconstruction when he contended that it imposed military domination not for the purpose of maintaining public order but rather "as a means of coercing the people into the adoption of principles and measures to which it is known that they are opposed." He went on to suggest that they had an undeniable right to exercise their judgment. That depends, however, on whether or not you accept the idea that civil government had actually been created acceptable to the United States—and the very fact that Congress had not accepted its representatives indicated that was not true. In short, Congress had imposed new rules for being part of the Union, and unless the South accepted those rules, it was clear that it would not be restored to the Union. Johnson issued his veto on March 2. Congress overrode his veto that same day, passing the bill by a vote of 135 to 48 in the House and 38 to 10 in the Senate. To ensure that the president could not interfere in any of this, Congress also passed laws that limited his power to remove federal officials, including cabinet members, until a new appointee was confirmed by the Senate and denied him the power to remove the general of army, Ulysses S. Grant, without the consent of the Senate. His efforts at defying these laws ultimately led to the president's impeachment.[23]

Congress imposed further demands on those states that remained unreconstructed after February 1869. As the first former Confederate states came back into the Union, members of Congress became increasingly concerned that the enfranchisement of African Americans, intended when blacks were registered to vote under the First Reconstruction Act, would not be guaranteed in the future. As a result, Congress began considering another amendment to the Constitution, an addition that would become the Fifteenth Amendment. Initially the Radicals in Congress proposed a simple statement saying that all citizens of the United States had the right to vote and no state could place any restrictions on that right. As a result of compromises with Moderate and Conservative Republicans, the bill was finally crafted to step back from the positive original statement and instead forbade states from denying any citizen the right to vote on the basis of race, color, or previous condition. This opened the possibility for the imposition of other sorts of restrictions such as the literacy, registration, and poll tax constraints used by Southern states in their efforts at disfranchising blacks later in the century. The already reconstructed states, controlled by Republican governments, quickly ratified the proposed amendment. Legislation passed by Congress after the amendment was submitted to the states required Georgia, Mississippi, Texas, and Virginia, still unreconstructed, to ratify the amendment before they were readmitted to the Union.[24]

Through the summer of 1867 Southerners began organizing under the requirements set by Congress. In most of the Southern states, leaders of the Democratic Party—in some states referring to themselves as Conservatives to attract former Whigs or Conservative Republicans—reorganized in an effort at controlling the constitutional conventions. Their goal was to meet the demands of Congress in as limited a manner as possible and produce conservative constitutions. On the other hand, a coalition of whites consisting of native Southerners and newcomers from the North began organizing state Republican parties.

Initially both the Democrats and the Republicans vied for black voters, but blacks indicated early that they would go with the Republicans. Their decision to align themselves with the Republicans unleashed a wave of violence and intimidation aimed at limiting their influence at the polls that continued across the South up to the end of Reconstruction. Violence against black tenant farmers and black churches and schools had been endemic from the very beginning of Reconstruction, but the enfranchisement of African Americans intensified attacks aimed at both black and white Republican leaders as well as party institutions such as the Union League. The emergence of the Ku Klux Klan reflected the increased use of violence in an effort by whites to keep blacks from achieving their full independence or exercising the rights they had gained under the Civil Rights Act and the Fourteenth Amendment. The Klan, born in secrecy in Tennessee in 1865, spread across much of the rest of the South after 1867, and the country's newspapers applied the Klan name to all groups that used violence to reassert white hegemony in the face of a potential social as well as political revolution.[25]

Registration initially indicated that the Democrat-Conservative parties might gain control of the constitutional conventions in some of the Southern states. In five of the states, more whites registered than blacks, a fact that contradicted the later assertion that Congressional Reconstruction disfranchised most whites. In the elections, however, black voters turned out in large numbers while many whites stayed away from the polls. As a result, Republicans carried all of the elections and controlled the state conventions. The men elected to the conventions constituted a new political leadership and included local whites, whites who had come to the South following the war, and blacks. In every state except South Carolina, whites who had been present prior to the war made up the majority of delegates.

The proportion of each group attending the Arkansas convention was relatively typical, with sixty-four percent being residents of the state before the war, twenty-four percent citizens who had arrived following the war, and eleven percent black. Their political opponents pinned the opprobrious labels of "scalawags" on the native whites and "carpetbaggers" on whites from the North. The Democrat-Conservative politicians characterized the so-called scalawags as vindictive people from the meanest element in Southern society, the so-called carpetbaggers as adventurers who came to the South to exploit the political situation, and black politicians as ignorant dupes of the whites. Revisionist scholarship, however, has shown the majority of these men to have been responsible politicians who sought political office to achieve a variety of goals, including preserving the results of the war and establishing more democratic and progressive governments in the South. The specific details of the reforms they sought emerged as they worked to form new state constitutions.[26]

Historian James McPherson called the constitutions written by this new political majority "among the most progressive in the nation." All of them contained provisions for universal male suffrage without regard to race, color, nationality, or previous condition, although Alabama and Georgia avoided these specifics by simply extending the suffrage to all adult male citizens. Five of the states added specific exceptions to this general enfranchisement, excluding all men who had been disfranchised by the Reconstruction Acts and the Fourteenth Amendment. The rest left disfranchisement in the hands of Congress and opened the way for former Confederate leaders to regain their voting rights when the national government removed its restrictions.

An additional requirement included in all of the new state constitutions was the stipulation that states create public school systems, a measure designed to appeal both to the former slaves and to the poor whites in the South. Debates over whether or not the schools should be racially separate were rancorous in many of the conventions, but most of the states ultimately produced constitutions that avoided the issue by simply requiring free public schools. Only the conventions in South Carolina and Louisiana specifically required integrated schools.

Other than provisions for the extension of the franchise and the mandate for public schools, the constitutions written in 1868 and 1869 primarily differed from earlier charters in their tendency to increase the power of the state government. In Arkansas, for example, the constitution empowered the state government to assist business development with state credit and also to develop other institutions that would promote social and economic causes. Additionally, the office of the governor in Arkansas received extensive authority to appoint notaries public, the chief justice of the Supreme Court, and state judges and court officers at the district level. On the whole, however, the new constitutions hardly represented the radical documents that the Conservative and Democratic opposition contended them to be.[27]

In elections held in 1868 and 1869 all of the former Confederate states approved their new constitutions, although once again the low turnout of registered white voters ensured this would happen. Arkansas was the first state to apply for restoration and have its congressmen seated, the state returning to its normal relationship in the Union on June 22, 1868. In Virginia and Mississippi, voters initially rejected the constitutions, whites protesting primarily against the clauses disfranchising former Confederates, but both of these states ultimately adopted their constitutions when voters were allowed to vote on the disfranchising stipulations separately from the constitution. In Georgia,

Conservatives gained control of the both houses of the state's General Assembly. They subsequently moved to expel all of the black members of the Senate and the House and also refused to adopt the Fifteenth Amendment. As a result, Congress restored military rule and the commander removed most of the Democrats from the legislature on the grounds that they were disfranchised under the Fourteenth Amendment. Congress finally readmitted Georgia after the General Assembly restored the black members and approved the required amendment. Texas was the last of the states to be restored, with Congress recognizing its reconstruction on March 30, 1870.[28]

As a result of the elections, in all of the Southern states except Georgia, a Republican majority based on the coalition of scalawags, carpetbaggers, and blacks gained control of the new governments. As in the case of the state conventions, the men who had been residents of their states before the war made up the majority of state legislators. Carpetbaggers successfully ran for the governorship in six of the ten state elections, with Powell Clayton, a native of Pennsylvania, securing that office in Arkansas. Given the later charges that blacks dominated these new governments, Republicans actually elected few blacks to any statewide offices. Only Louisiana's lieutenant governor, Oscar J. Dunn, and state treasurer, Antoine Dubuclet, and the secretaries of state from Florida, Mississippi, and South Carolina were black. The only black state officer in Arkansas was Superintendent of Education Joseph C. Corbin, although he was not elected until 1873. Blacks controlled no legislature during the entire Reconstruction period, although in the first election blacks gained a majority in the lower house of the South Carolina General Assembly. In Arkansas, voters sent only six blacks to the General Assembly in the 1868 election.[29]

The task confronted by these Republican governments was overwhelming. They faced the problem of rebuilding public buildings that had been neglected during the war. In most of the states, they also had to look to the funding of institutions mandated by the new constitutions, particularly public school systems. In a broader sense, they set out to meet the needs of what historian Eric Foner described as an "expanded citizenry." In part, this meant meeting the needs of the newly enfranchised black voters. Republicans could not, however, overlook the concerns of white voters, as more white voters than black registered in 1868 in five of the ten states reorganized under the congressional plan. Whites would constitute the majority in even more states after the adoption of the new state constitutions, since all but Arkansas provided for the re-enfranchisement of most former Confederates. A broader appeal was essential for the survival of the Republican regimes and also for the establishment of the party's political legitimacy. The Republican approach in every state was the creation of a more-activist government, a basic shift from the tradition of limited government that had characterized antebellum Southern government.[30]

Superintendent of Education Joseph C. Corbin was the only African American elected to a high state office in Reconstruction-era Arkansas, winning the office in 1873. "Joseph Carter Corbin, superintendent of public instruction, 1873-1874," ASA_Photo_G0158, Arkansas State Archives, Little Rock, Arkansas.

A commitment to the creation of public schools represented one of the more significant goals of the new governments. All Southern states had declared support for the idea of public schools, but before the war little had been done. Republicans, contending that public education was essential to an informed citizenry, and finding strong support for schools particularly among their black constituents and many poor whites, moved forward with the actual building of schools. By 1870, public schools existed in every Southern state, although all except for those of Louisiana and South Carolina were segregated, a fact that created significant financial problems for the schools going forward. South Carolina's schools evidenced the remarkable achievement of these schools. In 1870 that state's new school system consisted of 769 schools with a total of 30,448 children. By 1876, the number of schools had increased to 2,776 with 123,035 students. In the case of Arkansas, the drive for public schools and particularly for making education possible for blacks was less successful. The 1870 census reported that 30,138 white males attended the schools and 26,650 white females, but only 2,930 black males and 2,854 black females were enrolled. The Arkansas system was further burdened when the legislature allowed school taxes to be paid in treasury certificates that were virtually useless, leading many teachers to close their schools and leave the state after 1871.[31]

Every Southern state government also attempted to appeal to its state's business and commercial interests by pursuing aggressive programs of economic development. Most of the Southern states created state agencies that worked to promote their states, encouraging immigration and trying to attract new businesses. To encourage the latter, the states often provided tax exemptions and in some cases outright grants of monies for new industries. The most common government investment was in the construction of railroads. States underwrote the bonds of railroad companies or provided, in some cases, outright grants of public funds. Texas not only underwrote bonds but also provided land grants to the railroads. In Arkansas, the legislature created a railroad commission and supported construction with government bonds. The state chartered eighty-six railroads during Reconstruction, but ultimately it provided bonds to only a few of these. The drive for the building of railroads and the means of financing them were not unlike what was undertaken in the North at this time, and support was based on the optimistic belief that the railroads could revive and expand local economies.

The railroads not only provided jobs but offered the promise of integrating the South into the national economy. In Arkansas, this government support allowed the completion of rail connections between Memphis and Little Rock via the Memphis and Little Rock Railroad, northeastern Arkansas to southwestern Arkansas on the Cairo and Fulton, and Little Rock to Fort Smith on the Little Rock and Fort Smith Railroad. Politically all of these roads also had the potential, never realized, of converting white Democrats to the Republican Party. While the Southern Republican governments actually managed to build the roads they financed, their efforts had unanticipated consequences of increasing public debt and, in the long run, of making it easier for the South to be exploited by the industrializing Northeast and Midwest as a provider of agricultural products and raw materials such as timber and minerals rather than as an industrial power.[37]

Given the political violence that had broken out in 1868, most of the Southern states also implemented measures to restore law and order and particularly to protect Republican voters and political leaders. Political violence remained pervasive throughout the Reconstruction period and proved difficult to suppress, at least in

Francis P. Blair Jr., shown here in an 1859 congressional photograph, was the Democrats' vice-presidential candidate in the 1868 election. Courtesy of the Library of Congress Prints and Photographs Division.

part because the leadership of the Conservative and Democratic opposition often justified such activity in its rhetoric. When the Democratic vice-presidential candidate in 1868, Francis P. Blair of Missouri, attacked Republican governments as illegitimate regimes that allowed white men to be "trodden under foot by an inferior and barbarous race," he virtually sanctioned the use of any means possible for the removal of these governments by Democrats. He did not hesitate further, suggesting that the Democratic Party existed to restore whites to their birthright and that whites should "march to Washington…and take their seats, and re-inaugurate the white man's government." The editor of New York's *Evening Post* saw clearly the import of Blair's words, charging the candidate with proposing to inaugurate "government by assassination and violence, instead of government by law." The sanctioning of violence by a national leader as important as the Democratic Party's vice-presidential candidate sent clear signals to Southerners that any methods they used to regain power would be considered acceptable by their Northern political allies.[33]

As a political tool, violence was unquestionably effective, as it required the Republican governments to respond. In the 1868 presidential election, the Republican candidate, General Ulysses S. Grant, won the vote. In Georgia, however, Democratic suppression of the vote using violence and intimidation was remarkably successful. In twenty-two Georgia counties, with a registration of 9,300 black voters, Grant received only 87 votes. In eleven counties, he did not receive a single vote. Louisiana was the one state with a black majority population where violence proved particularly widespread. The Joint Committee on Reconstruction in Congress examined the situation in that state during the presidential election and concluded that at least one thousand blacks had been killed there between April and November 1868. A particularly brutal riot in the vicinity of Shreveport left more than a hundred blacks dead. Another in Opelousas in St. Landry Parish left two hundred blacks dead. The impact of such activity was as obvious in Louisiana as in Georgia. At Opelousas, no Republicans voted on the day of the election. In eleven parishes where 4,707 Republicans had voted in the April constitutional election, no Republican votes were cast in November. In another twenty-one parishes where 26,814 had voted for the constitution in 1868, only 501 cast their ballots for Grant in the November election. The message to Republican governments in the South was clear: Their survival depended on bringing about a restoration of law and order and an end to this type of electioneering.[34]

In response, all of the Southern states bolstered their court systems and in some cases actually expanded them. Realizing that the ordinary course of justice could be thwarted by the level of violence, they also at times used state militia forces. The most successful states at suppressing violence were Arkansas and Texas. In

Arkansas, the legislature authorized Governor Powell Clayton to raise the militia to use against the outbreak of violence that took place in 1868. Clayton was reluctant to use the militia, but the number of murders reached a point that in November of that year he declared martial law in ten counties where the Ku Klux Klan had operated most openly. He sent state troops into these counties and, despite provoking outrage among his political opponents, successfully crushed the Klan. Governor Edmund Davis of Texas also used the state militia with success, declaring martial law in four counties and threatening it in two more where white mobs disrupted the electoral process. Texas additionally raised a state police force that operated beyond local jurisdictions to arrest criminals and also men charged with the political violence. Most states attempted to use such methods. North Carolina's legislature not only allowed the governor to call out the state militia but also made wearing a mask a crime. While they at times suppressed violence, they also generated considerable hostility among white Conservatives and Democrats and garnered charges of government tyranny. Republicans proved particularly reluctant to use black troops against whites, fearing that any confrontations might lead to race war. Historian George Rable concluded that, in the end, none of the state governments ever succeeded in bringing a complete end to political violence on their own. This forced them to turn to the federal government.[35]

Initially Congress appeared willing to help. On May 31, 1870, it passed the Enforcement Act, justified by the Fourteenth and Fifteenth Amendments, giving Congress the power to pass legislation necessary to enforce its provisions. The Enforcement Act made incidents involving interference with voting rights a federal crime and placed such cases in federal courts. It also provided specific definitions of the crimes. In 1871, Congress went further and passed what was popularly known as the Second Enforcement Act or Ku Klux Act. This legislation established machinery the government could use to enforce the first act, allowing the president to go so far as suspending the writ of habeas corpus and using the military to enforce federal law in the states. Using these laws, the army was sent back into South Carolina, North Carolina, and Mississippi, where it was used to

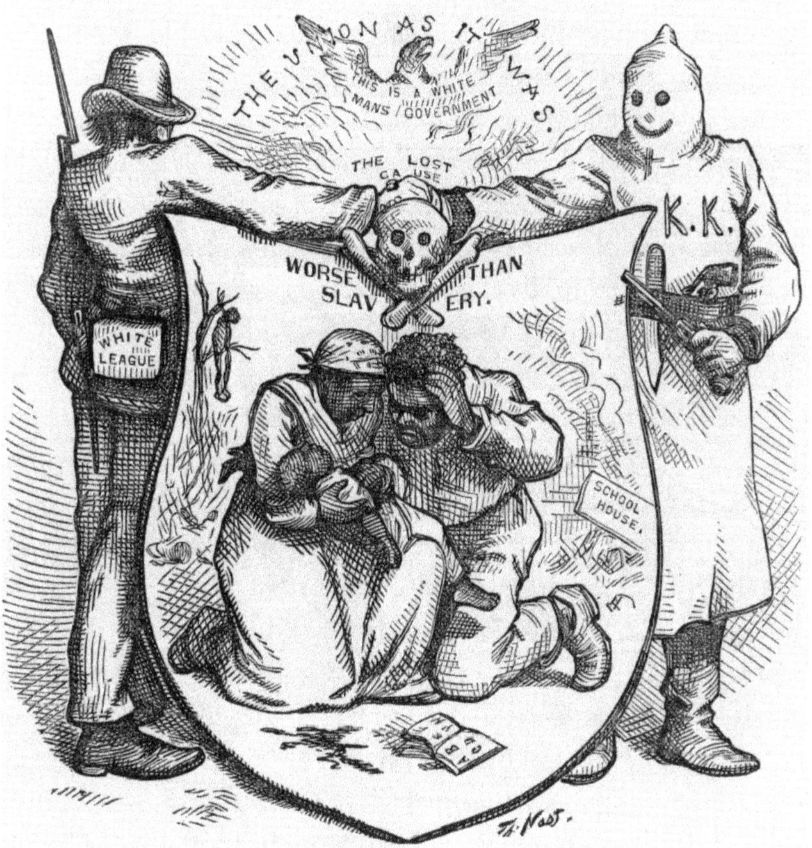

Organizations like the Ku Klux Klan, which formed in 1866, and the White Leagues of the 1870s used violence and murder to suppress the rights of African Americans and intimidate white Republicans. Courtesy of the Library of Congress Prints and Photographs Division.

round up thousands of Klansmen. A final measure, introduced by Senator Charles Sumner, was the Civil Rights Act of 1875, a law that guaranteed equal access to public accommodations, specifically inns, theaters, and places of public amusement, as well as transportation, including conveyances on land or water. It also prohibited the exclusion of citizens from jury duty on the basis of race, color, or previous condition of servitude. As a measure of suppressing discrimination, however, it was a weak one, naming any offenses under the act misdemeanors punishable by no more than a year's imprisonment. None of these measures proved successful in accomplishing their goals in the long run. Even the Civil Rights Act would be rendered ineffectual when the U.S. Supreme Court sustained its provisions regarding juries but ruled the guarantee of access to public accommodations unconstitutional in the *Civil Rights Cases* in 1883, concluding that Congress did not have the power to regulate private affairs.[36]

The progressive legislation implemented by the Republican governments had a major political drawback. Schools and railroads cost money. Public schools invariably segregated and were particularly costly because of the need for separate teachers, buildings, and administrations. Alabama spent nearly a million dollars in 1872 to educate a little more than 67,000 students, an amount equal to $14.51 per student. Louisiana, Arkansas's southern neighbor, spent more than a million dollars for 25,832 pupils, exceeding $46.00 per student. The Mississippi school system spent $780,339 in 1869 on 39,141 students. In Arkansas, the salaries of school teachers alone cost nearly $400,000 or approximately four dollars per student in 1869. By 1872 the schools had only 62,572 children and spent $681,962. These states had spent nothing on schools in the 1850s. Railroad funding was often in the form of bonds, instruments that technically indebted the state for the repayment of the bonds at some future time if the railroads did not pay the state. The increased cost of government could be seen in the rapid rise of state debts across the South. Florida's debt grew from $524,000 in 1868 to $5,621,000 in 1874. South Carolina's increased three fold from 1868 to 1871, from $5,403,000 to $15,768,000. Historian Kenneth Stampp suggested that the overall indebtedness of the Southern states increased by approximately $132,000,000 from the restoration of the Southern states to the Union to 1872.[37]

The cost of Republican economic and social programs forced state governments to search for revenue. Some states helped fund the expenses of their schools by requiring students to pay part of the cost. In Arkansas, for example, students paid $119,331 of the total $681,962 spent on schools. Inevitably, however, most of the cost fell on the state's taxpayers. This represented a political problem in states where tax levels had traditionally been low and most taxpayers were from the wealthier classes of whites. Mississippi's property tax rate increased fourteen hundred percent, from one to fourteen mills, between 1869 and 1874. South Carolina's tax rate doubled. That of Louisiana increased nearly four hundred percent. State governments looked to other sources of revenue as well, raising taxes on luxury items, occupations, and some businesses. Arkansas followed the general pattern. In 1868 the property tax was 1.425 percent of the assessed value of property, three times what had been levied by the previous General Assembly. County taxes allowed by the legislature were one and a half times the amount previously levied and the state also allowed municipalities to levy additional taxes. At the same time as taxes increased, state and local governments also raised the assessed value on property, creating even more problems for taxpayers unused to paying much in the way of taxes.[38]

Taxation provided Democrats and Conservatives in the South with a particularly powerful political tool to use against their opponents. Race had been useful in initial attacks on the Republicans, but after the Republican governments were in place, the opposition increasingly assailed the cost of Republican rule. Democratic and Conservative politicians joined with wealthy landowners and merchants in organizing taxpayers' conventions to condemn high taxes. South Carolinians held two conventions, the first in 1871 and the second in 1874. Louisianans formed the Tax Resisting Association in 1872. In Texas a taxpayers' convention in 1871 brought together Conservative Republicans and Democrats to criticize that state's expenditures. Republicans responded to these efforts by contending that the taxes were necessary for the state's growth, but their opponents argued that the expenses were unnecessary and resulted from bad government, appealing both to the racism of white voters and also to their feeling that they were not getting anything for the money they paid. The public schools were portrayed as a particularly egregious waste, mainly for their efforts at educating black children, and also for forming an expensive bureaucracy of teachers and administrators. The taxpayers undermined the legitimacy of government expenditures by alleging that many of them involved corruption on the part of Republican officials. There were enough such incidents to suggest the truth of such charges. In Arkansas, for example, a black politician allegedly was paid $9,000 for bridge repairs that should have cost $500. Still, relatively few proven incidents of corruption occurred and many of these were not uncommon to politics in the United States before the war and after Reconstruction.[39]

Factors such as violence, hostility to taxation, racism, and possibly, in the end, the absolute refusal of many whites to accept the new circumstances of the postwar South and particularly the aspirations of blacks in government and society ultimately began to bring down the Republican governments made possible by the intervention of Congress almost as quickly as they were in place. Of the ten organized under the congressional plan, only the governments in Florida, South Carolina, and Louisiana lasted for more than eight years. Victorious Democrats and Conservatives called the process of recapturing control of their state governments from Republicans "Redemption," and the Redemption process began as early as 1870 when factions within the Republican Party allowed Democrats to win control of the state legislature and governor's office in the first election after returning to the Union. The Radical Republicans also lost control of the state government in North Carolina that same year when Klan organizations suppressed the Republican vote enough to take back the state. In 1874 Democrats won both the legislature and governor's office in Alabama with the use of violence and intimidation to quash the Republican turnout. Mississippi Democrats ended the reconstruction process in the state in the election of 1875, using groups known as Red Shirts and White Leagues to keep Republican voters from the polls.[40]

The end of the Reconstruction era in two states, Texas and Arkansas, reflected another aspect of the fate of reconstruction in the South. After roughly eight years of intervention in Southern affairs, many Northerners had grown tired to the effort. The Grant administration also showed reluctance to intervene to support the faltering Republican governments. The point of reconstruction had not been just to restore the former Confederate states to the Union but also to secure the results of the war, particularly the establishment of a loyal federal government and the protection of the former slaves in their freedom. As one state after another fell into the hands of the Democratic

Party, however, the entire effort appeared fruitless. As early as 1867, Senator Carl Schurz had shown evidence of such disenchantment with efforts at protecting the freedmen and also a realization that a more radical solution was needed to secure Republican goals, writing, "There are many social disorders which it is very difficult to cure by law." In Texas, Democrats were swept into power in a general election in December 1873. The state Supreme Court subsequently ruled the election unconstitutional, but the newly elected Democratic legislature convened despite the ruling and then inaugurated their governor, despite the fact that the sitting governor, Edmund J. Davis, still had a claim to hold the office for several more months. Davis appealed to President Grant for troops to maintain the ruling of the court and force the Democrats to conform to the law. Grant refused, deciding that the question was too complicated to warrant intervention. The triumphant Democrats then forced Davis to abandon his office. Grant would act similarly in the Brooks-Baxter conflict in Arkansas, abandoning the regular Republican candidate in a disputed election with an opponent openly supported by the state's Democrats.[41]

No single factor satisfactorily explains the North's abandonment of the Republicans in the South, but a variety of forces appear to have influenced decision-making in Washington. Senator Schurz's realization that laws might not change conditions in the South certainly played a part. Historian James McPherson noted in his study of Reconstruction that the white North never had a strong commitment to black rights. Blacks secured their freedom and received suffrage in part as a result of the demands of the war and the immediate post-war years. Now many whites asked, what more should they receive? McPherson quoted the *Washington National Republican* to illustrate the disillusionment with the reconstruction process that had taken hold by the beginning of 1874. The editor wrote, "People are becoming tired of...abstract questions, in which the overwhelming majority of them have no direct interest. The negro question, with all its complications, and the reconstruction of the Southern States, with all its interminable embroilments, have lost much of the power they once wielded."

In addition, the presidential election in 1872 forced President Grant to confront a revolt within his own party. Liberal Republicans, seeking a coalition with moderate Democrats, proposed ending future national incursions into the South in return for the white South's acceptance of the Fourteenth and Fifteenth Amendments. The Liberals' party platform, even though it pledged support for securing the equality of all men before the law, also supported a return to local self-government and an end to the supplanting of civil authority by the military, a practical invitation to the white Democrats of the South to do what they wanted to regain power.

Further, national attention was refocused from wartime issues to a growing economy, increasing labor unrest. Then in 1873 an economic panic of worldwide proportions emerged in the United States due to the failure of Jay Cooke & Company and other banking firms that had over-invested in railroad construction. The failure of the banks led to other business failure, with thousands of businesses declaring bankruptcy by 1876. Eighty-nine railroads declared bankruptcy. National unemployment reached fourteen percent. The panic also helped Democrats secure control of the House of Representatives in the 1874 elections, which promised to reverse President Grant's monetary policies, making any further intervention in the South difficult if not impossible. Such conditions hardly promoted much concern in

Washington or elsewhere in the North for the plight of black and white Republicans in the South.[42]

The shifting interests among Northern politicians and their constituents established the framework within which the last stages of Reconstruction would be played out in Louisiana, South Carolina, and Florida. Political struggles in Louisiana had been a recurring problem that further worsened in 1872 following an election in which both Republicans and Democrats claimed victory. Two legislatures met, and the assemblies inaugurated two different governors: the Republican, William P. Kellogg, and the Democrat, John McEnery. Both sides appealed to the courts to decide who won, but when the courts found in favor of Kellogg, the Democrats still refused to accept the results. The Democrats maintained their own government and organized what came to be known as White Leagues to support their claims with violence: assassination of Republican leaders and black voters. On April 13, 1873, one of the worst confrontations took place in Colfax, Louisiana, when a black militia unit sent into the area to suppress the White League clashed with the league, with the result that at least a hundred men in the black militia were killed. In August 1874, at least six white Republicans and up to twenty blacks were killed in the Coushatta Massacre. The following September, the White League attacked the state militia and city police in a battle later memorialized as the Battle of Liberty Place. In 1876, only the presence of federal troops in New Orleans kept the Republican government in place. Federal troops also surrounded the statehouse in South Carolina, where Republican governor Daniel H. Chamberlain held on to the governor's office, claiming victory against former Confederate general Wade Hampton because of the fraud, violence, and intimidation that had been used by Hampton's supporters in the election.[43]

The Democrat-aligned White League attacked the state militia and city police in New Orleans in an altercation later sensationalized as the Battle of Liberty Place on September 14, 1874, after an election much like the one that led to Arkansas's Brooks-Baxter War. "Battle of Liberty Place," Louisiana Image Collection, Louisiana Research Collection, Tulane University.

The violence aimed at Republican governments in the South made it clear that they could be maintained only with the use of force. In Washington, for all the reasons already noted, the use of troops had lost its support. President Grant's intervention in Louisiana met widespread disapproval by 1875. Congress considered new legislation to protect citizens in their civil and legal rights by insisting on their equal access to public facilities and to seats on juries with the Civil Rights Act of 1875, but the final bill provided no means for its enforcement. An enforcement act stalled in Congress. In 1876 Republicans ran a candidate, Rutherford B. Hayes, who had assured a friend in Texas that, toward the South, "nothing but good will now exists" and that the policy he pursued was one of "let alone." Within this context, when a Democratic candidate's supporters used what was by now the well-tried formula of economic coercion and intimidation to defeat the Republican gubernatorial candidate, no appeal to Washington was made. Florida passed quietly into the hands of the Redeemer Democrats. After securing office in a disputed election, Hayes indicated there would be no more use of force to protect Republican governments in the South and he ordered the federal troops protecting Kellogg and Chamberlain back to the barracks, allowing the Redemption of Louisiana and South Carolina. The withdrawal of the troops effectively brought an end to the process of reconstruction.[44]

The era of Reconstruction ended leaving much of what it was intended to accomplish unfulfilled. With inadequate protection from the federal government and the collapse of Republican governments in the South, African American citizens were relegated to second-class citizenship, subordinated to whites in every aspect of life from economics to education. Historians almost universally see this era as one marked by potential to reshape race and even class relations in the South. In the end, however, too many factors conspired to bring about failure. William Gillette, a student of the end of Reconstruction, observed that Northern efforts had never truly reconstructed or reformed the South. In most respects the white South remained unchanged and the South was more "attached to, than severed from, the past." John Hope Franklin, the dean of African American historians, described the era as one in which both North and South suffered an "ignoble defeat." The Union had been preserved and slavery abolished as a result of the war, but the Union had "not made the achievements of the war a foundation for the healthy advancement of the political, social, and economic life of the United States." The failure to maintain the positive accomplishments of the reconstruction process left the nation faced with much undone business. Eric Foner noted that a century would lapse before the people of the United States would try again to "come to terms with the implications of emancipation and the political and social agenda of Reconstruction." He observed that, "In many ways, it has yet to do so," which remains as true today as when he wrote those words in 1988.[45]

Winthrop Rockefeller in 1966 became the first Republican to win Arkansas's governorship since Reconstruction ended in 1874, breaking a run of Democratic dominance that was fueled in part by the state's political memory of the post–Civil War era. Courtesy of the Arkansas Secretary of State's Office.

Chapter 2: An (Un)Exceptional Moment: The Politics of Reconstruction-Era Arkansas

By Jay Barth

For most of the years since its conclusion, a relatively simple story has been advanced regarding electoral politics in Arkansas during the Reconstruction era. In the most basic terms, the Reconstruction era is portrayed as a period of unique and thorough Republican electoral dominance. Following on this, the phrase "for the first time since Reconstruction" has been regularly employed to describe every new Republican Party success in Arkansas beginning with Winthrop Rockefeller's election as governor in 1966. Attached to this portrayal of GOP partisan dominance during Reconstruction is a consistent description of abuse of white Arkansas natives in the policies carried out by those empowered Republicans. The Arkansas history textbook from which the youth of Arkansas learned about Reconstruction for decades described Reconstruction as an era in which "carpetbaggers…stirred up trouble between the whites and the negroes… to advance their own selfish interests."[1] "The government in their hands was hurtful; for many of the officials were dishonest and extravagant," summed up John Hugh Reynolds about this distinctive period in Arkansas history in *Makers of Arkansas History*.[2]

Instead, as clearly shown in the rest of this volume, all things regarding the Reconstruction era in Arkansas are decidedly more complex than their traditional portrayal. In contrast with historians of the past such as Reynolds, more-contemporary historians, including those whose work is found elsewhere in this collection, have developed a richer, more nuanced, and more progressive understanding of the events of Reconstruction era in the state. In addition, the true picture of electoral politics in the aftermath of the Civil War in Arkansas is itself more complicated than traditionally portrayed in various respects.

To be certain, during the Reconstruction era, those identifying as some brand of Republican did win most of the elections for national and state office in Arkansas. That said, this success was fleeting. By the most generous of descriptions, the period of true GOP electoral dominance totaled eight years. Second, in federal races in particular, Republican victories were less overwhelming than is typically portrayed.

What is clear, however, is that ongoing, shifting factionalism within the majority party was the most important dynamic in elections during this period and, because of the chaos created through the Brooks-Baxter conflict in which electoral factionalism morphed into physical violence, a constitutional structure that promoted a culture of sharply limited government was established in the state as Arkansas ended Reconstruction. As a result, the Reconstruction era simply reflects the norm in Arkansas electoral politics across time. Before statehood, factionalism within the dominant Democratic Party was the key story in Arkansas politics. During one-party Democratic rule that returned following disenfranchisement of African Americans in the 1890s, a more fleeting factionalism defined by "friends and neighbors" voting was the driver of the state's messy election outcomes before more stable patterns of division in the Democratic Party emerged in the middle of the last century.[3] Finally, in the new era of Republican control of the state's politics in the 2010s, sharpening factionalism is increasingly the defining force in Arkansas elections. Thus, in this key respect, this "exceptional" period was quite "unexceptional" when it comes to electoral dynamics when viewed in the frame of the electoral history of the state from before statehood to the present.

A Brief Overview of Reconstruction-Era Electoral Dynamics

The electoral history of the Reconstruction era in Arkansas spans just over a decade, beginning with the March 1864 state constitutional ratification election and ending with the election ratifying a very different constitution in October 1874. Across that period, numerous elections took place, often including more than one major statewide election per year. This flurry of elections presents challenges for those wanting to present systematic analyses of electoral patterns, as the results are often contradictory. Moreover, the constant change in the composition of the electorate, often driven by the dynamics of state-federal relations, enhances this messiness, making the electoral period challenging to analyze in any systematic fashion. Finally, many of the key tools used by political scientists in such work—such as reliable county-level election data—are often missing or of dubious reliability, undermining the credibility of the analysis. While the period was "confused and confusing" as a result of these forces, it is possible to see some important trends in this decade of elections in Arkansas.

An Ever-Changing Electorate

Since who is actually casting votes is highly determinative of the ultimate results, the fact that the Arkansas electorate changed constantly and severely across this period is central to this puzzlement. These alterations of the electorate were driven mostly—but not entirely—by the shifting levels of engagement by the federal government in the South, including Arkansas. In the first key vote of this period, the 1864 Constitution was ratified by a thoroughly nonrepresentative electorate in the state. The Confederacy still controlled the southern portion of Arkansas, and the new constitution was voted on only in those portions of the state that had returned to Union control by that time. Only about 17,000 votes were cast on the measure and, indicative of the composition of the electorate, only approximately 200 votes opposed the new measure.[4]

Upon entering office, the new state government operating under the 1864 Constitution immediately passed a new "loyalty oath" for voters that required any Arkansas voter to swear that he had not supported the Confederacy after March 1864.[5] That constraint—termed the Iron Clad Oath—reduced turnout rates mightily in 1865; only approximately 6,500 votes were cast in the congressional elections. Late in 1865, however, the oath was struck down by the state Supreme Court in *Rison et al. v. Farr*. The court determined that the oath added a qualification to be a voter that was not found in the current state constitution.[6]

This key court decision significantly altered the dynamics for the 1866 elections as Confederate sympathizers swept back into the electorate to participate in that year's local and statewide elections. (The exact size of the electorate is not shown in the records maintained by the Arkansas Secretary of State, however.) Among the Old Guard, only three statewide elected officials not up for reelection until 1868—Unionist governor Isaac Murphy and Republicans in the roles of lieutenant governor (Calvin C. Bliss) and secretary of state (Robert J. T. White)—remained in power.

Once back in power, the Conservatives in the legislature passed a bevy of legislation that favored the traditional economic and social elites of the state. After several months, however, the game was quickly altered as a result of the legislature's emphatic rejection of the Fourteenth Amendment to the U.S. Constitution. This action in several Southern state legislatures, including Arkansas's, provoked a period of so-called "Congressional Reconstruction," a radicalization of federal policy toward the South.

In Arkansas, what was termed Congressional Reconstruction meant reinstatement of the Iron Clad Oath by federal law and its implementation by the military officials of the Fourth Military District. Under the federal statute, military officials—in Arkansas's case, led by General E. O. C. Ord—had the ultimate power to determine who could participate in state elections. Most relevantly, Ord determined participation in an election that would determine whether a fundamental overhaul of the state's constitution should occur.

In November 1867, 41,000 voters participated in a vote to determine whether a state constitutional convention should take place. Approximately two in three of those voters concurred in approving a convention. That convention, which took place in 1868, was dominated by Radical Republicans and, with eight African Americans serving as delegates, was biracial; this led to its being termed the "black and tan" convention. Written swiftly, the 1868 Constitution changed state government significantly by expanding gubernatorial powers markedly, establishing the first public education system in the state and redistricting the legislature in a manner that favored the Delta and southwestern

Arkansas, thus enhancing African American political power. Most relevantly, the constitution explicitly denied suffrage to those who had been disloyal or had "violated the rules of civilized warfare" during the Civil War.[7]

Major General E. O. C. Ord, commander of the Department of Arkansas and the Fourth Military District during Reconstruction, had the authority to determine who could vote in Arkansas elections. Courtesy of the Library of Congress Prints and Photographs Division.

The ratification vote on the new constitution was rushed to the state's voters in mid-March 1868 to take place alongside congressional and state elections. This new constitution was easily ratified, and Republicans were elected in the accompanying races with only token opposition. This number included several African Americans, including the first elected to the state legislature.[8] Most importantly, Republican Powell Clayton was elected governor in a system in which the individual serving in that role had elevated power over policymaking in the state. This elite power extended to control of voting processes in the state.

On occasion, Clayton used his powers assertively. For example, he was praised for successfully tamping down Ku Klux

Klan activity in the state, going so far as to place up to fourteen counties at one time under martial law to ensure the safety of African Americans, including protecting their right to participate in the electoral system. Clayton's controversial heavy-handedness clearly left white Confederate sympathizers—still mostly disenfranchised—bitter at the governor and his political party.

With over 20,000 African American voters newly registered, in 1868 Republican presidential candidate Ulysses Grant won the largest percentage of the two-party vote for a Republican presidential candidate (just under 54 percent) to that point, a record that would hold until Richard Nixon's dominant performance in 1972. Relatedly, the total electorate shrunk to 41,190 in the fall 1868 election. The shrinking of the electorate was driven by a combination of the new strictures on participation by white Confederate loyalists and by race-based political violence that Governor Clayton worked hard to stamp out.

Even with these advantages in the composition of the electorate, however, the 1868 GOP victory was not a landslide, especially when considering the deep conservatism of the national Democratic Party challenging Grant's GOP. The Democratic Party's national platform called for the "[i]mmediate restoration of all the States to their rights of the Union" and "[a]mnesty for all past political offenses, and the regulation of the elective franchise in the States, by their citizens." Moreover, it stated:

> Upon this platform the Democratic party appeals to every patriot, including all the Conservative element, and all who desire to support the Constitution and restore the Union, forgetting all past differences of opinion, to unite with us in the present great struggle for the liberties of the people; and that to all such, to whatever party they may have heretofore belonged, we extend the right hand of fellowship, and hail all such co-operating with us as friends and brethren.[9]

As shown in Figure 1, Grant ran up margins in the Ozarks, whose residents had objected to Arkansas's secession in the first place, the heavily African American Delta counties, and around the state capital of Little Rock. His Democratic opponent, New Yorker Horatio Seymour, overperformed in the southern and northeastern portions of the state.[10]

Four years later, Grant won the popular vote in Arkansas again, with just over 52 percent of the vote. The electorate in the state nearly doubled as compared to 1868—to just short of 80,000 votes. While much of the map of county-level returns shown in Figure 2 looks similar to 1868, Grant's vote share dropped significantly in northwestern Arkansas and in some southern counties with many shifting against the GOP nominee. While most official records of the 1872 election indicate a Grant victory in the state, Arkansas's electoral votes were not included in his national vote

Figure 1. 1868 Presidential Election

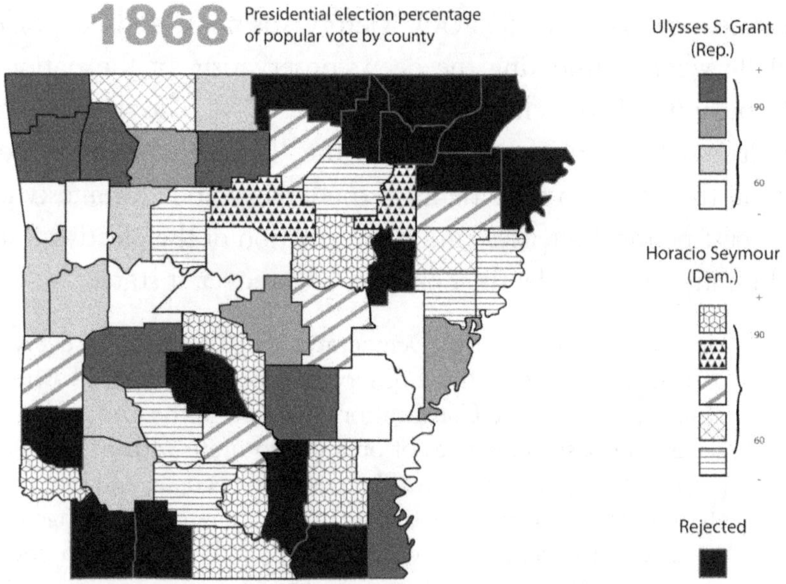

Map by Sarah Wells, Department of Arkansas Heritage

Figure 2. 1872 Presidential Election

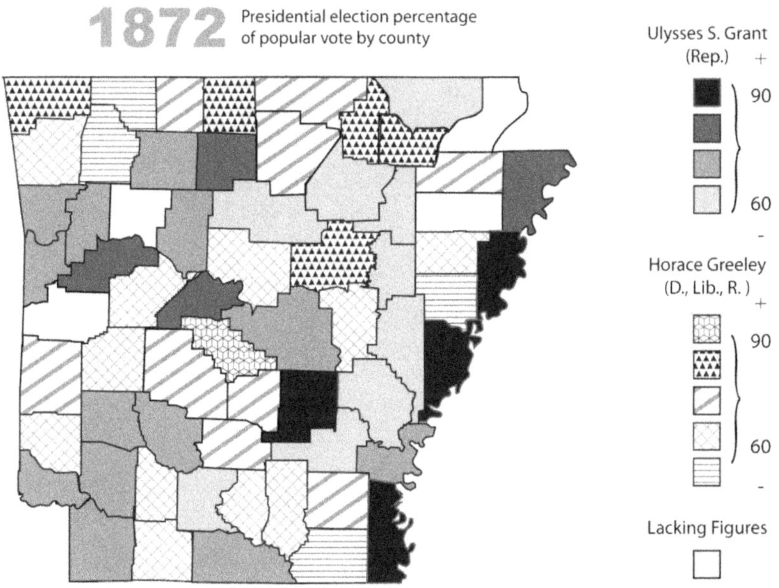

Map by Sarah Wells, Department of Arkansas Heritage

because of the U.S. Senate's questioning of the accuracy of the vote count in the Republican-controlled state.[11] No matter, at least in federal elections, the accepted notion that Republicans totally dominated the outcomes of elections in Arkansas is overstated.

Malleable Party Labels and the Rise of Factionalism

Across this period, not only were the size and composition of the Arkansas electorate shifting consistently, but the labels by which candidates for office advertised themselves to voters were also regularly changing, creating confusion for the voters—and for those whose job it is to analyze the elections 150 years later. While the label "Democrats" disappeared from the ballot immediately after Arkansas's return to the Union, former Democrats and Whigs did put together a slate of candidates for the state legislature in 1865 who identified themselves as "Conservatives."

Powell Clayton, shown here in his Civil War uniform, led the "Minstrel" faction of the Arkansas Republican Party and clashed with both the "Brindletail" faction and the former Confederates who sought a return to power in the state. Courtesy of Wilson's Creek National Battlefield.

The real electoral action, however, was in the Republican Party. After the rise of Governor Powell Clayton, his "Regular" Republicans (often called "Minstrels") faced opposition from "Liberal" Republicans (who went by the nickname "Brindletails"). This factional divide was generally non-ideological, in dramatic contrast to the very real ideological division between "Radical" Republicans and "Mainliners" exhibited in the debates in the halls of Congress. Although there were some patterns of support based on whether one was a native or non-native of the state, what divided the Arkansas Republican factions even more than that was personality, as adherents to each faction showed allegiance to their factional leaders. The factions, however, generally lacked any real policy differences.

The election of 1872 and the subsequent events that erupted ultimately into the Brooks-Baxter War marked the high point of this factionalism. In this battle to succeed Clayton as governor, Arkansas native Elisha Baxter represented the Regular Republicans and carpetbagger Joseph Brooks represented the Brindletails (which were by now a convoluted fusion of the

Liberal Republicans and the Democrats).[12] Baxter won a close election at the ballot box. The Secretary of State's *Historical Report* shows a 41,808 to 38,909 win for Baxter over Brooks (who is described as a "Democrat" in that official record). However, like many of the era, it was an election in which widespread irregularities were charged.

Baxter tried to calm the waters by committing to lead a period of "peace and good feeling" in the state in his early 1873 inaugural address. This spirit of reunification was symbolized by a state constitutional amendment put forward soon after the inauguration in March 1873 that removed limitations to the vote on former Confederates (making Arkansas the last Southern state to take such a step). Despite this, the Brooks forces did not give up the fight regarding what they considered the impropriety of the

The contested race for Arkansas's governor in 1872 ended with armed conflict in the state's capital city until President Grant ultimately decided that Elisha Baxter was the rightful chief executive. This illustration shows reinforcements crossing the Arkansas River to bolster Joseph Brooks's supporters at the capitol. Courtesy of the UA Little Rock Center for Arkansas History and Culture.

election outcome. A series of legislative appeals and court actions preceded the physical violence that ultimately became known as the Brooks-Baxter War, the most confusing event of a most confusing era in Arkansas history. (Thomas A. DeBlack describes these happenings in detail in Chapter 4 in this collection.)

The conflict was ultimately decided in Washington DC, with President Grant abiding by the judgment by Attorney General George H. Williams that Baxter was the rightful governor of the state. This action unofficially ended the Reconstruction era—and Republican electoral advantage—in the state. By that point in the process, Arkansans were less invested in the winner of the governorship than in the arrival of genuine "peace and good feeling" in the state. As Lee County sheriff W. H. Forbush wrote in a telegram to President Grant: "We do not care—and I speak the sentiments of the people of Arkansas without egotism—who is governor: All we want is peace."[13]

The way in which the Brooks-Baxter conflict ended Reconstruction in Arkansas was crucial in shaping Arkansas government for the century that followed. Specifically, it helped to create a severe bent toward a "do-little" government in the state of Arkansas and, over time, played a part in forging a political culture among Arkansans in which little was expected of government. This culture defined the state until the modern era.

The Constitution of 1874 and Its Aftermath

American Political Development (APD) is an analytical framework in political science that argues that America's institutions, not its ideology, explain the distinctive shape of the country's political outcomes. Moreover, it posits that these key institutions were shaped at "magic moments" often driven by the peculiarities of the time at which they were created. Such institutions then shape and truncate the policy decisions of later times. Because understanding these key moments in the past is so crucial, historical methodology is employed to understand the policy outcomes of today.[14] The events surrounding the Brooks-Baxter War emphatically influenced the nature of the Constitution of 1874 that followed quickly on its heels and therefore were crucial in shaping modern political inactivity in the state. While Arkansas's state government has become decidedly more activist in recent generations, it has done so while still shackled by the confines of the 1874 Constitution.

After the Brooks-Baxter factional conflict was resolved, the biggest winners in the state's politics were the re-enfranchised Redeemers who quickly returned to power at a moment when the perceived abuses of the Clayton governorship were fresh in the minds of Arkansas voters returning to the ballot box, driving their initial political actions. One of the Redeemers' first acts was to promulgate a new constitution. Just weeks after the end of the violence, well over 90 percent of voters in the state supported a constitutional convention. Showing their disempowered condition—partly manifested by their own divisions—less than a quarter of the delegates to the convention were Republicans. Within just a few months, the new document was easily passed by 76 percent of the state's electorate in October of 1874.

A pervasive distrust of government is expressed in almost every section of the 1874 document. To ensure popular control over officialdom, many offices previously appointive became elective, and terms were almost uniformly reduced from four to two years, giving voters, according to one estimate, forty-four rather than fourteen opportunities to exercise their electoral control in any four-year period. Formal gubernatorial powers were sharply reduced, including the fact that a simple majority of the legislature could overturn a veto. To prevent excessive and unwise lawmaking, the legislature was limited to one sixty-day session every other year. Maximum salaries for all state and county officials were specified and fixed. Elaborate statutory details on everything from the conduct of elections to the times and places of circuit court meetings and the procedures for letting state printing contracts were included to leave little leeway to any state official tempted to abuse his powers. Above all, the taxing and spending powers were circumscribed with every prohibitive device imaginable. Sixty-nine of the 261 sections of the original 1874 constitution dealt with financial matters, and most in a restrictive way: local governments were severely limited in their taxing powers, state tax and appropriations measures required extraordinary majorities, and there could be no extension of credit or assumption of debt for any purposes whatsoever. Finally, the 1874 Constitution was specifically designed to protect citizens from possible oppression by their own state government, with many of the duties previously held by state government transferred to the counties.[15]

To be fair, this negative and restrictive document reflects also the basic socioeconomic conditions of Arkansas in the 1870s. The state was relatively small (with a population of less than 500,000) and overwhelmingly rural (over 95 percent), and most of the people lived in impoverished circumstances. The state government spent only $320,000 in the fiscal year 1874–75, so a sixty-day biennial session might well have seemed adequate for determining allocation of the few state services offered. Fearing the rising tides of tenancy and economic dependency, it made sense to guarantee the people exemption from seizure of their homesteads and to specify a maximum interest rate of two percent on private loans. However, the social and economic context alone did not drive this document's form. Instead, revulsion against the perceived excesses of Reconstruction—and the Clayton governorship in particular—and the chaos exemplified in the Brooks-Baxter conflict were also at work in this important institution's creation.

Despite a flurry of constitutional amendments, which have not only created a more flexible document but also lengthened the already long document, many of the problems of the original document persist in limiting the effectiveness of state government in the present day to respond to the needs of the people of the state. The continuation of long, "bedsheet" ballots (seven separately elected state executive officials, as many as nine county executive officials, plus all state and local legislators and judges) constantly asks voters to fill offices whose functions are obscure with individuals whose qualifications are unknown—an open invitation to trouble. "Chief" executives find their administrative authority diminished by a host of separately elected executive officials (often potential political rivals). Because of the time restrictions on legislative sessions, grievous errors inevitably occur, and the requirement of a three-fourths majority for passage of appropriation measures gives obstructionist minorities golden opportunities for legislative mischief. But, more important, they interfere with Arkansas's government's ability to successfully deal with the issues facing the state's citizens in a comprehensive manner. The historically underfunded educational system of Arkansas, for example, was further harmed by the inability to raise the revenues at the state or local levels, and the ban on the state going into debt except through a vote of the people led to a "pay as you go" approach to transportation in a poor state. In 1949, the Chrysler automobile company touted its cars by celebrating that they had passed the "Arkansas Mud Test."

Even more crucial, as proponents of the historical institutionalist approach argue, such institutional arrangements begin to shape the cultural norms of the place: in this case, they truncated for generations Arkansans' notions of what is possible and what is appropriate for their government to do. Those institutional limitations began to seep deeply into the political culture of Arkansas, creating an assumption that government—and, by extension, the elections that placed governmental officials in power—just did not matter.

More immediately, however, the reentrance of white Confederate sympathizers into the state's elections shifted the balance of power in the Democrats' direction. In the fall elections in 1874, Democrat Augustus Garland was elected governor without opposition and Republicans were obliterated in legislative races (aside from a few pockets of the state). Until the populist revolt in the mid-1880s, Democrats again became dominant in all state elections. The rise of the Redeemer class in politics in a revitalized Democratic Party was shown not just in state elections but also in the presidential election of 1876. President Grant's success in 1868 and 1872 in the state was significantly reversed when Rutherford B. Hayes carried the GOP torch in 1876. Then, Democrat Samuel J. Tilden gained 59.9 percent of the state's popular vote (in an electorate that grew to 96,946, an increase of over 20 percent from 1872). As shown in Figure 3, only the counties of the Delta, Pulaski County (Little Rock), and a scattering of counties in southwestern Arkansas and deep in the Ozarks remained loyal to the Republicans. The disenfranchisement of African Americans through election "reforms" in the early 1890s would further reduce the GOP to an Ozarks-only party until the middle of the twentieth century.

Figure 3. 1876 Presidential Election

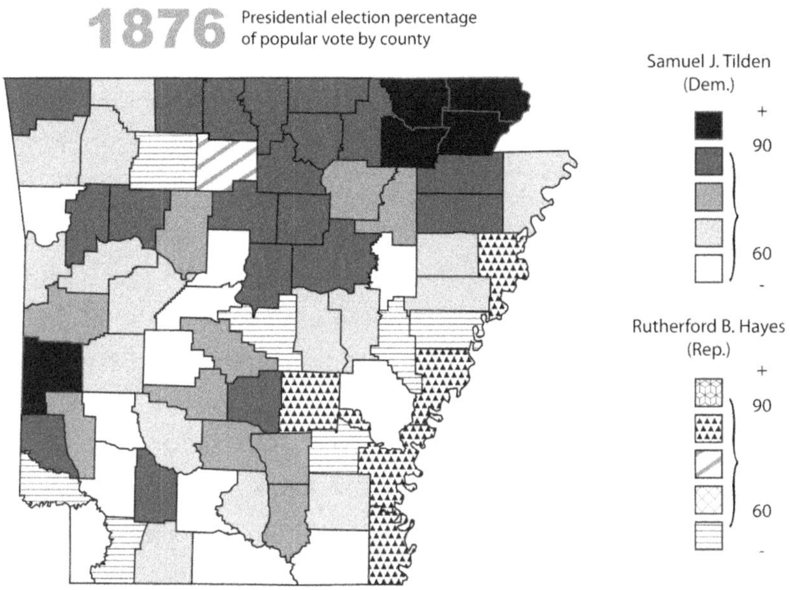

Map by Sarah Wells, Department of Arkansas Heritage

Reconstructing Reconstruction: The Dunning School

While this chapter and other pieces in this collection focus on the complicated story that was the Reconstruction period in Arkansas, at the time, it became crucial for newly empowered Conservative Democrats to develop and maintain a much simpler story: during Reconstruction, self-interested so-called carpetbaggers and scalawags manipulated ill-prepared black voters to ensure Republican domination in the state. Hence, the party, particularly an out-of-control central government, abused the rights and liberties of hardworking Arkansans.

Like Democrats across the region, Arkansas's Conservative Democrats had an unlikely ally in their efforts: the history profession—in particular, Columbia University professor William A. Dunning, who collaborated with a large cadre of his graduate students (mostly native white Southerners) to propagate the initial historical account of Reconstruction's role in American history.[16] In a series of documents, including analyses of the Reconstruction experience in each of the Southern states, the Dunning School scholars chronicled the utter failing of Reconstruction. At the heart of their worldview was the assumption that the granting of political and social rights to newly freed slaves was the fatal mistake, bringing "on the South an orgy of corruption of misgovernment," in the words of revisionist Reconstruction scholar Eric Foner.[17] Foner argued that "the writings of the Dunning School did more than reflect prevailing prejudices—they strengthened and helped perpetuate them."[18]

The Dunning School's Arkansas contributor was Thomas Starling Staples, who came to Hendrix College to teach history following his graduate work under Dunning's tutelage. Just after Dunning's death in 1922, Staples published *Reconstruction in Arkansas, 1862–1874*. In it, Staples tells the story of a Republican Party in Arkansas that was "a highly centralized organization, composed of three distinct elements, no one of which was representative of the intelligent tax-paying part of the population, and dominated by a single mind."[19] Those three elements, of course, were enfranchised African Americans, carpetbaggers, and scalawags, and the "single mind" was, of course, Governor Powell Clayton. Staples's work then chronicles the abuses of Clayton's martial law, his manipulation of the electoral systems in the state, and his government's heavy taxation rates with small benefits to the people in return. As Staples concluded the work: "Reconstruction and its first fruits were now in the past, and it was not yet revealed how long the people of Arkansas were to suffer from the years of Republican rule through which they had passed."[20]

Perhaps even more important than Staples's academic work, which few Arkansans actually read, were those textbooks from which thousands of Arkansans learned about Reconstruction for decades. This included *Makers of Arkansas History* by John Hugh Reynolds, one of the first Arkansas history textbooks available, which was first published in 1905 while Reynolds was teaching at the University of Arkansas (he would later join Staples at Hendrix College as president of the institution for over three decades). The textbook then went through two additional editions, the last in 1918. Reynolds's work portrays an even more cartoonish version of Reconstruction-era Republicanism. While Governor Clayton is described as a war hero with "great ability as a political leader," the political dynamic that Clayton was key to driving is portrayed quite differently:

> [The carpetbaggers] soon acquired a strong influence over the negro, who, on account of his ignorance, was easily duped. The carpet-baggers told him that they had come from the North, that they had freed him from bondage, and that they were going to see that he got justice. But most of these people were not the negro's friends, they were simply using him to advance their own selfish interests. They stirred up trouble between the whites and the negroes. The former slave was made to believe that his master had wronged him. He was told that the government was going to take his master's land, and that it would give to every negro a mule and forty acres of land. These promises spoiled the negro; for they made him impudent and idle. He turned to petty stealing for a livelihood. It was very unfortunate that Arkansas should have fallen into the hands of the carpetbaggers...

Even more problematic was Reynolds's racist justification for the rise of the Ku Klux Klan:

> If a negro gave any trouble by his impudence, idleness, or thieving, he was visited by the Klan, flogged, and warned of a worse punishment if the offense were repeated. Sometimes an obnoxious carpet-bagger was called upon and whipped. He was ordered to do right or to leave the country. Such visits were

> always made at night, and the men were always disguised. These steps were taken by the whites for the purpose of stopping many of the evils from which they were suffering.

Through the writings of Staples and Reynolds, Reconstruction's perceived evils became established truth in the minds of Arkansans, a view that was reinforced by portrayals of the Reconstruction era in popular books and films. Most important of these, of course, was the cinematically groundbreaking silent film *Birth of a Nation* (1915), an adaptation of the novel *The Clansman*.[21]

The Unexceptionalism of the Reconstruction Era

This telling of Arkansas's Reconstruction experience continued to impact electoral politics in Arkansas in the decades that followed. The brutality of the Republican rule during Reconstruction was regularly employed rhetorically by Conservative Democrats as a warning against white Arkansans' being tempted by populism, as a justification for election reforms that would disenfranchise many Arkansans, and as a cudgel that smacked down any efforts at Republican rebirth in the state for the generations that followed.

In this respect, Reconstruction was an era that had an ongoing exceptional impact on politics. However, it is also important to note the ways in which the electoral dynamics during Reconstruction in the state—a politics defined by factional divides within the majority party—were actually quite typical of those found in other periods of Arkansas's political history. With only a few inflections of genuine partisan conflict, factionalism has been the defining dynamic in Arkansas politics across time. Debates over public policy have rarely been between closely matched political parties; instead, the defining forces in those disputes have been factions within political parties.

With the revival of Redeemers following Reconstruction, of course, those meaningful factions came to exist within the Democratic Party. V. O. Key, the chronicler of Southern politics at the middle of the past century, argued that "fluid" factions defined the politics of the "pure one-party politics" of Arkansas. These "transient and amorphous" factions within the state's Democratic Party were typically tied to potent personalities rather than anything that smacked of ideological coherence. As Key wrote: "Whether Arkansas' fluid factionalism or its issueless politics came first, or whether each feeds on the other, the upshot is a politics singularly free of anything save the petty argument and personal loyalty of the moment."[22] Because Arkansas remained overwhelmingly Democratic later than any other state in the South, factionalism continued to dominate in the state, although, over time, a more coherent conflict between "modernizers" (who supported educational advancement and civil rights) and "traditionalists" (resistant to such change) began to emerge.[23]

Political scientist V. O. Key observed of Arkansas politics: "Whether Arkansas' fluid factionalism or its issueless politics came first, or whether each feeds on the other, the upshot is a politics singularly free of anything save the petty argument and personal loyalty of the moment." Courtesy of Ferdinand Hamburger Archives, Sheridan Libraries, Johns Hopkins University.

During Barack Obama's presidency, Democrats' stark advantages in Arkansas electoral politics faded and—for several legislative sessions—the two parties were closely matched in the state electoral and legislative arenas. The result was a unique period in which partisanship drove debates, as members of the Democratic and Republicans legislative caucuses rarely veered across partisan lines on major issues. Thanks to the GOP's supermajority status in both houses of the General Assembly following the 2016 election, however, factionalism within the Republican Party is again the most important force in Arkansas's public policy debates, with the current important factional divide being one between the GOP establishment and the conservative populists.[24]

The present-day establishment, led by Governor Asa Hutchinson, practices a form of "do no harm" conservatism that follows the traditional rules of the game in carrying out the duties of government. Although the establishment is certainly conservative on social issues, for instance, it becomes deeply concerned when proposals such as anti-immigrant or anti-LGBT legislation threaten the business climate in the state. In this climate, populists see themselves as activists rather than party loyalists. Indeed, some populists are actually fairly recent converts to Republicanism. This faction is impatient and wants to get immediate results on its priority issues, such as gun deregulation or religious freedom, even if it means blowing up the traditional norms of how government operates. The divide takes on a clear geographical dimension as the establishment hails primarily from the suburban areas of central and northwestern Arkansas while the populists are primarily rural in their origins. The populists see the establishment as privileged and elitist, and the establishment views the populists as reckless amateurs not ready for prime time. Because of the GOP's dominance in the state, all signs are that this party division will be the key political battle in the state in the coming years, and those Republicans who find a way to bridge it will have distinctive power.

The GOP factionalism of the Reconstruction era that ultimately led to armed conflict on the streets of Little Rock is indeed exceptional in the state's history, and the chaos of that period, particularly the Brooks-Baxter War, helped usher in a new constitution that has continued to constrain government in the state since 1874. However, the personality-based factionalism at work in Arkansas politics in that period is, indeed, quite normal when we think about Reconstruction in the context of Arkansas's electoral patterns across time.

In 1885, more than a decade after Reconstruction ended, seven African American legislators served in the Arkansas House, though none served in the Senate during the session. The men were farmers, teachers, ministers, and lawyers, and they represented cotton-producing counties in the east—Jefferson, Desha, Mississippi, Chicot, and Lincoln—and the southwest—Lafayette. Courtesy of the Old State House Museum, Little Rock, Arkansas.

Chapter 3: African American Legislators in the Arkansas General Assembly, 1868–1893: Another Look

By Blake Wintory

In 1860, a total of 111,115 men, women, and children of African descent in Arkansas were held in bondage. By the end of the decade, the Civil War and Reconstruction had transformed these chattel slaves into free citizens. This upheaval and reordering of the social and political order would eventually include black male suffrage. This new order also led to the election of African American officeholders to local and state offices. By 1893, eighty-six African American men had been elected to the Arkansas General Assembly.

A diverse group of former slaves and freeborn men, Arkansas's African American legislators were community leaders, farmers, merchants, and ministers who represented rural and urban areas. To aid researchers, two rosters have been assembled from primary sources and secondary works: a chronological listing of African American legislators in the Arkansas General

Assembly between Reconstruction and disenfranchisement (tables 1 and 2) and a biographical data set on them (table 3).[1]

Under Congressional Reconstruction, citizenship and voting rights for former slaves began to take shape with the passage of the Reconstruction Acts in March 1867. In May, Brevet Major General Edward O. C. Ord ordered the registration of eligible voters in the Fourth Military District of Arkansas. A total of 21,696 black men were added to the state's rolls. Voters then elected eight black men to the constitutional convention held in January 1868.[2] As a condition of the state's re-entering the Union, Arkansas's new constitution included black male suffrage. Ratification of the Fifteenth Amendment to the U.S. Constitution on February 3, 1870, solidified suffrage for black men, allowing citizens to vote without regard to "race, color, or previous condition of servitude."[3]

Taking an active role within the Republican Party, African Americans elected thirty-four African American men to forty-four positions in the General Assembly between 1868 and 1874. In the post-Reconstruction years, in which Democrats "redeemed" or regained political power, African American men continued to serve. A total of eighty-six African American legislators had served in the General Assembly by 1893. In the following years, however, disfranchisement through new election laws effectively ended political participation and representation for black residents, who made up over a quarter of the state's population.

Of the eighty-six African American legislators who served between 1868 and 1893, six made their careers in the Senate, seventy-six served exclusively in the House, and four were elected to both chambers. Black legislators came predominantly from counties dominated by plantation economies and possessing a growing number or actual majority of black citizens. But they also hailed from important urban centers like Pine Bluff, Helena, and Little Rock that supported the growing black middle class from which many of these leaders emerged.[4] Two cotton-producing regions elected the most black legislators. Eastern Arkansas accounted for forty-four of the eighty-six legislators, and the Jefferson County region (home to Pine Bluff) accounted for twenty-six. Pulaski County accounted for nine, while Lafayette and Hempstead counties in southwestern Arkansas totaled eight legislators during the period. Conway County, a white-majority county in the Arkansas River Valley, narrowly elected one black legislator in 1886 in a surge of populism that siphoned white voters away from Democrats.[5]

In historian Eric Foner's examination of black Reconstruction-era officeholders in the South, he found people of mixed black and white ancestry (called mulattos at the time) to be a slight majority. While the matter was highly subjective and potentially unreliable census data was used, so-called mulattos made up nearly half of Arkansas's eighty-six legislators. Foner noted, "Many freeborn blacks were of mixed ancestry." This is true of Arkansas's legislators who hailed from the North, but many legislators born into slavery were also of mixed ancestry.[6]

Reflecting their rural agricultural constituents, at least forty-six of the eighty-six legislators farmed at some point during their lifetime, and another three were termed "planters." However, community leaders also emerged from the nexus of church, school, and the growing urban black middle class. At least twenty-nine legislators had careers as ministers, twenty-seven as educators, eleven as lawyers, nine as merchants, and thirteen in other professions. Election to the General Assembly was likely the capstone for a modest political career, and thirty-five of the legislators are known to have served the public in other capacities at the county and state level or in federal appointments.[7]

The modest middle-class and even elite status of many in the group is apparent if the 1870 manuscript census and county tax rolls of the time are examined. Forty-five legislators appear in the 1870 census: sixteen claimed no property; fifteen claimed between $1 and $500; three claimed between $501 and $1,000; six claimed between $1,000 and $2,000; and five claimed over $2,000. County tax rolls reveal a similar pattern. Of the fifty-six legislators located on county tax rolls, seven reported no property, ten reported personal property between $1 and $50, fifteen reported between $51 and $100, thirteen reported between $101 and $200, five reported between $201 and $300, four reported between $301 and $400, and two reported over $400.[8] The average wealth of black legislators was higher than that of most black Arkansans generally, but probably less than that of most whites.[9]

African Americans were first elected to the Arkansas General Assembly in 1868. That year, seven black legislators served. Their numbers peaked in 1873 with sixteen in the House of Representatives and four in the Senate. As Reconstruction collapsed, the number dipped substantially, to four, in the extraordinary session called by conservative Governor Elisha Baxter just days after President Ulysses S. Grant sided with him in what became known as the Brooks-Baxter War.[10] Intimidation of white and black Republican voters in Delta counties like Phillips and Lee contributed to declines in 1879 and 1881. But, as historian Carl Moneyhon noted, "The end of Reconstruction, accompanied by violence against blacks, did not conclude with the removal of blacks from participation in southern politics."[11] Instead, Democratic leaders like Governor Augustus H. Garland supported black civil rights and encouraged fusion arrangements in Delta counties with large black electorates. Fusion guaranteed political offices for both parties and helped avoid political violence.[12] These arrangements during the 1870s and 1880s allowed the number of black legislators to grow to twelve during the 1891 session. The 1893 session of the General Assembly, the first following the Election Law of 1891, which increased Democratic control of polling places and screened out many illiterate voters, found only five black legislators present—two in the House and one in the Senate from eastern Arkansas and two in the House from Jefferson County. With the subsequent imposition of a poll tax and the establishment of the all-white Democratic primary, it would be another eighty years before the Arkansas General Assembly would again welcome black legislators.

With few exceptions, nineteenth-century black legislators aligned with the Republican Party. It appears that 1879 was the first year any black legislators were willing to break with the Republicans. Four had been elected on the Greenback ticket and one was elected as a Democrat. (An offshoot of the national Greenback Labor Party, the Arkansas Greenbackers believed that national monetary policy placed too much burden on the debtor, and they wanted to expand the national currency with paper money.) The early 1880s also saw a few Greenbackers elected, but fusion and Republican alliances with Greenbackers and members of the labor group the Agricultural Wheel seem to have kept black voters and candidates within the Republican fold. The final exception in the nineteenth century is Benjamin F. Adair, who served in the 1891 General Assembly as a Democrat.[13]

As many as seventy-three legislators (thirty with some certainty) were enslaved before the Civil War.[14] At least four legislators were born slaves, but they were free and living in the North during the antebellum period. Two of the four—James W. Mason and Benjamin F. Adair—were Arkansas natives and the sons of their masters. They led privileged lives in their fathers' households and never personally knew the hardships of slavery—the humiliation of the auction block, labor in the fields, an overseer's whip, or the fear and uncertainty of separated families.

Benjamin F. Adair, who served in the 1891 General Assembly, was one of the few African American legislators elected as a Democrat and the only black legislator to vote for the Separate Coach Law. Adair was born a slave in Phillips County in 1852—the son of a white master and one of his slaves. After free blacks were barred from Arkansas in 1859, the young Adair and his mother were relocated to Ohio and manumitted. "BF Adair, Pulaski County," ASA_Photo_G5401_4, Arkansas State Archives, Little Rock, Arkansas.

For the vast majority of the legislators who were enslaved, there is little record of their lives. However, for a few, historical records have left glimpses into their lives. One of the best documented, albeit not ordinary, is the life of James Milo Alexander. Historian Willard B. Gatewood Jr. described James and his wife Fannie as "favored slaves who enjoyed extraordinary privileges that set them apart from the masses of slaves who toiled in the cotton fields." Owned by Lawson H. Alexander, James arrived at his master's St. Francis County plantation in the 1830s from Virginia. Sometime in the early 1840s, James, a coachman, married Fannie Miller, a household servant. The couple, both of mixed race, learned to read and write while they were enslaved.[15]

The death of Lawson Alexander in 1842 precipitated the separation of the family by the late 1840s. Removed to Helena by one of Lawson's children, James was forced to leave his wife and two children behind on the plantation. In Helena, James led an extraordinary and independent life as a barber and merchant. Yet, James's pain is revealed in his letters to his wife.[16] In 1851, he wrote, "Dear Francis...you must talk with our little son about his father. Try and not let him forgit [*sic*] me." In 1854, he wrote, "I want to see you so very much, dear Fannie....I do not think it so very hard that we should be sepparated [*sic*] in this manner, but Dear Wife, I am not living in [a] world as those that have no hope…"[17]

The family was reunited in 1857, when Fannie and the children were purchased by a nearby Helena family. Though he was still enslaved, James's business prospered and he was likely able to purchase the freedom of some of his family.[18] The 1859 law against free blacks living in the state nullified their freedom, but the family's privileged status remained. After the Civil War, he was respected by whites and by blacks for his role in the Prince Hall Masons and as an African Methodist Episcopal minister. In addition to his one term in the House, he served as a justice of the peace, a school trustee, and a member of a grand jury. He died in 1871 at age fifty-six.[19]

Hempstead County's Daniel Hunt came to Arkansas from Virginia around 1859. During the Civil War, he was the foreman at a shoe shop near Washington. He was elected in 1869 to fill a vacancy in the House from Hempstead County, and a sketch that year described him as a farmer with a "good education."[20] Hunt also served as a constable, justice of the peace, and school board trustee.[21] Upon his death in 1887, the *Arkansas Democrat* wrote, "Dan Hunt our honored colored Justice of Peace...died last

Saturday night.... [He] was certainly an exception to his race, he was regarded by attorneys here as one of the best justices in Hempstead county."[22]

At least ten black legislators served in the Union army during the Civil War.[23] Pension files from the U.S. Pension Bureau and service records for three of them give insight into their lives during slavery and after.[24] In 1870, Americus Mayo was a Monroe County farmer and minister with $250 in personal property. He married Ellen Williams in Memphis on August 30, 1865. Ellen, likely a war-time refugee, hailed from Yazoo City, Mississippi, while he served in the Third U.S. Colored Cavalry. Both had children from previous relationships, but their families were broken up by the slave trade. In their 1870 household were his two Virginia-born teenagers, and two younger children, likely Ellen's. A year later, Americus Mayo represented Monroe County in the Arkansas House.[25]

Mayo died in 1890 and his widow filed for his Civil War pension. His pension file reveals some details of Mayo's life. Born in Norfolk, Virginia, around 1820, Mayo married Elizabeth Jones, a free woman of color, around 1848 in Norfolk's "old Colored Baptist Church." The couple "lived together like slave people," according to a witness, and had as many as eleven children. According to Elizabeth Mayo in an 1898 interview, the family was separated in 1857: "[He] was sold [by Jack Wilkins] and went away South long before the late war broke out. He was sold and sent from me before the yellow fever in Norfolk...1857, the year of the big snow." Records do not reveal how these events affected Mayo, but his loss was likely devastating to his young children and wife.[26] It is not clear where or to whom Mayo was sold, but perhaps he was enslaved on a steamboat that plied western waters. In September 1864, listing his occupation as a "boatman," Mayo joined the Third U.S. Colored Cavalry at Vicksburg, Mississippi. Discharged at Memphis in June 1866, he found work on steamboats on the Mississippi River and traveled back to Norfolk in the spring of 1870. Mayo, who had remarried in the summer of 1865, stayed two or three weeks with Elizabeth Mayo, and then returned to Arkansas with his teenage son and daughter.[27]

In 1880, Green Hill Jones was a thirty-eight-year-old, married farmer living near Grand Lake in Chicot County. Unlike other members of his household, Jones was literate, but there is little else in the census to distinguish him from the other farmers and sharecroppers near him. Nor is there anything to suggest that he would soon represent Chicot County in the Arkansas House in 1885 and 1889.

In a 1904 interview, Jones sketched out his life to a pension examiner:

> I[,] Hill Jones were born in the state of Tenn. in 1842 December 18. My age is 61 years & some months & brought to Arkansas when 4 years old & lived as a slave on Mr. K. R Rainer's [Rayner's] Place below Grand Lake untill [*sic*] when I went to Memphis Tenn & enlisted in Co F 3rd USC H[eavy] A[rtillery] as Hill Jones[.] I had a long name taken...My name were Green Hill Jones Haywood but I only went by Hill Jones in the service as I thought that part of my name were enough and after I learned to read & write prefixed G to my name for Green & left off Haywood all together. I have 3 scars under left thigh made by a whip before the war & 2 scars on top of left arm made by vaccinating before the war and one in right arm above elbow under neath. After my discharge on April 30, 1866, I left Memphis & went to Mound City, Ill & to New Madrid, Mo & from there to Hillsdale, Mich. and again to New Madrid, Mo. and in 1873 I moved back to Grand Lake Ark where I was before the war and have been living here every [*sic*] since.[28]

Jones's scars from the overseer's whip, his lack of an education, and his desire to escape testify to the exploitative nature of slavery.[29] In contrast, Jones's owner, Kenneth Rayner, masked exploitation with the rhetoric of a benevolent slaveholder. The North Carolina Whig Congressman married the wealthy Susan Polk in 1842 and claimed he "never bought any [slaves], except to bring man and wife together." Instead, his wife inherited many slaves from her father's estate, including Jones, who was sent, in 1846 at age four, to Rayner's newly purchased 538-acre Chicot County plantation.[30] Rayner believed slavery to be an "evil," but he felt there was little he could to change the institution. Instead, the self-described "negro-spoiler" emphasized the "humanity" of slavery, making sure slaves were decently fed, clothed, and housed.[31] Jones, unfortunately, did not comment on Rayner's ideas of humanity.

Green Hill Jones, a Baptist minister and farmer living near Grand Lake in Chicot County, would serve in the Arkansas House of Representatives in 1885 and 1889. Enslaved in Chicot County, he joined the Third U.S. Colored Heavy Artillery in 1863. After the Civil War, he went north and was educated at Hillsdale College in Michigan before returning to Chicot County in 1873. "Green Hill Jones," ASA_Photo_G2864OV_14, Arkansas State Archives, Little Rock, Arkansas.

Following his discharge, Jones spent time in Missouri and was ordained a Baptist minister in Mound City, Illinois, in 1869. Illiterate before the war, it was likely through his connection to the Baptist church that Jones began to learn to read and write. In Michigan, from 1870 to 1873, he continued his studies as a preparatory student at Hillsdale College, a Free Will Baptist institution.[32] Jones returned to Chicot County in 1873, and was soon elected county treasurer (1874–1876) and county assessor (1876–1878).[33] At his death in 1924, he proudly owned 120 acres of farmland and town lots in Eudora.[34]

George Washington Lowe came to Monroe County in 1881 from Marshall County, Mississippi. He was part of a wave of African American migrants into the state in the 1880s.[35] Lowe, a Baptist minister and a teacher, told his story to a special examiner from the pension office:

> Am a regularly ordained minister of the Bethel Chapel and have been for the past 26 years...I would sometimes teach school and work on [the] farm, but am now, and have been for the past 3 years giving my entire attention to my duties as a district missionary. I am the same and identical person who served in Co F 5th U.S.C.H.A. during the late Civil War under the name of George Washington.
>
> I was born in Hardeman Co., Tenn. as a slave of Mr. Sam Bunting near Panthers Creek, our nearest town was Saulsbury. I have been told and have always understood that I was born on March 22, 1847. While I was an infant[,] Mr. Bunting died and I became the property of his estate. My last owner was Mr. M. C. Pierce of Memphis who acquired me through the inheritance of his wife who was a daughter of Mr. Bunting....During the time that I was in slavery I had no surname, but was known as Mr. Bunting's boy or Mr. Pierce's boy George Washington. "George Washington" was my given name. My father belonged to Mr. Ezekiel Lowe who lived near Saulsbury, Tenn. and his name was Kendrick and he was

known as Lowe's Kenrick, and after freedom he took the name Kendrick Lowe.[36]

By the end of the decade, as populism peaked in the rural South, Lowe was elected president of the Colored Agricultural State Wheel and to two terms in the Arkansas House, 1889 and 1891. The special examiner, impressed with Lowe, explained his prominence in the community in a 1902 memo:

> This claimant is a man of great prominence in his community and is regarded as one of the best and most reliable negroes in the state. He was so well thought of for honesty and intelligence that he was elected some years ago by a fusion party of whites and blacks to represent Monroe Co. in the State Legislature and served one year and this subsequent to the reconstruction period following the close of the civil war. He is said to be quite an orator and is a regularly ordained minister of the Baptist Society in good standing assigned to missionary work among his race. He has a formal education, and he impressed me with his thorough honesty and sincerity in the assigning of his identity with the soldier of record.[37]

George Washington Lowe, a farmer and Baptist minister, emerged as a populist leader after he arrived in Monroe County from Mississippi in 1881. A former slave in Tennessee, he joined the Fifth U.S. Colored Heavy Artillery at age fifteen as a musician and displayed a drum tattoo on his left arm. Lowe, who lost his left eye in a farming accident, is photographed in profile. Courtesy of the UA Little Rock Center for Arkansas History and Culture.

During the Twenty-Eighth General Assembly, Lowe voted against the 1891 election law that would soon end black voter participation. During that shameful time, he supported constituents' desire to move to Liberia with a letter to the American Colonization Society. He wrote: "There is a great restlessness among [my people] on accoun[t] of discriminating laws that are being made." Lowe stayed in Monroe County and died at Holly Grove on February 16, 1920.[38]

Of the nineteen legislators who were free or possibly free prior to the Civil War, ten were born in the North, five were born in border states or Washington DC, and four were born in Southern states. At least two of the five born in border states were slaves who later attained their freedom.[39] Of the four born in the South, they all later lived in the North or a border state.[40] Fourteen of these men served terms during Reconstruction.

The North provided freedom, but it was no escape from racism. African Americans in the North had opportunities to carve out economic success, but they were subjected to economic segregation and pushed into menial and service positions. Many of the ambitious African American men who came to Arkansas from Midwestern cities and river towns held positions of status and influence within their home communities as teachers, ministers, barbers, and boat stewards.[41] Attracted by opportunity, they were able to channel status and education into leadership positions in Arkansas.

The most prominent of the free-born legislators were William H. Grey and James T. White. Both arrived in Union-occupied Helena in 1865. Grey, born free in Washington DC, where he attended a "pay school," had lived in Pennsylvania and Ohio, and, in 1860, worked on steamboats out of St. Louis, Missouri. The future legislator had also spent time as a servant and gained political experience with Virginia governor and congressman Henry A. Wise. In the fall of 1865, he, along with James T. White, participated in the Little Rock Convention of Colored Citizens, the "first colored convention ever held in the state of Arkansas." Elected to the 1868 Constitutional Convention, he became a fierce proponent of black suffrage during the proceedings. Upon his election to the House from Arkansas in 1868, the Little Rock *Morning Republican* described him as a "first class representative of his race." In 1874–1875, he filled a Senate seat after the death of Senator John Willis Williams and later held a cabinet-level position in the state government. In 1878, Grey suffered a series of debilitating strokes from which he never recovered. He died in Helena on November 8, 1888.[42]

The free-born William H. Grey arrived in Helena in 1865 and served in both the Arkansas House of Representatives and the Arkansas Senate. Grey was the first Grand Master of the Most Worshipful Grand Lodge (Colored) of Free and Accepted Masons of Arkansas. "William H. Grey, ASA_Photo_PS02_01," Arkansas State Archives, Little Rock, Arkansas.

James T. White, with a common school education in Indiana, joined his two brothers in the ministry in 1858 at age twenty-one. As a twenty-six-year-old missionary, he arrived in Helena in 1865 to perform missionary work among the throngs of newly free men and women who flocked to the Union-occupied city. In 1870, the Baptist minister reported $9,500 in personal property and real estate, making him one of the wealthiest black men in the state. The *Morning Republican* described him in 1869 as a "zealous Republican" with a "considerable amount of political ability."[43] White served one term in the House (1868–1869) and two terms in the Senate (1871, 1873). His brother, Rev. Reuben B. White, arrived in Little Rock around 1870 and served in the Senate in 1873 and the extraordinary session of 1874.[44] The brothers remained mainstays in the Baptist Church and their communities until the death of Reuben in 1886 and James in 1892.[45]

James T. White arrived in Helena 1865 to perform missionary work among the freedmen and freedwomen who flocked to the Union-occupied city. White served one term in the House (1868–1869) and two terms in the Senate (1871, 1873). "James T. White," ASA_Photo_PS44_02, Arkansas State Archives, Little Rock, Arkansas.

Northern men like Grey and the White brothers had access to educational opportunities from common schools and colleges not available to blacks bound to the South. The *Memphis Daily Appeal* seemed shocked by Phillips County representative George H. W. Stewart's "excellent English and classical education." The Indiana-born teacher, it reported, "is said to be addicted to books."[46]

Several legislators went beyond common school to attend college. Richard A. Dawson, the son of a wealthy Chicago barber and minister, graduated from the University of Chicago Law School.[47] Attending Oberlin College were James W. Mason, the son of Elisha Worthington, Arkansas's largest planter; William L. Copeland, the son of John Anthony Copeland, an abolitionist and militant who joined John Brown at Harper's Ferry; and Benjamin F. Adair, son and namesake of a Phillips County planter and ginner.[48] Henry A. Johnson and R. C. Weddington, both born in Mississippi, attended Alcorn University in that state.[49] George W. Bell, perhaps the most studied legislator white or black, attended Southland College, Lincoln University, National University in St. Louis, and Dartmouth Medical College.[50]

Critics of nineteenth-century black politicians often charged that they were illiterate and unsuited for office. Illiteracy was certainly a problem, since there was a near total ban on educating slaves. That ban pushed adult illiteracy rates for African Americans in the South in 1860 above ninety percent.[51] However, contemporary descriptions, interviews, and census data paint a picture of black legislators in Arkansas as educated men or at least men seeking an education.

Jerome Riley, an African American Democrat and critic, wrote in 1895: "At the head of the [Jefferson County] republican legislative ticket in 1875 was Mr. Ned Hill, colored, who could neither read or write, but whose fighting weight was two hundred pounds, drunk or sober." A Ned Hill in the 1870 Census in Pulaski County is listed as unable to read or write. However, Riley may have only been partially right about Hill. A reporter with the *Fort Wayne Gazette* who visited Little Rock in 1875 suggested a range of literacy and education when he noted, "all [nine of the 1875 black legislators] can read print, but only four can write."[52]

Freedmen and freedwomen, in a rejection of slavery, embraced education as a new and empowering right of their freedom.[53] Future legislators were no different, and evidence shows many sought and acquired an education.[54] Abraham H. Miller, born a slave in St. Francis County in 1851, came to Union-occupied Helena with his mother during the Civil War. The former Phillips County representative (1874–1875), described his post-war opportunities in his 1911 autobiography:

> I have never had more than a common school education. In 1872 I attended public schools of Helena, Arkansas, for only one session, under Prof. Geo. H. W. Stewart. I attended the Southland College, a school which the Quakers established in the county, about nine miles from Helena. I would have attended that school much longer, but my money gave out and I returned home and went to work.[55]

Chicot County's Green Hill Jones, mentioned earlier, was illiterate when he joined the Union army and learned to read and write in his role as a Baptist minister and then at a Northern college. Anderson L. Rush, representing Pulaski and White counties in 1868, was born a slave at Arkansas Post in 1838, according to his Civil War service record. In 1869, the *Morning Republican* noted, the former field hand was a merchant with "a fair education—self acquired." A year later, the 1870 Census showed Rush as a school teacher with $900 in real estate.[56]

Thomas Kersh was likely a slave when he enlisted at Pine Bluff in the Second U.S.C. Light Artillery on April 15, 1864. Born in South Carolina in the mid-1840s, Kersh was listed as illiterate in the 1870 Census, but literate in the 1880, 1900, and 1910 censuses. The farmer and minister, who represented Lincoln County in 1885 and 1887, told the pension office in 1902, "When I joined the army in 1861 I could neither read nor write...since 1864 I have learned to read and write."[57]

Slaves who managed to escape and make their way North often found educational opportunities. Edward A. Fulton, born in 1833, escaped enslavement in Missouri before 1851. He emerged in Chicago and was educated in the city's schools. While he was representing Drew County in the House in 1871, the *Morning Republican* called Fulton "a man of considerable intelligence and fair education." Yet years later, in a call of solidarity with blacks denied an education, he would write "[I] was born a slave and [have] been robbed of years of toil and opportunity of getting an education."[58]

Abraham H. Miller was born a slave in St. Francis County in 1851 and came to Union-occupied Helena with his mother during the Civil War. He served Phillips County in the House of Representatives in 1874–1875. He later wrote a book titled How I Succeeded in my Business. "Abraham Miller," ASA_Photo_PS44_01, Arkansas State Archives, Little Rock, Arkansas.

Until recently, little attention has been paid to the actual legislative work performed by African American legislators. A recent analysis of Arkansas House and Senate journals during Reconstruction by Chris W. Branam sheds light on their work.[59] Branam wrote, "They introduced bills that eventually became laws…made points-of-order and proposed amendments." In short, they were active and capable members of the legislature as "likely to take the floor as their white colleagues."[60] While not of a single mind, they legislated a Southern Republican agenda of civil rights, public education, economic development, and law and order. While passing legislation in 1868 and 1873, civil rights unified black lawmakers throughout Reconstruction. With little division, they supported free public schools and the establishment of Arkansas Industrial University in Fayetteville and Branch Normal in Pine Bluff. Black legislators supported Republican policy to rebuild the state's economy by encouraging immigration and through investments in railroads, roads, and levees. Governor Powell Clayton's use of the state militia to fight the lawless terrorizing of black communities by the Ku Klux Klan also found strong support among black legislators.[61]

These issues largely united African American legislators, but strong divisions emerged in 1871 between Regular Republicans, aligned with Governor Clayton, and Liberal Republicans, who increasingly voted with Conservative Democrats. While divisions over restoring ex-Confederate voting rights seemed to be about wealthier mixed-race legislators aligned with white interests, the messy and failed impeachment proceedings against Lt. Gov. James M. Johnson, Clayton, and Supreme Court Justice John McClure had everything to do with politics.[62]

Similar analysis has yet to be undertaken for the legislative sessions following Redemption: the defeat of Radical Republicans (white and black) by white Democrats ("Redeemers"), marking the end of the South's Reconstruction era. In this new era, black legislators were still active participants, but as Branam stated, they became "members of a powerless Republican minority."[63] In the early years of Redemption, Governor Garland and his successor supported black civil and voting rights, but by the late 1880s and early 1890s Democrats' support for black rights had evaporated; support had even eroded with some Republicans. The passage of the Election Law of 1891 effectively ended black suffrage by removing local control of polling places and screening out illiterate voters. In 1893, only five black legislators remained in the General Assembly.[64] The poll tax and the all-white Democratic primary ensured that another eighty years would pass before the Arkansas General Assembly would have black legislators among its ranks.

Author's Note on Methods for Tables

When party affiliation is known, it is in bold. When it is not known, it is assumed to be Republican, unless the legislator was a member of a different party in a previous term. I have attempted to make the columns listing primary and secondary sources as comprehensive as possible; however, I have omitted some sources that recycle earlier material. City directories were cited only when they added details not available elsewhere.

Table 3 provides biographical data derived from the sources listed in the first two tables. Few contemporary biographies survive for nineteenth-century legislators, so the bulk of the biographical data is pulled from U.S. Census manuscript records (nativity, color, occupation, and literacy), legislative directories that appeared in the Arkansas Secretary of State's *Biennial Report*, the *Arkansas Gazette*, the *Morning Republican*, a few surviving directories that accompany composite photographs of legislators, and two rule books for the General Assembly. The slave or free status prior to the Civil War is uncertain for many of the legislators. When it is known, the information came from a contemporary biography or from a secondary source. An exception is William A. Marshall, who was described as a "freeman" in the 1868 Hempstead personal property tax records. I cautiously assumed that legislators born in the South prior to 1861 were born into slavery. These individuals are listed as "Slave (?)." On similar grounds, I treated the Northern-born legislators as free, regardless of their birth year. Northern-born legislators located in an antebellum census are listed as "Free"; otherwise they are listed as "Free (?)." An "x" appears when property value information was unavailable or not applicable. For tax records, a "?" appears where records were available, but the individual was not found.

Arkansas's African American Legislators, 1868–1893

Table 1: African Americans in the Arkansas Senate, 1868–1893

Year(s)	Legislator	Party	District	Sources
Reconstruction (1867–1874)				
1868–1869	James W. Mason	**Rep.**	22 (Ashley, Chicot, Drew, Desha)	1870 Census (Chicot); *Debates* (1868); *Morning Republican*, Mar. 13, 1868, Mar. 25, 1871; *New York Tribune*, May 26, 1869; *Helena Daily Independent*, Dec 4, 1874; *Ark. Gaz.*, Dec. 13, 1874; Oberlin (1919); Hume (1973); St. Hilaire (1974); Gatewood (1993); Foner (1996); Graves (1990); DeBlack (1995, 2003); Harrison (2008); Griffin (2017)
1871	James W. Mason	**Rep.**	22 (Ashley, Chicot, Drew, Desha)	See 1868–1869 Senate
1871	James T. White	Rep.	11 (Phillips, Monroe)	1860 Census (Marion, IN); 1870, 1880 Census (Phillips); *Rules for the Government* (1873); Simmons (1887); Hickman (1967); Hume (1973); St. Hilaire (1974); Graves (1990); Foner (1996); Rosen (2009); *Morning Republican*, Mar. 13, 1868, Mar. 25, 1871; *Chicago Tribune*, Mar. 16, 1892
1873	Richard A. Dawson	Rep.	20 (Jefferson, Bradley, Grant, Lincoln)	1870 Census (Cook, IL); *Rules for the Government* (1873); *Ark. Gaz.*, Feb. 1, 2, 1873 TWD Coll [*NY Tribune*, July 8, 1879]; Leslie (1978); Graves (1989, 1990); Smith (1993); Foner (1996); Kilpatrick (2003); Wintory (2004)

Abbreviations: Dem.=Democrat; GB=Greenback; Rep.=Republican; UL=Union Labor.

1873	Samuel H. Holland	Rep.	22 (Ashley, Chicot, Drew, Desha)	1860 Census (Hamilton, OH); 1870 Census (Pulaski); *Rules for the Government* (1873); 1880 Census (Chicot); *1871 Little Rock City Directory*; Moneyhon (1991); Foner (1996); *Peoples Advocate*, Oct. 6, 1883; *Ark. Gaz.*, Aug. 5, 1886; *Christian Recorder*, Mar. 10, 1887
1873	James T. White	Rep.	11 (Monroe, Phillips)	See 1871 Senate
1873	Reuben B. White	Rep.	10 (Pulaski, White)	Sometimes spelled Ruben. 1860 Census (Marion, IN); *Rules for the Government* (1873); 1880 Census (Pulaski); Foner (1996); *Ark. Gaz.*, Aug. 26, 1886
1874 Extra	Richard A. Dawson	Rep.	20 (Jefferson, Bradley, Grant, Lincoln)	See 1873 Senate
1874 Extra	Samuel H. Holland	Rep.	22 (Ashley, Chicot, Drew, Desha, Lincoln)	See 1873 Senate
1874 Extra	Reuben B. White	Rep.	10 (Pulaski, White)	See 1873 Senate
Post-Reconstruction/Redemption				
1874–1875	John Willis Williams (died in office, replaced by William H. Grey)	Rep.	14 (Phillips, Lee)	1870 Census (Phillips); *Rules for the Government* (1873); *Ark. Gaz.*, Feb. 1, 1873; Graves (1990); Foner (1996); Wintory (2004); For Grey, see 1868–1869 House

1877	Anthony L. Stanford	**Rep.**	14 (Phillips, Lee)	1850 Census (Cumberland, NJ); 1870 Census (Philadelphia, PA); *Ark. Mansion*, Aug. 11, 1883; Moneyhon (1985); Patton (1992); Barnes (2004)
1879	Anthony L. Stanford	**GB**	14 (Phillips, Lee)	See 1877 Senate
Between 1881 and 1885 no African Americans served in the Arkansas Senate				
1887	William H. Logan	**Rep.**	15 (Desha, Chicot)	1860 Census (Ross, OH); 1880, 1900 Census (Chicot); 1886, 1888 *Biennial Report*; *Ark. Dem.*, Jan. 12, 1887
1889	William H. Logan	**Rep.**	15 (Desha, Chicot)	See 1887 Senate
1891	George W. Bell	**Rep.**	15 (Desha, Chicot)	1880 Census (Desha); 1880 Census (Chester, PA); 1900, 1910 (Jefferson); TWD Coll [*Ark. Mansion*, July 14, Nov. 3, 1883]; *Pine Bluff Commercial*, July 17, 1883; 1890, 1892; *Freeman*, Feb. 21, 1891; *Pine Bluff Daily Graphic*, Jan. 25, 1901; Ark. *Gaz.*, Aug. 4, 1925; *Biennial Report*; Gaines (1898); Henderson (1906); *Lincoln University Herald*, Feb. 1917; *Lincoln University* (1918); Gatewood (1972, 1974); Graves (1973, 1990); Kousser (1975); Moneyhon (1985); Gordon (1995); Barnes (2004); Kennedy (2009)
1893	George W. Bell	Rep.	15 (Desha, Chicot)	See 1891 Senate

Table 2: African Americans in the Arkansas House of Representatives, 1868–1893

Year	Legislator	Party	District	Sources
Reconstruction (1867–1874)				
1868–1869	William H. Grey	**Rep.**	11 (Phillips, Monroe)	1860 Census (St. Louis, MO); 1870, 1880 Census (Phillips); *Debates* (1868); *Morning Republican*, Mar. 13, 1868; Jan. 8, 1869; *Freeman*, Mar. 2, 1889; *Ark. Gaz.*, Nov. 11, 1888, Dec. 21, 1958; Hume (1969, 1973); St. Hilaire (1974); Williamson (1979); Dillard (1980/81, 2003b); Simpson (1985); Graves (1990); Foner (1996); Kilpatrick (2003); Wintory (2004)
1868–1869	Monroe E. Hawkins	**Rep.**	15 (Lafayette, Little River)	1870 Census (Lafayette); 1880 (Miller); *Debates* (1868); *Rules for the Government* (1873); *Ark. Gaz.*, Feb. 1, 1873; Hume (1973); Foner (1996); *Morning Republican*, Mar. 13, 1868; Jan. 8, 1869; *Ark. Hist. Commission News*, Sept. 2013
1868–1869	Daniel Hunt	**Rep.**	14 (Hempstead)	Hunt replaced Rep. S. D. Belden. 1870, 1880 Census (Hempstead); *Morning Republican*, Jan. 8, 1869; *Washington Telegraph*, May 31, 1871; *Ark. Dem.*, Oct. 3, 1887; McKenzie (1906)
1868–1869	Anderson L. Rush	**Rep.**	10 (Pulaski, White)	Often misidentified "Bush," see "Rush, Anderson L.," Vertical File in Butler Center; 1870 Census (Pulaski); Julia Rush (widow) in 1880 Census (Pulaski); Foner (1996); *Morning Republican*, Mar. 13, 1868; Jan. 8, 1869; Service Record (RG 94); Pension File (RG 15)

Abbreviations: Dem.=Democrat; GB=Greenback; Rep.=Republican; UL=Union Labor.

1868–1869	Richard R. Samuels	**Rep.**	14 (Hempstead)	*Debates* (1868); *Morning Republican*, Mar. 13, 1868, Jan. 8, 1869; Hendron (1922); Williams (1951); Hume (1973); St. Hilaire (1974); Graves (1990); Foner (1996); *Ark. History Commission News* (Sept. 2013); Bob Samuels, Hempstead Co., Arkansas, WPA Slave Interview
1868–1869	James T. White	Rep.	11 (Phillips, Monroe)	1860 Census (Marion, IN); 1870, 1880 Census (Phillips); *Rules for the Government* (1873); Simmons (1887); Hickman (1967); Hume (1973); St. Hilaire (1974); Graves (1990); Foner (1996); Rosen (2009); *Morning Republican*, Mar. 13, 1868, Mar. 25, 1871; *Chicago Tribune*, Mar. 16, 1892
1871	James M. Alexander Sr.	Rep.	11 (Monroe, Phillips)	James M. Alexander Jr. in *Historical Report*, but see Gatewood (1982; 1990); 1870 Census (Phillips); *Cleveland Gazette*, Nov. 29, 1884; Foner (1996)
1871	Conway Barbour	Rep.	15 (Lafayette, Little River)	1860, 1870 (Alton, IL); 1870 Census (Lafayette); *Morning Republican*, March 25, 1871; *Ark. Gaz.* May 9, 1871, July 8, 1876; Foner (1996); Harrison (2008, 2010)
1871	Austin Barrow	**Rep.**	11 (Monroe, Phillips)	Austin Barrows in 1870 Census (Phillips); *Morning Republican*, Mar. 25, 1871; *Ark. Gaz.*, July 11, 1872; John Patterson, Helena, Arkansas, WPA Slave Interview; Staples (1920); Wintory (2004); Barnes (2004)
1871	Edward A. Fulton	**Rep.**	22 (Ashley, Chicot, Drew, Desha)	1860 Census (Cook, IL); 1870 Census (Drew) 1880, 1900 Census (St. Louis, MO); *Ark. Gaz.*, Nov. 19, 1870; *Morning Republican*, Mar. 25, 1871; *Cleveland Gazette*, Dec. 3, 1887; Riley (1895); Staples (1920); Graves (1990); Foner (1996); Wintory (2004)
1871	Jeff Haskins	Rep.	9 (Crittenden, St. Francis, Woodruff)	1870, 1880 Census (St. Francis); *Morning Republican*, Mar. 25, 1871; Staples (1920); Foner (1996)

1871	Adam R. Johnson	Rep.	9 (Crittenden, St. Francis, Woodruff)	1870 Census (Crittenden); *Rules for the Government* (1873); *Morning Republican*, Mar. 25, 1871; *Ark. Gaz.*, Feb. 1, 1873; Staples (1920); Foner (1996)
1871	Americus Mayo	Rep.	11 (Monroe, Phillips)	1870, 1880 Census (Monroe); *Morning Republican*, Mar. 25, 1871; *Ark. Gaz.*, April 21, 1871; Staples (1920); Service Record (RG 94); Pension File (RG 15)
1871	Carl R. Polk	**Rep.**	20 (Bradley, Jefferson, Grant)	Carl Pope in *Historical Report*; 1870 Census (Pulaski); 1880 Census (Jefferson); 1880 *Biennial Report*; Roster (1881); *Pine Bluff City Directory* (1881); *Morning Republican*, Mar. 25, 1871; *Ark. Gaz.*, April 21, 1871, Jan. 17, 1872; Leslie (1978); Staples (1920); Service Record (RG 94); Pension File (RG 15)
1871	James A. Robinson	**Rep.**	22 (Ashley, Chicot, Drew, Desha)	A. J. in *Historical Report*; 1870 Census (Desha); *Ark. Gaz.*, Nov. 19, 1870; Robinson (1876); *Morning Republican*, Mar. 25, 1871; *Ark. Gaz.*, April 21, 1871; Staples (1920)
1871	John W. Webb	**Rep.**	22 (Ashley, Chicot, Drew, Desha)	1870, 1880, 1900 Census (Chicot); *Ark. Gaz.*, Nov. 19, 1870; *Morning Republican*, Mar. 25, 1871; Staples (1920); Foner (1996)
1871	William H. Young	Rep.	22 (Bradley, Jefferson, Grant)	1870, 1880 Census (Jefferson); *Morning Republican*, Mar. 3, 25, 1871; Staples (1920); 1882 *Biennial Report*, *Ark. Gaz.*, Sept 30, 1882, Jan. 7, 1883; Leslie (1978)
1873	Charles Brown	Rep.	9 (Crittenden, St. Francis, Woodruff)	Likely Charley Brown in 1870 Census (St. Francis); *Rules for the Government* (1873); *Ark. Gaz.*, Feb. 1, 1873; Foner (1996)

1873	Cornelius "Neal " Brown	Rep.	10 (Pulaski, White)	1870 Census (Pulaski); *Rules for the Government* (1873); *Ark. Gaz.*, Feb. 1, 1873; Foner (1996)
1873	William L. Copeland	Rep.	9 (Crittenden, St. Francis, Woodruff)	1870 Census (Lorain, OH); 1880 Census (Pulaski); *Rules for the Government* (1873); *Ark. Gaz.*, Feb. 1, 1873, July 29, 1876; Robinson (1876); Goodspeed (1890); Oberlin (1919); Moneyhon (1985); Rector (1997); Lubet (2015); General Index to Pension Files (T288)
1873	William "Willis" Hines Furbush	Rep.	11 (Phillips, Monroe)	Forbush in 1870 Census (Phillips); *Rules for the Government* (1873); *Ark. Gaz.*, Feb. 1, 1873; *Memphis Daily Appeal*, Feb. 22, 1873; Riley (1895); Graves (1990); Gordon (1995); Foner (1996); Wintory (2004)
1873	Toney Grissom	Rep.	11 (Phillips, Monroe)	Grisham in 1870 Census (Phillips); 1880 Census (Phillips); *Rules for the Government* (1873); Robinson (1876); *Ark. Gaz.*, Feb. 1, July 30, 1873; Foner (1996)
1873	Ferdinand "Ferd" Havis	Rep.	20 (Bradley, Jefferson, Grant, Lincoln)	1870, 1880, 1900, 1910 (Jefferson); *Rules for the Government* (1873); *Ark. Gaz.*, Feb. 1, 1873; Goodspeed (1890); (Riley 1895); Gatewood (1974); Leslie (1978); Gordon (1995); Foner (1996); Barnes (2004)
1873	Monroe E. Hawkins	Rep.	15 (Lafayette, Little River)	See 1868–1869 House
1873	Adam R. Johnson	Rep.	9 (Crittenden, St. Francis, Woodruff)	See 1871 House

1873	John H. Johnson	Rep.	9 (Crittenden, St. Francis, Woodruff)	Johnston in 1870 Census (Vanderburgh, IN); *Rules for the Government* (1873); 1880 Census (Woodruff); Williamson (1979); *Ark. Gaz.*, Feb. 1, 1873, July 14 1885; *Freeman*, Mar. 2, 1889; J. M. Johnson in Foner (1996); Kilpatrick (2003)
1873	William A. Marshall	Rep.	14 (Hempstead, Nevada)	1870 Census (Lafayette); *Rules for the Government* (1873); *Ark. Gaz.*, Feb. 1, 1873; Foner (1996)
1873	William Murphy	Rep.	20 (Bradley, Jefferson, Grant, Lincoln)	1870, 1880 Census (Jefferson); *Debates* (1868); *Rules for the Government* (1873); *Rules of the House* (1877); *Washington Telegraph*, April, 24, 1872; *Ark. Gaz.*, Feb. 1, 1873; Hume (1973); Leslie (1978); Moneyhon (1985); Foner (1996)
1873	Henry H. Robinson	Rep.	11 (Phillips, Monroe)	*Rules for the Government* (1873); *Ark. Gaz.*, Feb. 1, 1873; Barnes (2004)
1873	John C. Rollins	Rep.	22 (Ashley, Chicot, Drew, Desha)	John C. Collins in *Historical Report*; J. C. Rawlins in *Ark. Gaz.*, Feb. 1, 1873; John Rollens in 1870 Census (Ashley); *Rules for the Government* (1873); Georgianna Rollins (widow) in 1880 Census (Ashley)
1873	Archie/Archer Shepperson	Rep.	14 (Hempstead, Nevada)	1870, 1880 Census (Hempstead); *Rules for the Government* (1873); 1880 Census; *Ark. Gaz.*, Feb. 1, 1873, Jan. 22, 1967; Williams (1951); Foner (1996); *Ark. Hist. Commission News*, Sept. 2013
1873	George H. W. Stewart	Rep.	11 (Phillips, Monroe)	1870 Census (Marion, IN); *Rules for the Government* (1873); 1880 Census (Phillips); 1900 Census (Pulaski); *Ark. Gaz.*, Feb. 1, 1873; *Memphis Daily Appeal*, Feb. 22, 1873; TWD Coll [*Arkansas Mansion*, Aug. 25, 1883; *Baptist Vanguard*, June 15, 1894]; Foner (1996); Wintory (2004)

1873	John Willis Williams	Rep.	11 (Phillips, Monroe)	1870 Census (Phillips); *Rules for the Government* (1873); *Ark. Gaz.*, Feb. 1, 1873; Graves (1990); Foner (1996); Wintory (2004)
1874 Extra	Monroe E. Hawkins	Rep.	15 (Lafayette, Little River)	See 1868–1869 House
Post-Reconstruction/Redemption				
1874–1875	Levi B. Boston	**Rep.**	Jefferson	Levi Baston in 1880 Census (Jefferson); L. B. Boston in *Pine Bluff Weekly Graphic*, Aug. 18, 1888; *Pine Bluff Eagle Press*, Aug. 21, 1888; *Pine Bluff Press*, Oct. 22, 1874; Robinson (1876)
1874–1875	Berry Coleman	Rep.	Phillips	1870, 1900, 1910 Census (Phillips); *Rules of the House* (1877); Robinson (1876); Moneyhon (1985)
1874–1875	William L. Copeland	Rep.	Crittenden	See 1873 House
1874–1875	Toney Grissom	Rep.	Phillips	See 1873 House
1874–1875	Ned Hill	**Rep.**	Jefferson	1870 (Pulaski); Robinson (1876); Riley (1895); Moneyhon (1985); Graves (1990)
1874–1875	L. J. Maxwell	**Rep.**	Jefferson	Likely Jessy L. Maxwell in 1880 Census (Jefferson) [same township as L. J. Maxwell in 1877 Tax Roll]; *Pine Bluff Weekly Press*, Aug. 3, 1876; TWD Coll [*Arkansas Mansion*, Sept. 1, 1883]; Robinson (1876)
1874–1875	Abraham H. Miller	Rep.	Phillips	1880, 1900, 1910 Census (Phillips); Robinson (1876); Morris (1901); Miller (1911); Abraham H. Miller Papers, 1889–1928 (UALR.MS.0096); Delta Cultural Center (1993); Woodward (2016)

1874–1875	Burns Polk	Rep.	Lee	1870 Census (Phillips); Robinson (1876); U.S. House (1907)
1874–1875	James A. Robinson	Rep.	Desha	See 1871 House
1877	Crockett Brown	**Rep.**	Lee	*Rules of the House* (1877); 1880, 1900 Census (Lee); Moneyhon (1985); Wintory (2004)
1877	Berry Coleman	**Rep.**	Phillips	See 1874–1875 House
1877	Jacob N. Donohoo	**Rep.**	Phillips	1880, 1900, 1910 Census (Phillips); *Rules of the House* (1877); 1888, 1890 *Biennial Report*; Arkansas House (1891); *Ark. Gaz.*, Sept. 19, 1886, Nov. 4, 1893; *Ark. Dem.*, Oct. 14, 1890; *Indianapolis Freeman*, April 4, 1891; Moneyhon (1985); Gatewood (1972, 1974); Kousser (1975); Dillard (1980/1981); Graves (1990); Gordon (1995); Barnes (2004); Wintory (2004)
1877	Anderson Ebberson	**Rep.**	Jefferson	1870 Census (Jefferson); Epperson in 1900, 1910 Census (Jefferson); *Rules of the House* (1877); 1880 *Biennial Report*; Roster (1881); Leslie (1978); Moneyhon (1985); Service Record (RG 94); Pension File (RG 15)
1877	William Murphy	**Rep.**	Jefferson	See 1873 House
1877	Patrick T. Price	**Rep.**	Lee	1870 Census (St. Francis); 1880 Census (Lee); *Rules of the House* (1877); Wintory (2004)
1877	Francis "Frank" H. Sawyer	**Rep.**	Lincoln	1860 Census (St. Louis, MO); 1870 Census (Arkansas); 1880 Census (Lincoln); *Rules of the House* (1877); T. H. Sawyer in *Historical Report*; Moneyhon (1985)

1877	James Wofford	**Rep.**	Crittenden	1880 Census (Crittenden); *Rules of the House* (1877); *Ark. Gaz.*, Nov. 22, 25, 1876, Sept. 11, 1884
1879	Richard A. Dawson	**GB**	Jefferson	See 1873 Senate
1879	William "Willis" Hines Furbush	**Dem.**	Lee	See 1873 House
1879	Isaac Gillam	**GB**	Pulaski	1870, 1880, 1900 Census (Pulaski); *Little Rock City Directory, 1893–1894*; TWD Coll [*NY Tribune*, July 8, 1879]; Dillard (1973, 1976, 2000a, 2003a 2006); Gatewood (1990); Graves (1990)
1879	William C. Payne	**GB**	Jefferson	1880 Census (Jefferson); 1880 *Biennial Report*; Roster (1881); *Pine Bluff Weekly Press*, Aug. 3, 1876; TWD Coll [*Ark. Gaz.*, March 5, 1879; *NY Tribune*, July 8, 1879]; Leslie (1978)
1881	Anderson Ebberson	Rep.	Jefferson	See 1877 House
1881	William "Willis" E. Gray	Rep.	Pulaski	1870, 1880, 1900 Census (Pulaski); 1880 *Biennial Report*; Roster (1881); Morris (1901)
1881	Carl R. Polk	Rep.	Jefferson	1880 Census (Jefferson); 1880 *Biennial Report*; Roster (1881); *Pine Bluff City Directory, 1881;* Leslie (1978); Service Record (RG 94); Pension File (RG 15)
1881	William C. Payne	GB or Rep.	Jefferson	See 1879 House

1883	Daniel W. Lewis	**Rep.**	Crittenden	1880 Census; 1882 *Biennial Report*; Officers (1883); *Ark. Gaz.*, Sept. 30, 1882, Jan. 7, 1883; Daniel W. Lewis, Sr. Papers (MC 516); Bogle (1994); Kilpatrick (2003)
1883	Marshall M. Murray	**Rep.**	Lafayette	N. M. in *Historical Report*; 1900 Census (Lafayette); 1882 *Biennial Report*; Officers (1883); *Ark. Gaz.*, Sept. 30, 1882; Jan. 7, 1883, May 25, 1903; TWD Coll [*Colored American*, Nov. 14, 1903; *Arkansas Mansion*, Jan. 5, 1884]; Moneyhon (1991)
1883	Granville Ryles	**Rep./ GB**	Pulaski	1870 Census (Sebastian); 1880 Census (Pulaski); 1900 Census (Creek Nation, Indian Territory); *Ark. Gaz.*, Sept. 30, 1882; 1882 *Biennial Report*; Officers (1883); Wright (1916); Foreman (1978)
1883	Rusty Sherrill	**Rep.**	Jefferson	1870, 1880 Census (Jefferson); 1882 *Biennial Report*; Officers (1883); *Ark. Gaz.*, Sept. 30, 1882; Leslie (1978)
1883	Blackstone Waterhouse	**Rep.**	Jefferson	1870, 1880, 1900, 1910 Census (Jefferson); 1882 *Biennial Report*; Officers (1883); *Ark. Gaz.*, Sept. 30, 1882, Jan. 7, 1883; TWD Coll [*Arkansas Mansion*, Aug 11, 1883]; *Pine Bluff City Directory* (1881, 1883–1884); Leslie (1978)
1883	Francis "Frank" W. White	**Rep./ GB**	Pulaski	1880, 1900 Census (Pulaski); 1882 *Biennial Report*; Officers (1883); *Ark. Gaz.*, Sept. 30, 1882; Claimed to be a Democrat in "Opportunity School Is Conducted By Cherokee," *Ark. Gaz.*, June 29, 1930
1883	William H. Young	**Rep.**	Jefferson	See 1871 House
1885	Isaac G. Bailey	**Rep.**	Desha	1870 Census (Chicot); 1880 Census (Desha); 1900 (Jefferson); Officers (1885); *Ark. Gaz.*, Sept. 11, Dec. 2, 1884, Feb. 19, 1914; Morris (1901); Eatmon (1982)

1885	Joseph H. Bradford	**Rep.**	Mississippi	J. H. Bradford in *Historical Report*; 1880 Census (Mississippi) or Joseph Bradford in 1880 Census (Mississippi); Officers (1885); *Ark. Gaz.*, Sept. 11, 1884
1885	Joseph B. Brooks	**Rep.**	Lafayette	J. B. Brooks in *Historical Report*; 1880, 1900 Census (Lafayette); 1884 *Biennial Report*; Officers (1885); *Ark. Gaz.*, Sept. 11, 1884, Dec. 2, 1884
1885	Ed Glover	**Rep.**	Jefferson	1880, 1900 Census (Jefferson); 1884 *Biennial Report*; Officers (1885); *Ark. Gaz.*, Sept. 11, 1884
1885	William B. Jacko	**Rep.**	Jefferson	W. E. in *Historical Report*; 1880 Census (Jefferson); William B. Jacko in 1900, 1910, 1920 Census (Jefferson); 1884 *Biennial Report*; Officers (1885); *Ark. Gaz.*, Sept. 11, 1884, Sept. 17, 1886
1885	Green Hill Jones	**Rep.**	Chicot	1880, 1900, 1910 Census (Chicot); 1884, 1888 *Biennial Report*; Officers (1885); *Ark. Gaz.*, Sept. 11, 1884; Service Record (RG 94); Pension File (RG 15)
1885	Thomas R. Kersh	**Rep.**	Lincoln	Kirsh in *Historical Report*; 1870, 1880, 1900, 1910 Census (Lincoln); 1884, 1886 *Biennial Report*; Officers (1885); *Ark. Gaz.*, Sept. 11, 1884; Service Record (RG 94); Pension File (RG 15)
1885	Samuel H. Scott	**Rep.**	Jefferson	Sam H. Schott in 1880 Census (Shelby, TN); 1884 *Biennial Report*; Officers (1885); *Pine Bluff City Directory, 1883–1884*; *Ark. Gaz.*, Sept. 11, 1884; White (1986); Kilpatrick (2003); Payne (2009)
1887	Hal B. Burton	**Rep.**	Jefferson	1880, 1910 (Jefferson); 1886 *Biennial Report*; *Pine Bluff City Directory* (1883, 1894, 1898, 1908); *Ark. Gaz.*, Sept. 17, 1886
1887	Jacob N. Donohoo	**Rep.**	Phillips	See 1877 House

1887	W. E. Jacko	**Rep.**	Jefferson	See 1885 House
1887	Ed Jefferson	**Rep.**	Jefferson	1870, 1900 Census (Jefferson); 1886, 1888 *Biennial Report*; *Ark. Gaz.*, Sept. 17, 1886; TWD Coll [*Freeman*, May 30, 1891]; Gatewood (1974)
1887	Thomas R. Kersh	**Rep.**	Lincoln	See 1885 House
1887	Hugh L. Newsome	**Rep.**	Chicot	H. C. in *Historical Report*; 1870, 1900 Census (Pulaski); 1880 Census (Chicot); *Ark. Gaz.*, Sept. 17, 1886; TWD Coll [*Arkansas Mansion*, Sept. 1, 1883, Jan. 12, 1884]; Ella Newsome (widow) in 1920 Census (Pulaski)
1887	Sandy Shepard Odum	**Rep.**	Crittenden	1880 Census (Crittenden); 1900, 1910 Census (Monroe); *Ark. Gaz.*, Sept. 17, 1886, June 19, 1892; TWD Coll [*Cleveland Gazette*, Oct. 2, 1886]; Graves (1990)
1887	George W. Trower	**Rep.**	Conway	1900 Census (Burleson, TX); 1910 Census (Clay, KS); 1886 *Biennial Report*; Barnes (1998); Matkin-Rawn (2013)
1889	John H. Carr	**Rep.**	Phillips	1870, 1880, 1900 Census (Phillips); *Ark. Gaz.*, Nov. 4, 1891; *Indianapolis Freeman*, April 4, 1891; 1888, 1890, 1892 *Biennial Report*; Arkansas House (1891); Moneyhon (1985); Gatewood (1972, 1974)
1889	Sebron Williams Dawson	**Rep.**	Jefferson	1880, 1900, 1910 Census (Jefferson); 1888, 1890 *Biennial Report*; Arkansas House (1891); *Indianapolis Freeman*, April 4, 1891; *Ark. Gaz.*, Nov. 4, 1892; *Pine Bluff Commercial*, Feb. 3, 1989; Gatewood (1972, 1974); Moneyhon (1985); Graves (1990); Gordon (1995); Matkin-Rawn (2013)
1889	Jacob N. Donohoo	**Rep.**	Phillips	See 1877 House

1889	Ed Jefferson	**Rep.**	Jefferson	See 1887 House
1889	Green Hill Jones	**Rep.**	Chicot	See 1885 House
1889	George Washington Lowe	**Rep.**	Monroe	1870 Census (Hardeman, TN); 1900, 1910 Census (Monroe); 1888, 1890 *Biennial Report*; Arkansas House (1891); *Ark. Gaz.*, Nov. 4, 1890; *Indianapolis Freeman*, April 4, 1891; Morris (1901); Gatewood (1972); Barnes (2004); Ali (2010); Service Record (RG 94); Pension File (RG 15)
1889	Green W. Thompson	**Rep.**	Pulaski	1880, 1900 Census (Pulaski); Graves (1967, 1990); Gordon (1995); Dillard (2000b, 2004a, 2004b, 2011)
1889	Henry W./N. Williams	**Rep.**	Lincoln	H. N. in *Historical Report*; H.W. marries Louise Green recorded March 14, 1879, Lincoln County Marriage Records; Henry Williams married to Lewusie Williams in 1880 Census (Lincoln); 1888, 1890 *Biennial Report*; Arkansas House (1891); *Ark. Gaz.*, Sept. 14, 1888, Nov. 4, 1890; Gatewood (1972, 1974); Moneyhon (1985)
1889	Samuel L. Woolfork	**Rep.**	Jefferson	S. S. Woolfork in *Historical Report*; 1880, 1920, 1930 Census (Jefferson); *Ark. Gaz.*, Nov. 4, 1890; 1888, 1890 *Biennial Report*; Arkansas House (1891); *Indianapolis Freeman*, April 4, 1891; Moneyhon (1985); Gatewood (1972, 1974); Matkin-Rawn (2013)
1891	Benjamin F. Adair	**Dem.**	Pulaski	1860, 1870 Census (Lorain, OH); 1880 Census (Woodruff); 1890 *Biennial Report*; Arkansas House (1891); *Ark. Gaz.*, July 28, 1888, Nov. 4, 1890; *Pine Bluff Daily Graphic*, Mar. 30, 1902; Oberlin (1919); Moneyhon (1985); Gatewood (1972, 1974); Graves (1990); Gordon (1995); Kilpatrick (2003); Barnes (2004); Mitchell (2017)
1891	John H. Carr	**Rep.**	Phillips	See 1889 House

1891	Sebron Williams Dawson	**Rep.**	Jefferson	See 1889 House
1891	Jacob N. Donohoo	**Rep.**	Phillips	See 1877 House
1891	Henry A. Johnson	**Rep.**	Chicot	1880, 1900, 1910 Census (Chicot); 1890 *Biennial Report*; Arkansas House (1891); *Ark. Gaz.*, Nov. 4, 1894; TWD Coll [*Arkansas Mansion*, Sept. 1, 1883]; *Indianapolis Freeman*, April 4, 1891; *Texarkana Gazette*, July 9, 2017; Gatewood (1972); Moneyhon (1985); Gordon (1995)
1891	George Washington Lowe	**UL/ Rep.**	Monroe	See 1889 House
1891	John Gray Lucas	**Rep.**	Jefferson	1900, 1910, 1920, 1930 Census (Cook); 1890 *Biennial Report*; Arkansas House (1891); *Ark. Gaz.*, Nov. 4, 1890; *Indianapolis Freeman*, April 4, 1891; Moneyhon (1985); Gatewood (1972, 1990); Graves (1973, 1989, 1990, 2000); Kousser (1975); Gordon (1995); Luker (1998); Kilpatrick (2003); Barnes (2004)
1891	George W. Watson	**Rep.**	Crittenden	1880, 1900, 1910 Census (Crittenden); 1890 *Biennial Report*; Arkansas House (1891); *Ark. Gaz.*, Nov. 4, 1890; *Indianapolis Freeman*, April 4, 1891; Moneyhon (1985); Gatewood (1972, 1974)
1891	Henry N./W. Williams	**Rep.**	Lincoln	H. W. in *Historical Report*; See 1889 House
1891	R. C. Weddington	**Rep.**	Desha	1900 Census (Desha); 1890 *Biennial Report*; Arkansas House (1891); *Indianapolis Freeman*, April 4, 1891; Moneyhon (1985); Gatewood (1972); Kousser (1975)

1891	Samuel L. Woolfork	**Rep.**	Jefferson	See 1889 House
		Disfranchisement		
1893	Peter H. Booth	**Rep.**	Jefferson	1870, 1880 Census (White); 1900, 1910 Census (Jefferson); 1920 Census (Hempstead); 1892 *Biennial Report*; TWD Coll [*Arkansas Mansion*, Dec. 8, 1883]; *Ark. Gaz.*, Feb. 19, 1917; *Osceola Times*, Feb. 23, 1917; Graves (1967)
1893	Howard McKay	**Rep.**	Jefferson	1900 Census (Jefferson); 1892 *Biennial Report*; 1894, 1903 *Pine Bluff City Directory*; Graves (1967)
1893	John H. Carr	**Rep.**	Phillips	See 1889 House
1893	Nathan E. Edwards	**Rep.**	Chicot	N. E. in *Historical Report*; 1880, 1900 Census (Chicot); 1892 *Biennial Report*; *Ark. Gaz.*, June 4, 1904; White (1986)

Figure 1: African American Legislators in the Arkansas General Assembly, 1868-1897

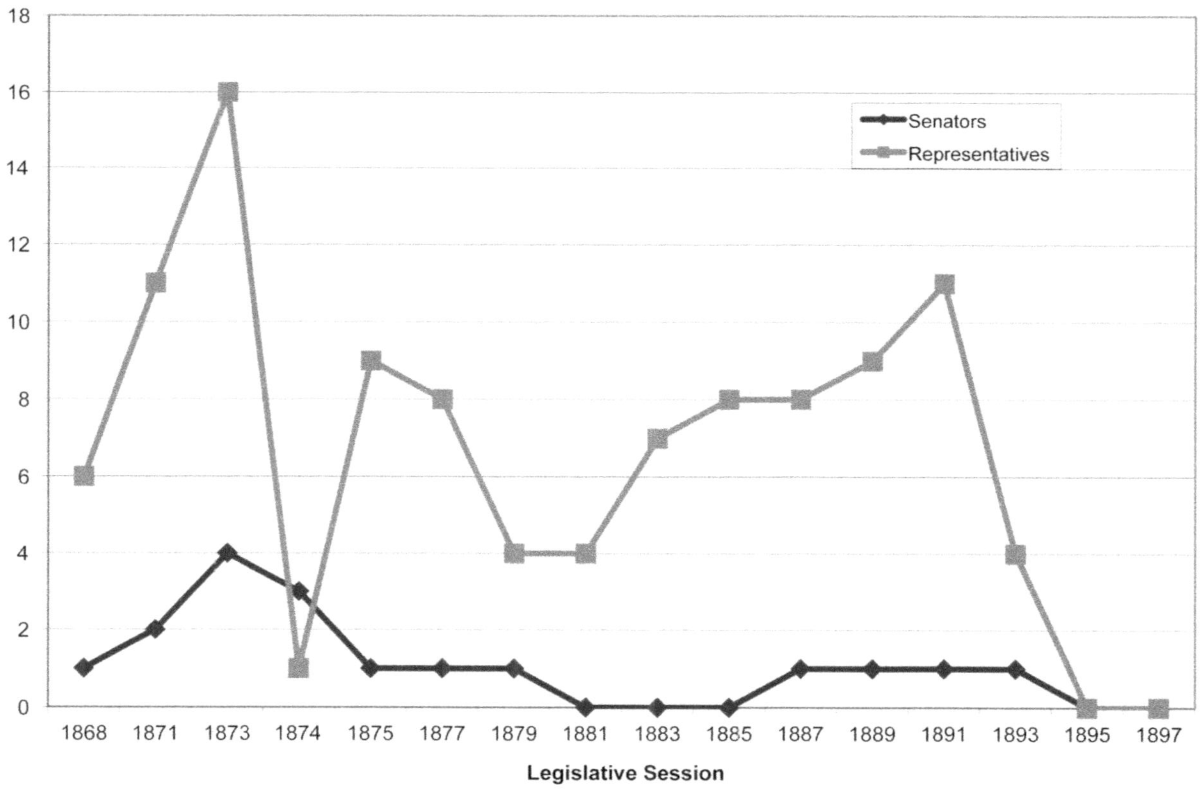

Table 3: Biographical Data

Legislator	Term	Birth	Antebellum Status	Black or "Mulatto"	Occupation	Literate	Property Value ($) (Co. Tax or Census)
Adair, Benjamin F.	1891 (H)	Phillips Co., AR (1853); d. 1902	Slave, Free	MU	Lawyer Oberlin College	Y	0 (1870 Census, Lorain, OH), 35 (Pulaski, 1893)
Alexander, James M., Sr.	1871 (H)	VA (ca. 1815); d. 1871	Slave	MU	Barber, Grocer, Justice of the Peace, AME Minister	Y	0 (1870 Census)
Bailey, Isaac George	1885 (H)	Chicot Co., AR (1846); d. 1914	Slave	MU/B	Baptist Minister, Educator	Y	x
Barbour, Conway	1871 (H)	VA (1818); d. 1876	Slave(?), Free	MU	Insurance Agent, Boatman/Steward, Cook, Restaurateur	Y	3,500 (1870 Census, Madison, IL), 0 (1870 Census, Lafayette, AR)
Barrow, Austin	1871 (H)	NC (1838)	Slave(?)	MU	Blacksmith, Sheriff, Co. Assessor	Y	3,800 (1870 Census)

Bell, George Walthal	1891 (S) 1893 (S)	MS, TN, "Abyssinia" (ca. 1855); d. 1927	Slave(?)	B	Traveling Book Salesman, Insurance Agent, President of Southland College, Teacher, Doctor National University (St. Louis), Dartmouth, Lincoln University	Y	290 (Jefferson, 1899), 330 (1900)
Booth, Peter H.	1893 (H)	TN, "America" (ca. 1851)	Slave(?)	B	Shoe shop, Blacksmith, Farmer, Farm Laborer	Y	0 (White, 1878), 48 (1879), 125 (1880), 98 (1881)
Boston, Levi B.	1874–1875 (H)	AR (ca. 1846)	Slave	B	Farmer, Co. Coroner	Y	170 (Jefferson, 1880)
Bradford, Joseph H.	1885 (H)	TN (ca. 1854)	Slave(?)	B	Teacher, Lawyer	Y	x
Brooks, Joseph B.	1885 (H)	MO (ca. 1840)	Slave(?)	B	Teacher, Preacher	N-1880 Y-1900	x
Brown, Charles F.	1873 (H)	MS (1840)	Slave(?)	B	Farmer (?)	N?	500 (?) (1870 Census)
Brown, Cornelius "Neal "	1873 (H)	TN (1845)	Slave(?)	B	Constable	Y	139 (Pulaski, 1871), 0 (1870 Census)
Brown, Crockett	1877 (H)	TN (1856)	Slave(?)	B	Farmer	Y	155 (Lee, 1875)

Burton, Hal B.	1887 (H)	AR (1851/1854)	Slave(?)	B	Farmer, Clerk, Merchant, Saloon Keeper, Porter	Y	15 (Jefferson, 1886), 20 (1887)
Carr, John H.	1889 (H) 1891 (H) 1893 (H)	Phillips Co., AR (1849)	Slave(?)	B	Farmer, Militia Member	Y	x
Coleman, Berry	1874–1875 (H) 1877 (H)	SC (1845)	Slave	B	Farmer	N-1870 Y-1900 Y-1910	0 (1870 Census)
Copeland, William L.	1873 (H) 1874–1875 (H)	OH (ca. 1846); d. 1885	Free	MU	Teacher, Union Soldier, Lawyer, Co. Assessor, Postal Clerk, Policeman Oberlin College	Y	0 (1870 Census, Lorain, OH), 0 (Crittenden, 1880, 1881)
Dawson, Richard A.	1873 (S) 1874–Extra (S) 1879 (H)	VA (1848); d. IL (1896)	Slave(?) Free	MU	Barber, Lawyer, Co. Clerk University of Chicago Law School	Y	0 (1870 Census, Cook, IL), 528 (Jefferson, 1873), 220 (1877), 250 (1879)
Dawson, Sebron W.	1889 (H) 1891 (H)	Baker Co, GA (1857)	Slave(?)	B	Farmer, Teacher	Y	50 (Jefferson, 1887), 80 (1889), 170 (1892)

Donohoo, Jacob N.	1877 (H) 1887 (H) 1889 (H) 1891 (H)	Bradley Co., TN (1854); d. 1917	Slave(?)	MU/B	Farmer, Lawyer, Grocer, Editor, Bank President, Real Estate	Y	x
Ebberson, Anderson	1877 (H) 1881 (H)	Jefferson Co., AR (1843); d. 1916	Slave(?)	MU/B	Farmer, Union Soldier	Y	230 (1870 Census) 50 (Jefferson, 1877)
Edwards, Nathan E.	1893 (H)	AL (1855); d. 1908	Slave(?)	B	Farm Laborer, Farmer, Baptist Minister	Y	0 (Chicot, 1883), 240 (1892) 179 (1894)
Fulton, Edward Allen	1871 (H)	KY (1833); d. 1906	Slave, Free	MU	Abolitionist, Tailor, Intelligence Officer, Census Taker (1870), Editor, Postmaster, Farmer, Laborer	Y-1860 N [*sic*]-1870 Y-1880	1250 (1870 Census), 0 (Drew, 1870), 205 (1871)
Furbush, William "Willis" Hines	1873 (H) 1879 (H)	Carroll Co., KY (1839); d. 1902	Slave, Free	MU	Photographer, Steamboat Porter, Union Soldier, Barber, Sheriff, Editor, Assayer	Y	2,500 (1870 Census), 210 (Lee, 1878)
Gillam, Isaac	1879 (H)	Hardin Co., TN (1840); d. 1904	Slave	MU/B	Horse Raising, Horse Shoer, Jailer, Policeman, Blacksmith, Alderman, Coroner	Y	400 (1870 Census), 75 (Pulaski, 1879)

Glover, Ed	1885 (H)	KY (1851)	Slave(?)	B	Farmer, Day Laborer	Y	55 (Jefferson, 1885), 10 (Jefferson, 1886)
Gray, William "Willis" E.	1881 (H)	AL (1848)	Slave(?)	B	Minister	Y	169 (Pulaski, 1882)
Grey, William H.	1868–1869 (H) 1874–1875 (S)	Washington DC (1829); d. 1888	Free	MU	Boatman, Minister, Grocer, Commissioner of Immigration and State Lands, U.S. Assessor, Farmer	Y	500 (1870 Census)
Grissom, Toney	1873 (H) 1874–1875 (H)	AR (1841/1850)	Slave	B	Farmer, Overseer, Preacher, Editor	Y	3,800 (1870 Census)
Haskins, Jeff	1871 (H)	NC (1820)	Slave(?)	B	Farmer, Minister	Y	1,320 (1870 Census)
Havis, Ferdinand "Ferd"	1873 (H)	Desha Co., AR (1847); d. 1918	Slave	MU	Barber, Grocer, County Clerk, Co. Assessor, Saloon Owner	Y	1,150 (1870 Census), 200 (Jefferson, 1873), 290 (1875), 550 (1900)
Hawkins, Monroe E.	1868–1869 (H) 1873 (H) 1874 (H)	NC (ca. 1832)	Slave	B	Baptist Minister, Farmer, Farm Laborer	Y	0 (1870 Census) 44 (Miller, 1875), 811 (1876)
Hill, Ned	1874–1875 (H)	AR (ca. 1845)	Slave	B	Farm Laborer	N	0 (1870 Census), 10 (Jefferson, 1877)
Hunt, Daniel	1868–1869 (H)	VA (1828/1834); d. 1887	Slave	B/MU	Farmer, School Board Trustee, Justice of the Peace, Constable	N-1870 Y-1880	0 (1870 Census)

Holland, Samuel H.	1873 (S) 1874–Extra (S)	Cincinnati, OH (ca. 1844); d. 1886	Free	B	Porter, Pullman Conductor, Sheriff, Jailor, Principal, Teacher, Planter	Y	300 (1870 Census) 80 (Chicot, 1873, 1874)
Jacko, William B.	1885 (H) 1887(H)	AR (1857)	Slave	B	Farmer, Teacher	Y	90 (Jefferson, 1883)
Jefferson, Ed	1887 (H) 1889 (H)	Memphis, TN (1861)	Slave(?)	B	Collector, Dep. Sheriff, U.S. Marshal	N-1870 Y-1880	0 (1870 Census), 75 (Jefferson, 1886), 65 (1887)
Johnson, Adam R.	1871(H) 1873(H)	MS (1825/1830)	Slave(?), Free(?)	B	Farmer, Lawyer, Teacher, Justice of the Peace, Business	Y	380 (1870 Census)
Johnson, Henry "Hal" Augustus	1891(H)	Johnson, MS (1855)	Slave	B/MU	Farm Laborer, Farmer/Planter, Sheriff, Justice of the Peace Alcorn University	Y	?
Johnson, John H.	1873(H)	Columbus, OH (1840); d. 1885	Free(?)	MU	Steward on Boat, Teacher, Union Soldier, Lawyer, Commissioner of Internal Revenue, Prince Hall Grand Master, Co. Assessor	Y	100 (1870 Census, Vanderburgh, IN) 0 (Woodruff, 1873)

Jones, Green Hill	1885 (H) 1889 (H)	Maury Co., TN (1842); d. 1924	Slave	MU/B	Sharecropper, Farmer Co. Treasurer, Minister, Assessor, Union Soldier Hillsdale College	Y	211 (Chicot, 1893) 204 (1894)
Kersh, Thomas R.	1885 (H) 1887 (H)	SC (1844/1847); d. 1916	Slave(?)	B	Farmer, Minister, Union Soldier	N-1870 Y-1880 Y-1900 Y-1910	150 (1870 Census), 215 (Lincoln, 1881, 1882)
Lewis, Daniel W.	1883 (H)	Frankfurt, KY (1851); d. 1932	Slave	B	Teacher, Lawyer, Judge, Justice of the Peace, Merchant, Co. Clerk	Y	91 (Crittenden, 1877) 0 (1879, 1880, 1884)
Logan, William H.	1887 (S) 1889 (S)	OH (1850/1855)	Free(?)	MU/B	Justice of the Peace, Preacher, Teacher, Farmer, Laborer	Y	325 (Chicot, 1894)
Lowe, George W.	1889 (H) 1891 (H)	Hardeman Co., TN (1847); d. 1920	Slave	B	Teacher, Minister, Farmer, Justice of the Peace, Pres. of the Colored Agricultural Wheel, Union Soldier	Y	200 (1870 Census, Hardeman, TN)

Lucas, John Gray	1891 (H)	Marshall, TX (1864); d. 1944	Slave(?)	MU	Lawyer, Prosecuting Attorney, U.S. Commissioner for Eastern Ark.	Y	30 (Jefferson, 1889),80 (1892)
Marshall, William A.	1873 (H)	SC (1843)	Slave	MU/B	Farmer, Justice of the Peace	N	0 (1870 Census),150 (Hempstead, 1868)
Mason, James W.	1868–1869 (S) 1871 (S)	Chicot Co., AR (1842); d. 1874	Slave, Free	MU	Planter, Postmaster, Sheriff, Judge Oberlin College	Y	12,000 (1870 Census), 1,300 (Chicot, 1873)
Maxwell, L. J.	1874–1875 (H)	SC (1851)	Slave	B	Farmer	Y	142 (Jefferson, 1877)
Mayo, Americus	1871 (H)	Norfolk, VA (1820/1834); d. 1891	Slave	B/MU	Farmer, Minister, Union Soldier	Y-1870 N-1880	250 (1870 Census)
McKay, Howard	1893 (H)	KY (1858)	Slave(?)	B	Teacher, Merchant, Grocer	Y	x 100 (Jefferson, 1892)
Miller, Abraham H.	1874–1875 (H)	St. Francis County, AR (ca. 1851); d. 1913	Slave	B	Farmer, Real Estate Agent, Preacher	Y	x
Murphy, William	1873 (H) 1877 (H)	KY (ca. 1810)	Slave(?)	B/MU	Farmer, Preacher	Y	400 (1870 Census), 80 (Jefferson, 1879)
Murray, Marshall M.	1883 (H)	AL (1856)	Slave(?)	B	Teacher, Professor, Real Estate	Y	x

Newsome, Hugh L.	1887 (H)	Nashville, TN (1849); d. 1900–1910	Slave(?)	MU	Teacher, Postal Clerk, City Marshal	Y	400 (1870 Census), 35 (Chicot, 1883)
Odum, Sandy Shepard	1887 (H)	MS (1852/1858)	Slave(?)	B	Teacher, Baptist Minister	Y	0 (Crittenden, 1880, 1881, 1882, 1884), 100 (1887)
Payne, William C.	1879 (H) 1881 (H)	Marion, TN (ca. 1841)	Slave(?)	MU	Teacher	Y	100 (Jefferson, 1880)
Polk, Burns	1874–1875 (H)	NC (1820)	Slave	MU	Farmer, Minister, Justice of the Peace	Y	0 (1870 Census), 0 (Lee, 1874)
Polk, Carl R.	1871 (H) 1881 (H)	AR/MS/VA (1841); d. 1926	Slave(?)	B	Farmer, Union Soldier	Y	0 (1870 Census)
Price, Patrick T.	1877 (H)	AL (1845-1848)	Slave(?)	B	Farmer, Minister	N-1870 Y-1880	0 (1870 Census), 20 (Lee, 1874), 155 (1875), 106 (1878)
Robinson, Henry H.	1873 (H)	AR (1847)	Slave(?)	B	Farmer, Teacher, Co. Assessor	Y-1878/1879	?
Robinson, James A.	1871 (H) 1874–1875 (H)	AR (ca. 1836)	Slave	B	Merchant	Y	500 (1870 Census) x
Rollins, John C.	1873 (H)	GA (1832/1835); d. before 1880	Slave(?)	B	Farmer	Y	0 (1870 Census), 9 (Ashley, 1873), 10 (1874)
Rush, Anderson L.	1868–1869 (H)	Arkansas Post, AR (1838); d. 1879	Slave	MU	Merchant, Teacher, Union Soldier	Y	900 (1870 Census), 135 (Pulaski, 1869)

Ryles, Granville	1883 (H)	KY (1831); d. 1909	Slave(?)	MU	Carpenter, Farmer, Mechanic, Minister	Y	100 (1870 Census), 130 (Pulaski, 1882)
Samuels, Richard R.	1868–1869 (H)	KY (ca. 1844); d. 1878	Slave	B or MU	Farmer, Blacksmith, Methodist Minister, Co. Clerk	?	160 (Hempstead, 1869)
Sawyer, Francis "Frank" H.	1877 (H)	MA/IL/OH (1831/1835)	Free	MU	Boat Steward, Teacher, Lawyer, Co. Assessor	Y	200 (1870 Census), 150 (Lincoln, 1876)
Scott, Samuel H.	1885 (H)	MA/NY (1840/1851)	Free(?)	MU	Lawyer, Editor	N [*sic*]-1880	?
Shepperson, Archie/Archer	1873 (H)	AR (1850); d. 1901	Slave	MU	Teacher, Sheriff, Farmer	Y	0 (1870 Census), 48 (Hempstead, 1877)
Sherrill, Rusty	1883 (H)	SC (1832/1835)	Slave(?)	MU	Farmer	N	285 (1870 Census), 400 (Jefferson, 1883)
Stanford, Anthony L.	1877 (S) 1879 (S)	NJ (1830); d. 1883	Free	B	Minister, Doctor, Liberia Immigration Leader, Liberian Judge	Y	1000 (1870 Census) x
Stewart, George H. W.	1873 (H)	IN (1839)	Free	MU	Editor, Teacher, Co. Assessor	Y	1800 (1870 Census, Marion, IN)
Thompson, Green W.	1889 (H)	Ouachita Co., AR (1847); d. 1902	Slave	MU/B	Grocer/Merchant, Landlord, City Alderman	Y	?

Trower, George E.	1887 (H)	AL (1855)	Slave(?)	B/MU	AME Minister	Y	?
Waterhouse, Blackstone	1883 (H)	LA/AL/AR (1840/1844)	Slave(?)	B	Grocer, Restauranteur, Saloon Keeper, Minister	Y	500 (1870 Census), 80 (Jefferson, 1887)
Watson, George W.	1891 (H)	Holly Springs, MS (1861)	Slave(?)	MU	Dep. Sheriff, Magistrate, Teacher, Farmer	Y	100 (Crittenden, 1891), 65 (1892), 135 (1893)
Webb, John W.	1871 (H)	KY (1824)	Slave(?), Free(?)	MU	Justice of the Peace, Business, Farm Laborer, Farmer	Y	1311 (1870 Census), 115 (Chicot, 1873, 1874)
Weddington, R. C.	1891 (H)	Rodney, MS (1866)	NA	B	Farmer, Teacher, Principal Alcorn University	Y	x
White, Francis "Frank" W.	1883 (H)	GA (1855)	Slave(?)	MU	Teacher, Farmer	Y	0 (Pulaski, 1882)
White, James T.	1868–1869 (H) 1871 (S) 1873 (S)	New Providence, IN (1840/1841); d. 1892	Free	MU	Baptist Minister, Editor	Y	9,500 (1870 Census)
White, Reuben B.	1873 (S) 1874–Extra (S)	IN (1845/1848); d. 1886	Free	MU	Minister	Y	0 (Pulaski, 1870, 1871)
Williams, Henry W./N.	1889 (H) 1891 (H)	TN (1844/1850)	Slave(?)	B	Farmer	N	111 (Lincoln, 1877)

Williams, John Willis	1873 (H) 1874–1875 (S)	MO (1835)	Slave	MU	Justice of the Peace	Y	0 (1870 Census)
Wofford, James	1877 (H)	GA (1843/1846)	Slave(?)	B	Farmer, Principal, Co. Assessor	Y	0 (Crittenden, 1877) 75 (1880)
Woolfork, Sam L.	1889 (H) 1891 (H)	Houston Co., KY [GA in Census] (1858)	Slave(?)	B	Farmer, Laborer, Teacher, Minister	Y	x 300 (Jefferson, 1887) 280 (Jefferson, 1889)
Young, William H.	1871 (H) 1883 (H)	TN/KY (ca. 1844)	Slave(?)	B	Minister	Y	600 (1870 Census) 25 (Jefferson, 1883)

Research Sources for Tables

Primary Sources, Collections, and Newspapers

Abraham H. Miller Papers, 1889–1928 (UALR.MS.0096), UA Little Rock Center for Arkansas History and Culture.

Arkansas Black History Online, Butler Center for Arkansas Studies, Central Arkansas Library System.

Arkansas Democrat-Gazette (Little Rock).

Arkansas Gazette (Little Rock).

"Arkansas House of Representatives, 1891." Photograph File, Arkansas State Archives, OV 2857.

"Arkansas House of Representatives, 1893" [Fragment]. Photograph File, Arkansas State Archives, OV 2858.

Arkansas State Gazetteer and Business Directory, 1884–5. St. Louis: R. L. Polk.

Arkansas State Gazetteer and Business Directory, 1892–3. Detroit: R. L. Polk.

Arkansas Weekly Mansion (Little Rock).

Baptist Vanguard (Little Rock).

Biennial Report of the Secretary of State of the State of Arkansas. 1880, 1882, 1884, 1886, 1888, 1890, 1892. Little Rock.

Biographical and Historical Memoirs of Central Arkansas. Easley, SC: Southern Historical Press, 1890.

Butler Center for Arkansas Studies. Vertical Files, "Bell, Sen. (Dr.) George Waltham" and "Rush, Anderson L." Central Arkansas Library System, Little Rock.

City Directory of Little Rock, 1871. R. L. Polk.

Christian Recorder (Philadelphia, PA).

Cleveland (OH) *Gazette*.

Colored American (Washington DC).

Compiled Military Service Records of the Office of the Adjutant General, 1780–1917, RG 94, National Archives and Records Service, Washington DC.

Debates and Proceedings of the Convention which Assembled at Little Rock, January 7, 1868… 1868. Little Rock: J. G. Price.

Dillard, Tom W., Black Arkansiana Collection. Biographical Files, "Adair, B. F."; "Bailey, I. G."; "Bell, George"; "Booth, P. H."; "Brown, Charles F."; "Brown, Neal"; "Carr, John H."; "Copeland, William L."; "Dawson, R.

A."; "Dawson, S. W."; "Donohoo, J. N."; "Fulton, E. A."; "Gillam, Isaac T."; "Grey, William H."; "Grissom, Tony (Attorney; Editor, *Arkansas Freeman Newspaper*)"; "Hawkins, Monroe"; "Holland, S. H."; "Jefferson, Ed"; "Johnson, Adam"; "Johnson, H. A."; "Kirsch, T. R."; "Lewis Sr., Daniel Webster (Attorney, Judge)"; "Logan, W. H."; "Lowe, G. W."; "McKay, Howard"; "Maxwell, L. J."; "Murray, M. M."; "Murphy, W. M."; "Newsome, H. C."; Odum, S. S."; "Payne, W. C."; "Price, Patrick L."; "Robinson, H. H."; "Rawlins, J. C."; "Shepperson, Archie"; "Stanford A. L."; Stewart, George H. W."; "Thompson, Green"; "Waterhouse, B."; "Watson, G. W."; "Weddington, R. C."; "White, J. T. (Reverend)"; "White, R. B."; "Williams, H. N." Butler Center for Arkansas Studies, Central Arkansas Library System, Little Rock.

Foreman, Grant, ed. 1978. *Indian Pioneer History Collection*, Vol. 111. Indian Archives Division, Oklahoma Historical Society, Microform Publications; transcribed by Gay Wall.

Freeman (Indianapolis).

Gaines, D. B. *Racial Possibilities as Indicated by the Negroes of Arkansas*. Little Rock: Philander Smith College, 1898.

General Index to Pension Files, 1861–1934. Washington DC: National Archives and Records Administration. T288, 546 rolls. [database accessible on Ancestry.com].

Goodspeed's Biographical and Historical Memoirs of Central Arkansas. Chicago: Goodspeed Publishing Co., 1889.

Henderson, Frank N., comp. *Illustrated Industrial Souvenir of Pine Bluff and Jefferson County, Arkansas*. Pine Bluff: George Adams, 1906.

Lewis, Daniel Webster, Jr. "Judge Daniel Webster Lewis, Sr., Early Arkansas Magistrate." *The Boulé Journal* 5–7 (ca. 1975). Copy located in Daniel W. Lewis, Sr. Papers (MC 516), Special Collections, University of Arkansas Libraries, Fayetteville.

Lincoln University. *Lincoln University: College and Theological Seminary Biographical Catalogue*, 1918.

Lincoln University Herald.

Little Rock City Directory, 1893–1894.

Marriage Records, Lincoln County, Book C, 373, Microfilm Reel 3 in Arkansas State Archives.

Miller, Rev. A. H. *How I Succeeded in my Business*, ca. 1911. Copies can be found at the Arkansas State Archives, Butler Center for Arkansas Studies, and Special Collections, University of Arkansas Libraries.

Morning Republican (Little Rock).

Morris, E. C. *Reflections from the Public Service of E. C. Morris, D.D.* Nashville, TN: National Baptist Publishing Board, 1901.

New York Tribune.

Oberlin. *General Catalogue of Oberlin College, 1833–1908*. Oberlin, OH, 1909.

O'Dougherty, Terence, and Frank M. Sarchet. *Combined Directory of Little Rock, Hot Springs, Pine Bluff, Eureka Springs, and Fort Smith: 1881–2*. Little Rock: Union Print and Pub. Co., 1881.

"Officers and Members of the Arkansas House of Representatives, 24th Session, 1883." Photograph File, Arkansas State Archives.

"Officers and Members of the Arkansas House of Representatives 25th Session, 1885" [1883 Members on reverse]. Photograph File, Arkansas State Archives.

Osceola Times.

Patterson, John, Helena, Arkansas, WPA Slave Interview, 1972. In *The American Slave: A Composite Autobiography*, edited by George P. Rawick, Vol. 10, *Arkansas Narratives*, Parts 5 and 6, 284–285. Westport, CT: Greenwood Press, 1941.

Personal Property Tax Records, Ashley County, Microfilm Reel, 40; Chicot County, Reels 71, 73; Crittenden County, Reels 52, 54; Desha County, Reel 70; Drew County, Reel 75; Hempstead County, Reel 76; Jefferson County, Reels 143, 144, 145, 148, 152, 156, 161; Lee County, Reels 34, 35; Lincoln County, Reels 46, 49; Miller County, Reel 41; Pulaski County, Reels 177, 178a, 179, 183, 184, 191; White County, Reel 59; Woodruff County, Reel 53—all in Arkansas State Archives.

Pine Bluff City Directory, 1881, 1883–1884, 1894, 1898, 1903, 1908. [1881, 1883–1884 at Butler Center for Arkansas Studies; 1894, 1898, 1903, 1908 in Pine Bluff/Jefferson County Library].

Pine Bluff Commercial.

Pine Bluff Weekly Graphic.

Pine Bluff Weekly Press.

Records of the Veterans Administration, Pension Case Files of the Bureau of Pensions and Veterans Administration, 1881–1942, Record Group 15. National Archives and Records Service, Washington DC.

Richardson, Clement. *National Cyclopedia of the Colored Race*. Montgomery, AL: National Publishing, 1919.

Riley, Jerome. *The Philosophy of Negro Suffrage*. Hartford, CT: American Publishing Co., 1895.

Robinson, H. H. "From the *Fort Wayne Gazette*" in *A History of the North-Western Editorial Excursion to Arkansas*, 198–212. Little Rock: T. B. Mills & Co., 1876. Edited and reprinted in Margaret Smith Ross, "Visiting Press Finds Legislature of 1875 Comfortably Housed, with Men of Note." *Arkansas Gazette*, December 21, 1958, p. 3E.

"Roster of the Officers and Members of the Arkansas House of Representatives, 23rd Session, 1881" [1879 Roster on reverse]. Photograph File, Arkansas State Archives.

Rules of the Government of the General Assembly of Arkansas. Little Rock: Little Rock Printing and Publishing Company, 1873. [Copies located in Butler Center for Arkansas Studies, UA Little Rock Center for Arkansas History and Culture, and University of Arkansas at Monticello Taylor Library Special Collections].

Rules of the House of Representatives and Joint Rules of the Senate and House of Representatives. Little Rock: Gazette Job and Book Printing House, 1877. [Copy located in University of Central Arkansas Archives].

Simmons, William J. *Men of Mark: Eminent, Progressive and Rising*. Cleveland, OH: Geo. M. Rewell & Co., 1887.

United States Census. Manuscript Returns. 1850–1930. Schedule of Population, various states and counties.

United States House. "Heirs of Burns Polk, Sr." *House Documents*, 59th Congress, 2d Session, Document No. 713. Vol 53, 1907.

"Untitled." Photograph File, Arkansas State Archives. Identified as "Arkansas House of Representatives, 1877" by White (1986) but could be "Arkansas House of Representatives, 1879."

Washington Telegraph.

Wright, Richard R. 1916. *Centennial Encyclopaedia of the African Methodist Episcopal Church*. Documenting the American South. University Library, The University of North Carolina at Chapel Hill, 2001. Online at http://docsouth.unc.edu/church/wright/wright.html (accessed January 23, 2018).

Secondary Sources

Arkansas History Commission Newsletter.

Ali, Omar H. *In the Lion's Mouth: Black Populism in the New South, 1886–1900*. Jackson: University Press of Mississippi, 2010.

Barnes, Kenneth C. *Who Killed John Clayton?: Political Violence and the Emergence of the New South, 1861–1893*. Durham: Duke University Press, 1998.

———. *Journey of Hope: The Back-to-Africa Movement in Arkansas in the Late 1800s*. Chapel Hill: University of North Carolina Press, 2004.

Bogle, Lori. "On Our Way to the Promised Land: Black Migration from Arkansas to Oklahoma, 1889–1893." *Chronicles of Oklahoma* 72 (Summer 1994): 160–177.

DeBlack, Thomas A. "A Garden in the Wilderness: The Johnsons and the Making of Lakeport Plantation, 1831–1876." PhD diss., University of Arkansas, 1995.

———. *With Fire and Sword, Arkansas, 1861–1874*. Fayetteville: University of Arkansas Press, 2003.

Delta Cultural Center. *A Land Given: 19th Century African-Americans in the Arkansas Delta*. Helena, AR, 1993.

Dillard, Tom W. "Enigmatic Black Pol Bucked Post Civil War System." *Arkansas Democrat-Gazette*, November 21, 2004.

———. "The Gilliam [*sic*] Family, Four Generations of Black Arkansas Educators." *Journal of Arkansas Education* 45 (April/May 1973): 19, 22.

———. "Gillam, Isaac T." In *Arkansas Biography: A Collection of Notable Lives*, edited by Nancy A. Williams and Jeannie M. Whayne, 122–123. Fayetteville: University of Arkansas Press, 2000.

———. "Gillam, Isaac Taylor." *Encyclopedia of Arkansas History & Culture*. http://www.encyclopediaofarkansas.net/encyclopedia/entry-detail.aspx?entryID=70 (accessed January 23, 2018).

———. "Isaac Gillam: Black Pulaski Countian." *Pulaski County Historical Review* 24 (March 1967): 6–11.

———. "No One Ever Stood Trial for Killing Green Thompson." *Arkansas Democrat-Gazette*, November 28, 2004.

———. "Thompson, Green Walter." *Encyclopedia of Arkansas History & Culture*. http://www.encyclopediaofarkansas.net/encyclopedia/entry-detail.aspx?entryID=1783 (accessed January 23, 2018).

———."Thompson, Green Walter." In *Arkansas Biography: A Collection of Notable Lives*, edited by Nancy A. Williams and Jeannie M. Whayne, 290–291. Fayetteville: University of Arkansas Press, 2000.

———. "Three Important Black Leaders in Phillips County History." *Phillips County Historical Quarterly* 19 (December/March 1980/1981): 10–23.

———. "William H. Grey Was Eloquent Advocate of Equality." *Arkansas Democrat-Gazette*, December 28, 2003.

Eatmon, Chris. *I. G. Bailey*. Little Rock: Self-Published, 1982. Copies located in Arkansas State Archives and the Mosaic Templars Cultural Center Research Collection.

Foner, Eric. *Freedom's Lawmakers: A Directory of Black Officeholders during Reconstruction*. Rev. ed. Baton Rouge: Louisiana State University Press, 1996.

Gatewood, Willard B., Jr. *Aristocrats of Color: The Black Elite, 1880–1920*. Bloomington: Indiana University Press, 1990.

———. "Arkansas Negroes in the 1890s: Documents." *Arkansas Historical Quarterly* 33 (Winter 1974): 293–325.

———. "John Hanks Alexander of Arkansas: Second Black Graduate of West Point." *Arkansas Historical Quarterly* (Summer 1982): 103–129.

———. "Negro Legislators in Arkansas, 1891: A Document." *Arkansas Historical Quarterly* 31 (Autumn 1972): 220–233.

———. "Sunnyside: The Evolution of an Arkansas Plantation, 1840–1945." In *Shadows over Sunnyside: An Arkansas Plantation in Transition*, 1830–1945, edited by Jeannie M. Whayne, 3–24. Fayetteville: University of Arkansas Press, 1993.

Gordon, Fon Louise. *Caste and Class: The Black Experience in Arkansas, 1880–1920*. Athens: University of Georgia Press, 1995.

Graves, John William. "The Arkansas Separate Coach Law of 1891." *Arkansas Historical Quarterly* 32 (Summer 1973): 148–165. Originally published in *Journal of the West* 7 (October 1968): 531–541.

———. "Lucas, John Gray." In *Arkansas Biography: A Collection of Notable Lives*, edited by Nancy A. Williams and Jeannie M. Whayne, 175–176. Fayetteville: University of Arkansas Press, 2000.

———. "Negro Disfranchisement in Arkansas." *Arkansas Historical Quarterly* 26 (Autumn 1967): 199–225.

———. "Jim Crow in Arkansas: A Reconsideration of Urban Race Relations in the Post-Reconstruction South." *Journal of Southern History* 55 (August 1989): 421–448.

———. *Town and Country: Race Relations in an Urban-Rural Context, Arkansas, 1865–1905*. Fayetteville: University of Arkansas Press, 1990.

Griffin, Nancy Snell. "Mason, James W." *Encyclopedia of Arkansas History & Culture*. http://www.encyclopediaofarkansas.net/encyclopedia/entry-detail.aspx?entryID=7547 (accessed January 23, 2018).

Harrison, Victoria L. "Man in the Middle: Conway Barbour and the Free Black Experience in Antebellum Louisville." *Ohio Valley History* 10 (Winter 2010): 25–45.

———. "Over the Horizon: Free Black Americans and Geographic Mobility in the Mid-Nineteenth Century, the Case of Conway Barbour." PhD diss., Saint Louis University, 2008.

Historical Report of the Arkansas Secretary of State. Little Rock: Secretary of State, 1998.

Hickman, Dale P. "The House at 928 Beech Street." *Phillips County Historical Quarterly* 5 (September 1967): 22–24.

Hume, Richard L. "The Arkansas Constitutional Convention of 1868: A Case Study in the Politics of Reconstruction." *Journal of Southern History* 39 (May 1973): 183–206.

Kilpatrick, Judith. *Arkansas' Early African-American Lawyers: A History*. 2nd ed., Fayetteville: University of Arkansas Law School, 2003.

Kousser, J. Morgan. "A Black Protest in the 'Era of Accommodation': Documents." *Arkansas Historical Quarterly* 34 (Summer 1975): 149–178.

Leslie, James W. "Ferd Havis: Jefferson County's Black Republican Leader." *Arkansas Historical Quarterly* 37 (Autumn 1978): 240–251.

Lubet, Steven. *The "Colored Hero" of Harper's Ferry: John Anthony Copeland and the War Against Slavery*. New York: Cambridge University Press, 2015.

Luker, Ralph E. *The Social Gospel in Black and White: American Racial Reform, 1885–1912*. Chapel Hill: University of North Carolina Press, 1998.

Matkin-Rawn, Story. "'The Great Negro State of the Country": Arkansas's Reconstruction and the Other Great Migration." *Arkansas Historical Quarterly* 72 (Spring 2013): 1–41.

McCaul, Robert L. *The Black Struggle for Public Schooling in Nineteenth-Century Illinois*. Carbondale: Southern Illinois University Press, 1987.

McKenzie, H. B. "Confederate Manufactures in Southwest Arkansas." In *Publications of the Arkansas Historical Association*, Vol. 2, 199–210. Fayetteville: Arkansas Historical Association, 1906.

Mitchell, Brian K. "Adair, Benjamin Frank." *Encyclopedia of Arkansas History & Culture*. http://www.encyclopediaofarkansas.net/encyclopedia/entry-detail.aspx?entryID=12339 (accessed January 23, 2018).

Moneyhon, Carl H. "Black Politics in Arkansas during the Gilded Age, 1876–1900." *Arkansas Historical Quarterly* 44 (Autumn 1985): 222–245.

———. "First Freedom, 1860–1900." In *Persistence of the Spirit: The Black Experience in Arkansas*, edited by Tom Baskett Jr., 18–27. Helena: Delta Cultural Center, 1991 [1986].

Patton, Adell, Jr. "The 'Back to Africa' Movement in Arkansas." *Arkansas Historical Quarterly* 51 (August 1992): 164–177.

Payne, Darwin. *Quest for Racial Justice: Louis Bedford Jr. and the Struggle for Equal Rights in Texas*. Dallas, TX: Southern Methodist University Press, 2009.

Rector, Theresa A. "William L. Copeland (ca. 1845–1885) of Ohio and Arkansas: Finding Him and Telling His Story." *Journal of the Afro-American Historical and Genealogical Society* 16 (1997): 21–35.

Simpson, Craig M. *A Good Southerner: The Life of Henry A. Wise of Virginia*. Chapel Hill: University of North Carolina Press, 1985.

St. Hilaire, Joseph M. "The Negro Delegates in the Arkansas Constitutional Convention of 1868: A Group Profile." *Arkansas Historical Quarterly* 33 (Spring 1974): 38–69.

Staples, Thomas S. "Negro Politics in Arkansas during Reconstruction." In "Some Negro Members of Reconstruction Convention and Legislatures and of Congress." Compiled by Monroe N. Work, *Journal of Negro History* 5 (January 1920): 68.

Texarkana (TX) *Gazette*.

White, Dena, comp. "Photographs of Black Legislators from Composites Available at the Arkansas History Commission." Arkansas State Archives, 1986.

Williams, Charlean Moss. *The Old Town Speaks: Recollections of Washington, Hempstead County, Arkansas*. Houston, TX: Anson Jones Press, 1951.

Williamson, Llewellyn W. *Black Footprints around Arkansas*. Hope, AR: Etter Printing, 1979.

Wintory, Blake. "William Hines Furbush: African-American Carpetbagger, Republican, Fusionist, and Democrat." *Arkansas Historical Quarterly* 63 (Summer 2004): 107–165.

Woodward, Colin Edward. "Miller, Abraham Hugo." *Encyclopedia of Arkansas History & Culture*. http://www.encyclopediaofarkansas.net/encyclopedia/entry-detail.aspx?entryID=9036 (accessed January 23, 2018).

"A PLAGUE O' BOTH YOUR HOUSES!"

Harper's Weekly *addressed the Brooks-Baxter War in its May 16, 1874, edition, characterizing the Arkansas drama as* "*A Plague O' Both Your Houses.*" Courtesy of the UA Little Rock Center for Arkansas History and Culture.

Chapter 4: Brindletails, Minstrels, Hercules, and Lady Baxter: The Brooks-Baxter War and the End of Reconstruction in Arkansas

By Thomas A. DeBlack

Since his election as governor of Arkansas in 1868, Powell Clayton had run the state much as he had run his cavalry regiment in the Civil War. Clayton was a man of unquestioned courage, but he was also a confrontational and polarizing figure. As governor, he made full use of the expanded appointive powers granted him by the new constitution of 1868, held the state for Ulysses Grant in that fall's presidential election, and, immediately following that election, declared martial law in a number of Arkansas counties to suppress Klan-inspired violence against freedmen and Republican officeholders. One prominent historian has argued that Clayton "accomplished more than any other Southern governor in suppressing the Ku Klux conspiracy."[1]

Clayton's harsh policies only added to the hatred that many of his former Confederate enemies had for him. But Clayton's troubles were not limited to his former foes. Even within the

Republican Party, the governor had serious enemies. Native Unionists, whom former Confederates referred to as "scalawags," chafed at the control of the Reconstruction process in Arkansas by Clayton and other "outsiders," the group that their opponents called "carpetbaggers." As early as April 1869, Lieutenant Governor James Johnson and a group of so-called Liberal Republican state legislators met to organize opposition to the Clayton regime, charging the governor with extravagance, mismanagement, corruption, and abuse of power. Clayton's Regular Republicans still controlled both houses of the legislature and the election machinery, and they were able to hold Liberal Republican gains in the 1870 elections to a minimum and to fend off an attempted impeachment attempt that same year.[2]

Governor Powell Clayton was a polarizing figure who struggled politically not only with Democrats and former Confederates but also with factions within his own Republican Party. Courtesy of the Old State House Museum, Little Rock, Arkansas.

There were other problems for the governor, however. That same election had seen Conservative-Democrats emerge as a legitimate force in both houses of the state legislature. It was clear to Clayton and other Republicans that the end of voting restrictions on former Confederates would place the Republican Party in Arkansas in dire straits. In the January 1871 session of the new legislature, Clayton pursued the U.S. Senate seat that was up for grabs. He was overwhelmingly elected, garnering not only the votes of his Republican supporters but also those of Conservative-Democrats who wanted him out of the state. He took his seat in March 1871, and a fierce new battle soon developed for political ascendancy in Arkansas.[3]

The Liberal Republican ranks included several major party figures, including U.S. Senator Benjamin Rice, but the man who came to lead the insurgents was a more minor figure named Joseph Brooks. Born in Cincinnati, Ohio, in 1821, he became an ordained Methodist preacher at age eighteen and a circuit rider in Iowa and Indiana. In 1856, he settled in St. Louis and became editor of the *Central Christian Advocate*, a Methodist anti-slavery newspaper, which gave him a forum for his own strong abolitionist sentiments.[4]

Lieutenant Governor James Johnson led the Liberal Republican state legislators who opposed the Clayton regime, charging the governor with extravagance, mismanagement, corruption, and abuse of power. "James M. Johnson, Secretary of State, 1873-1874," ASA_Photo_G5499OV, Arkansas State Archives, Little Rock, Arkansas.

He came to Arkansas in 1863 as chaplain of a black Union regiment whose colonel was his brother, William Brooks. William Brooks was killed in the action at Wallace's Ferry in Phillips County in July 1864. After the war, Joseph Brooks remained in Phillips County and made a considerable sum of money in the cotton business. He became a member of the Republican Party and was a dominant figure at the constitutional convention of 1868, where he was perhaps the most forceful and outspoken advocate for full civil rights for African Americans.[5]

Later that year, he was wounded in the ambush assassination attempt that took the life of Republican congressman James Hinds when they were traveling together to Monroe County. He had supported Governor Clayton's deployment of the militia in the state before later falling out with the governor and becoming the leader of the Reform or Liberal wing of the Republican Party. Brooks was a powerful speaker, leading another Liberal Republican and noted African American orator in Little Rock to declare that Brooks's voice reminded him of an old brindletail bull from his childhood that bellowed so loudly that he scared the other cattle half to death. Hence Brooks's faction would come to be called the Brindletails.[6]

Joseph Brooks was a member of the Liberal wing of Arkansas's Republican Party and claimed that he was the winner of the 1872 gubernatorial election, igniting the bizarre series of events known as the Brooks-Baxter War. "Joseph Brooks," ASA_Photo_PHC2733, Arkansas State Archives, Little Rock, Arkansas.

In 1871, Brooks announced his intention to seek the governorship the following year, and the Liberal Republican convention meeting in Little Rock made him its nominee in May 1872. The convention that nominated Brooks was made up of about half black members and about half white. He opened his campaign in June in a speech on the grounds of the state house in which he castigated Clayton and his administration in the strongest possible language. Promising that, if elected, he would launch an investigation into the various "crimes" of the administration, he added that, if he could find juries to present indictments and attorneys to prosecute the perpetrators, "I will fill the penitentiary so full of them that their legs and arms will be sticking out the doors and windows!"[7]

Four days later, Clayton confronted Brooks at a campaign stop at Lewisburg in Conway County, the scene of major disturbances during the postwar era. Speaking to the large crowd assembled there, Brooks repeated the charges made in his earlier address. Clayton listened intently until Brooks had finished. When his turn came to speak, he responded with a biting invective that matched or exceeded his opponents'. Calling the Liberal leaders "as scurvy a set of knaves and thieves as ever plunged their hands into the public treasury, and eluded the walls of the penitentiary," Clayton charged them with being participants in the very corruption they professed to deplore.[8]

He personally singled out Brooks, James Hodges, and Benjamin Rice as "thieves and scoundrels, reeking with corruption," charging that they had "stolen not only $500,000 from the Cairo and Fulton railroad company, but nearly everything else in the State." Addressing Brooks directly, he concluded his remarks with a "fable": "There was once an old brindle bull," the governor intoned, "which had been driving the small game into the lion's mouth, by bellowing up and down; and in turn the lion permitted him to graze a little, unmolested. But we shall not let the old brindle play his little game any longer. In November, we will strip his hide off, and hang it up for a warning."[9]

Despite this prediction, Clayton and his supporters knew that Brooks was a formidable candidate and that stripping his hide off would be no easy task. Brooks's strong record on civil rights drew support from black Arkansans, and his platform of "universal suffrage, universal amnesty, and honest men in office," combined with his opposition to Clayton, gave him strong appeal to many Conservative-Democrats. In the end, however, that support would cost him dearly among Republicans.[10]

Confronted by a candidate with wide appeal and great political skills, the Regular (pro-Clayton) Republicans faced the greatest challenge in their brief history. Meeting in convention in August, they dumped the colorless Ozro Hadley and nominated in his place the Batesville merchant and lawyer Elisha Baxter. Baxter was a native of North Carolina who had moved to Batesville in 1852 and served two terms in the state legislature in the 1850s. His exact political position before the war is difficult to determine. A onetime Whig, he had supported Thomas Hindman in the congressional elections of 1858 and 1860 but had opposed secession.[11]

Baxter's wartime experiences were the stuff of adventure novels. When Federal forces occupied Batesville in 1862, he was offered a commission in the Union army but declined. When Confederate forces reoccupied the area, Baxter fled to Missouri, where he took a job as a schoolteacher. In 1863, he was captured by a Confederate raiding party led by Colonel Robert C. Newton and returned to Arkansas to stand trial for treason. Friends in Little Rock helped him to escape (a fellow inmate's wife smuggled in a key), and he began a long and dangerous flight to Union lines in Missouri, surviving on little more than corn and berries. Arriving in Springfield, he recruited a mounted infantry regiment and became its colonel.[12]

After the fall of Little Rock to Union forces in September 1863, Baxter served the Isaac Murphy government as a member of the Arkansas Supreme Court and was later elected by the Unionist legislature to the U.S. Senate, although that Radical-controlled body refused to seat him. Governor Clayton later appointed him as judge for the Third Judicial District. John G. Price, a prominent member of the of the Regular Republicans and a one-time editor of the *Daily Republican* newspaper, had once been connected to a minstrel troop, and hence the Regulars soon became known as the "Minstrels." In actuality, the platform of the Regular Republicans differed little from that of the Brooks "Brindletail" faction. Like the convention that had nominated Brooks, the convention that nominated Baxter was about half white and half black in composition.[13]

Elisha Baxter became governor of Arkansas in 1872 and occupied that position until April 15, 1874, when Joseph Brooks and a group of armed men, citing a court ruling, threw him out of his office at the capitol. "Elisha Baxter, Governor," ASA-Photo_G0028-2, Arkansas State Archives, Little Rock, Arkansas.

The nomination of Brooks and Baxter by the opposing factions within the Republican Party began one of the most confused and confusing episodes in all of Arkansas history. As historian Michael Dougan noted, "That carpetbagger Brooks ran with Democratic and scalawag support against a scalawag nominated by a Party composed almost exclusively of carpetbaggers was enough to bewilder most voters as well as the modern student." Baxter could not match Brooks's oratorical ability, but he had his own advantage, namely control of the election machinery. In the end it proved decisive.[14]

The election in early November 1872 was marred by the now all-too-familiar pattern of fraud, intimidation, and stuffed ballot boxes. "Official" returns revealed that Baxter had won by a vote of 41,681 to 38,415. In Lincoln, Perry, Van Buren, and Arkansas counties, a number of votes were "disqualified," allowing Baxter to claim those counties by the remarkable tally of 465 to 0. In Jefferson County, however, some 400 Baxter votes were disqualified.

Brooks supporters fiercely contested the results, claiming that their candidate had actually won by 1,598 votes.[15] But they were frustrated in their attempts to have the election overturned. The legislature, dominated by Regular Republicans loyal to Baxter, offered little hope for a successful appeal, so the Brooks forces turned to the courts. In June 1873, the state attorney general initiated a *quo warranto* proceeding against Baxter, requiring the governor to prove the validity of his claim to the office. The Brooks forces hoped for a favorable ruling from the state supreme court, which was headed by Chief Justice John McClure, who had been a former Clayton ally and appointee but was now a Brooks supporter. The court denied the writ over McClure's dissent.[16]

That same month, Brooks filed a complaint against Baxter in the Pulaski County Circuit Court, claiming that Baxter had usurped the governor's office without authority. In response, Baxter filed a *demurrer*, and no further action was taken for a time. Having won a bitterly contested, divisive, and controversial election, Baxter immediately began to reach out to the opposition. In his brief inaugural address, he expressed the hope that his election would "mark the commencement of a new era of peace and good feeling in the history of Arkansas," and he appealed for a swift end to all voting restrictions on former Confederates. "The disfranchisement of certain classes for participation in the rebellion is a great impediment in the way of restoring fraternal feeling among the people," he noted. "It is needless for me to say that I desire the immediate enfranchisement of those persons who are now denied a voice in the selection of their rulers."[17]

Baxter moved quickly to make good on that pledge. An amendment restoring the vote was put to the voters in March 1873 and passed overwhelmingly. Thus Arkansas became the last state to remove voting restrictions on former Confederates. The new governor also appointed Democrats, Conservatives, and Liberals as well as Regular Republicans to government positions.[18]

After the legislature adjourned in April, a combination of gubernatorial appointments and resignations resulted in almost forty legislative vacancies, necessitating a special election in November 1873. The results of that election reflected the changes wrought by the recent passage of the new franchise amendment. Democrats were elected to fill practically all the legislative vacancies, giving them control of the state legislature for the first time since the advent of Congressional Reconstruction. The governor continued to broaden his appeal to all factions, and by the end of 1873, the *Daily Republican* reported that there had not been such peace and contentment in Arkansas since the beginning of Reconstruction. Historian Thomas Staples noted that by the close of that year, Brooks "was deserted by all but a few disgruntled Republican leaders and his reform party was all but dead."[19]

But in broadening his appeal to Democrats and Liberal Republicans, Baxter had begun to alienate his own base. U.S. Senators Powell Clayton and Stephen F. Dorsey continued to support Baxter, though they expressed their disapproval of many of his actions and were increasingly concerned by what his future course might be.[20]

The following year, however, a major schism developed that severely threatened the future of the Baxter administration. Democratic success in the special election gave rise to a call for a special convention to draft a new constitution more in line with Democratic principles. The prospect of a new charter that threatened to undo all that Republicans had worked for since 1868 sent shock waves through Republican ranks. When it became apparent that Baxter favored the calling of a convention, Senators Clayton and Dorsey hurried to Little Rock to attempt to exert their influence on the governor.[21]

That same month, Baxter further alienated many of his supporters over the issue of railroad bonds. In early 1873, he had helped quash an attempt by the railroads to require the state to accept company stock in payment for the bonds the state had issued to the companies and to impose a tax of three mills to pay off the interest and principal on the bonds (in effect, transferring the railroad companies' debts to the state). Now, in 1874, he opposed a request by the Arkansas Central Railroad (of which Senator Dorsey was a major official) for more state bonds. He then announced that he believed that the railroad bonds issued by the Reconstruction government (apparently including $400,000 worth of bonds that had been issued by him personally) had been issued in violation of the constitution and indicated that he would not issue any more such bonds.[22]

This action by the governor not only put the financial future of some major Republicans (including Dorsey and Clayton) in jeopardy, but it threatened to undermine the very foundation of the Republicans' plan for economic Reconstruction. For Dorsey and Clayton, this was the last straw. Deserting Baxter, they allied themselves with Brooks and persuaded a friendly Pulaski County circuit judge to bring up the case of *Brooks v. Baxter* (filed ten months previously). On April 15, 1874, the judge voided Baxter's *demurrer* and declared Brooks the legal governor of Arkansas, in effect overruling the previous decision of the Arkansas Supreme Court.[23]

Brooks was sworn in by Chief Justice McClure, and shortly thereafter, Brooks and more than a dozen armed men marched to the statehouse and forced the startled Baxter to vacate the governor's office. Baxter and his supporters established themselves at the Anthony House, a local boarding house located less than three blocks east of the capitol at the intersection of Markham and Scott streets. There they laid plans to retake the office. Main Street became the dividing line between the two opposing forces, and federal troops served as a peacekeeping force by attempting to keep the two sides apart.[24]

In preparation for such a circumstance as he found himself in, Baxter had mobilized the state militia in 1873 when he heard reports that an alliance of Regular Republicans, Liberal Republicans, and Democrats was planning to oust him. Ironically, he had chosen former Confederate colonel Robert Newton (the same Robert Newton who had arrested him for treason in 1863) to head the force. This militia failed to prevent his ouster a year later, but it now became the armed force behind his government in exile. To increase the surreal nature of the conflict, Brooks's militia was led by former Union colonel Robert Catterson and former Confederate general James Fagan. The Brooks forces soon erected earthworks and established a strong defensive position on the capitol grounds.[25]

In late April, Brooks sent an aide to St. Louis to purchase arms and ammunition for his troops. The agent purchased about 2,000 rifles, 13,000 rounds of ammunition, and a large quantity of other supplies. Anxious to avoid a repeat of the *Hesper* incident of 1868, the Brooks forces arranged to have the weapons shipped to Little Rock in small units in boxes labeled "whisky" or "Arkansas State Reports." Baxter's forces likewise fortified their position near the Anthony House, bringing in several small artillery pieces and salvaging a 64-pound cannon that had been positioned along the riverbank during the Civil War. The large gun was quickly nicknamed "Lady Baxter." (The cannon today sits on the grounds of the Old State House Museum.[26])

Though the controversy affected the whole state, Little Rock remained the center of the conflict. Volunteers for both sides rushed to the city until the number of armed men reached about 3,000, with each faction seeking desperately to secure weapons and ammunition. Among the Baxter supporters arriving in the city were about 300 black troops from Pine Bluff. They were led by a white officer who quickly established a reputation as one of the most colorful characters of the Reconstruction era: Hercules King Cannon White, a man whom historian John Harrell called "the most conspicuous figure, next to Brooks and Baxter, who took part in the Brooks and Baxter War."[27]

White was a Kentucky native who had run away from home at age fifteen to fight for the Confederate army. During the course of the war, he fought in both the regular Rebel army and with Confederate guerrillas. White moved to Pine Bluff to live with relatives. He served as a private tutor and studied law, obtaining his license to practice in 1868. Harrell described White as follows: "He was about twenty-eight years of age in 1874, rawboned, red-haired, and freckled….He married in Pine Bluff soon after the surrender, a granddaughter of ex-Gov. Roane….He allied himself with Powell Clayton in the early days of reconstruction and was made prosecuting attorney of his district by Clayton, entering with apparent zest into the organization of the Republican party in his county, the large majority of whom were negroes. He acquired an ascendancy of the people of that race in Arkansas." Harrell went on to say that White was "a man of unusual strength of intellect and originality, full of resources, energy, and audacity" and "so frank and fearless in his manner with men that he controls them by sheer force of will and dash—he runs over them, as it were, if he can." He concluded that White was "a ready and impressive speaker and skillful debater at the bar or in the party convention."[28]

Hercules King Cannon White, shown here as mayor of Pine Bluff in 1892, led militia troops loyal to Elisha Baxter and pledged that "Joseph Brooks will either be in hell, or the archives." Photo by R. W. Dawson, Little Rock; from the collection of Nathaniel Terry and Florence White Roberts's papers in the possession of great-niece Lela Roberts Murray.

When the Brooks-Baxter controversy broke out, the charismatic White tendered his services to Baxter, raised three companies of black troops, and on April 18 steamed with his command to Little Rock. Two days later, an additional 500 black men arrived by steamboat from Pine Bluff to reinforce Baxter. That same day, a large contingent of white citizens arrived from Pope and Johnson counties to lend their support to the exiled governor. Around five p.m., White turned out his command, accompanied by a brass band, for a parade. The parade ended at the Anthony House, where many Baxter supporters had gathered.[29]

Though claiming to be ill, Baxter appeared on the balcony to greet and address his supporters. White informed Baxter that he had not come to make a speech and then proceeded to make a speech. He told Baxter that he and his men were prepared to surrender their lives if necessary to reinstate the lawful authority of the state government. "Furnish us, simply, with the means—give us the authority—pronounce the order," White told Baxter, "and I will guarantee to you, sir, that in twenty-five minutes from the time the order is written, Joseph Brooks will either be in hell, or the archives." It was a bold pledge, particularly in light of the fact that many of White's "soldiers" were unarmed.[30]

Both the supporters of Joseph Brooks, who occupied the State Capitol (now the Old State House), and the supporters of Elisha Brooks fielded troops during the tense period when the governorship of Arkansas was disputed. "Old State House, Showing Troops during Brooks-Baxter War," ASA_Photo_G1746, Arkansas State Archives, Little Rock, Arkansas.

To his credit, Baxter urged patience until less drastic measures could be attempted. Unfortunately, when the commander of the federal troops tried to approach White to ask him not to move against Brooks's forces at the capitol, he inadvertently ran into one of White's black musicians. A disturbance broke out, shots were fired, and one man who was standing near a window in the Anthony House was killed by a stray bullet before order was restored. In an effort to calm the situation, Baxter requested that White return his men to Pine Bluff. White complied, but his involvement in the controversy was far from over.[31]

A bystander was killed during a scuffle following a speech by Elisha Baxter at Little Rock's Anthony House hotel in which he urged calmness and patience. "Street Clash in Brooks-Baxter War," ASA_Photo_G1776, Arkansas State Archives, Little Rock, Arkansas.

The conflict divided Arkansans of all political persuasions. That division, along with racial division, was reflected in the state's newspapers. Staples noted that twelve Republican and nine Democratic newspapers supported Brooks, while three Republican and fourteen Democratic newspapers supported Baxter. Another three Republican and five Democratic newspapers remained neutral.[32]

As were the other citizens of the state, black Arkansans were divided over the Brooks-Baxter conflict. Many were sympathetic to

Brooks because of his strong stand for civil rights, and a large part of Brooks's forces at the state capitol were African Americans. Others supported Baxter. African Americans from both camps would soon be involved in one of the war's major "battles."[33]

Shortly after Hercules King White's black militia returned to Pine Bluff, word reached him that another force of some 200 black Brooks supporters were organizing under the command of Captain J. M. Murphy at the community of New Gascony, about sixteen miles below the town. On April 30, White promptly embarked a command composed of white and black troops aboard the steamboat *Hallie* and proceeded downriver. Their arrival caught Murphy by surprise, and in the brief engagement that followed, White's forces routed the Brooks supporters, killing seven and wounding thirty. In later years, White would serve a term in the Arkansas Senate and six turbulent terms as mayor of Pine Bluff, but his greatest mark on Arkansas history was made during his brief involvement in the Brooks-Baxter War.[34]

Brooks's forces also scored victories in the conflict. On May 7, a week after the incident at New Gascony, forty Baxter supporters boarded the steamboat *Hallie* at Little Rock and started upriver to intercept a shipment of arms that was rumored to be headed down the Arkansas River from Fort Smith. The *Hallie* was captained by Sam Houston, the same man who had been the captain of the ill-fated steamer *Hesper* when it was intercepted by anti-Clayton forces on the Mississippi River in 1868. At a bend in the river near the community of Palarm (south of present-day Mayflower), 200 Brooks supporters who had concealed themselves along the riverbank waited to intercept it. When the *Hallie* hove into view, the Brooks men appeared and demanded its surrender. Houston refused, and the Brooks forces opened fire, killing Houston and piercing one of the *Hallie*'s steam pipes. The firing continued for half an hour as the stricken vessel drifted out of control. By the time the Baxter supporters on board finally surrendered, over half of their number were either dead or wounded.[35]

Despite the growing tensions between the rival camps in the capital, many local residents found the affair immensely entertaining. Bands played outside both the Brooks and Baxter headquarters, vendors hawked their wares, and the city's saloons did a roaring business. On April 21, police arrested a drunken woman who appeared near the contested area wearing men's clothing, sporting a large revolver, and declaring that she wanted to join the army.[36]

The schism in Republican ranks posed a dilemma for many Democrats and other Conservatives. Some had supported Brooks in

In this painting by James M. Fortenbury, supporters of Joseph Brooks open fire on the steamboat Hallie *at Palarm on the Arkansas River west of Little Rock, killing the vessel's captain and many of Elisha Baxter's supporters on board.* "The Battle of Palarm," ASA_Photo_G4543_44, Arkansas State Archives, Little Rock, Arkansas.

the election as the best hope of unseating the hated Regular Republicans, and they welcomed his *coup d'état*. Others, including prominent Little Rock attorneys Augustus Garland and U. M. Rose, remembered Brooks's staunch radicalism in the early days of the Clayton regime and feared his ascension to the governor's chair.[37]

Garland, a former Whig and Confederate senator, understood that the Conservative-Democratic element in the state could be a critical swing vote in the struggle between opposing factions in the Republican Party and that Baxter could be the instrument of the state's deliverance from Reconstruction. He and Baxter had become friends, and the embattled governor sought to bolster his position through Garland's standing in the community and his keen legal mind.[38]

Augustus Garland, a former Confederate senator, supported Elisha Baxter in the contested election, though he wrote, "It is small moment really who is Govr. of these two, but it is of great moment to settle these troubles and get a government by & from the people." Garland would himself be elected governor in 1874. "Augustus Hill Garland, Governor of Arkansas," ASA_Photo_PHC3048_01, Arkansas State Archives, Little Rock, Arkansas.

For Baxter, Garland was a major weapon in his struggle to retain his office, but for Garland, Baxter was only the means to an end. In a revealing letter to former Confederate governor Harris Flanagin, Garland candidly admitted, "It is small moment really who is Govr. of these two, but it is of great moment to settle these troubles and get a government by & from the people." These sentiments were shared by Robert Ward Johnson and Albert Pike, now residents of Washington DC who supported Baxter's cause in the nation's capital.[39]

In the final analysis, most Arkansans cared less about who occupied the governor's office than they did about the restoration of stability and order to state government. They joined the warring factions in appealing to President Grant to intervene. In September 1873, Grant had promised Baxter that the federal government would protect his claim to the governorship against any attempt to overthrow it. But Grant had been severely criticized for using the military to help settle a disputed gubernatorial election in Louisiana in 1872 and had done nothing since the crisis began. Instead he suggested that the state should settle the matter itself. Baxter contended that this meant that the state legislature should settle it. Brooks, on the other hand, maintained that the matter should be settled by the state courts. Finally, on May 15, 1874, one month to the day after Brooks seized the office, President Grant, convinced that serious violence was imminent, telegraphed his support for Baxter and ordered the Brooks forces to disband. He cushioned the blow by appointing Brooks to the position of postmaster at Little Rock.[40]

The following month, voters went to the polls to decide whether to hold a convention to write a new constitution and to choose delegates to that convention. This first statewide election since the end of restrictions on former Confederates gave clear evidence of a decisive shift in Arkansas politics. The convention was approved by a margin of almost ten to one (80,259 to 8,547), and Conservative-Democrats won more than seventy of the ninety-one delegate positions. Staples, in his landmark 1923 work *Reconstruction in Arkansas, 1862–1874*, wrote, "The Democratic members were elected and came together under the impression that they were to be the chief actors in a work of reform. That reform, as they understood it, was to be the undoing of the work of the Republican Party in Arkansas as far as the state constitution was concerned."[41]

The convention assembled on July 14, 1874, and remained in session until early September. The document it produced accomplished most of the "reforms" that the Conservative-Democrats had sought, which is to say that it precluded the kind of strong executive leadership and activist government that Powell Clayton and the Republicans had pursued. The governor's term was shortened to two years, his powers were dramatically reduced, and his salary, along with those of other state officials, kept very low. Gubernatorial vetoes could be overridden by a simple majority vote, and most state offices were made elective rather than appointive. In addition, the state's power to tax was severely limited. The document also provided for the civil and political rights of all citizens regardless of race, a necessary concession to prevent the possibility of federal intervention.[42]

On October 13, 1874, the voters went to the polls to vote for or against ratification of the proposed constitution and to elect officials to serve under the new document if adopted. Arkansas Republicans, their hopes for maintaining their hold on power tied to the increasingly unlikely prospect of federal intervention, did not put forward candidates for state offices. In the largest voter turnout in Arkansas history up to that time, the Democrats not only won control of those offices but also returned overwhelming majorities in the state legislature (thirty-one Democrats to two Republicans in the Senate, eighty Democrats to ten Republicans in the House) and elected Augustus Garland governor.[43]

A prominent Whig attorney in the antebellum period, Garland had supported John Bell of the Constitutional Union Party for president in 1860. Elected to represent Pulaski County in the secession convention of 1861, he had opposed secession until President Lincoln's call for troops. Through a combination of personal magnetism and ability, he had risen rapidly through the ranks of the Confederate government, serving first as a representative and later as a senator in the Confederate congress.[44]

Disfranchised by the Fourteenth Amendment, he had, through the influence of powerful friends, obtained a pardon from President Johnson in July 1865, only seventeen days after submitting his request. Garland then returned to his law practice. Though he had been admitted to the bar of the U.S. Supreme Court in 1860, his inability to take the Iron Clad Oath that he had never borne arms against the United States nor held office in a government hostile to it, prevented him from arguing cases before the court. In the case of *Ex Parte Garland* (1866), he successfully challenged the prohibition as unconstitutional and regained the right to appear before the Court. When Governor Baxter declined the Democratic Party's nomination for governor in 1874, the convention turned to Garland, and he won easy nomination and election.[45]

Only the long-anticipated report of a special committee of the U.S. House of Representatives charged with investigating the Brooks-Baxter controversy stood between the Conservative-Democrats and their goal of reclaiming control of the state government. The committee's majority report, submitted in early February 1875, concluded that the federal government should not interfere with the existing state government. The full House officially accepted the report on March 2.[46]

Three days later, Senator Clayton, who had labored diligently to overturn the Baxter government, conceded defeat, telling his followers, "The action of Congress on Arkansas affairs is conclusive. The validity of the new constitution and the government established thereunder ought no longer to be questioned. It is the duty of Republicans to accept the verdict, and render the same acquiescence which we would have demanded had the case been reversed."[47] Reconstruction in Arkansas was over, and the Brooks-Baxter War had, in effect, provided the means by which it was ended. In so doing, it marked the death knell for the constitution of 1868 and paved the way for the constitution of 1874.

By 1874, then, the old prewar planter class had largely realized its plan to "recover by the ballot what it had lost by the sword," as Colonel Willoughby Williams expressed it. These citizens had emerged from the struggles of the Reconstruction era weaker and poorer than before the war, but with their dominant position in Arkansas society restored. Nowhere was this more apparent than in the election of Garland and the men who followed him to the governor's office in the next two decades. William Miller (1877–1881) had been the Confederate state auditor; Thomas Churchill (1881–1883), a major general in the Confederate army; James Berry (1883–1885), a second lieutenant; Simon Hughes (1885–1889) and James Eagle (1889–1893), lieutenant colonels. Even had these men been disposed to assume an activist, progressive stance, the new constitution's reduction of the powers of the governor and its strict limits on the ability to raise taxes thwarted any serious attempt to promote the general welfare of the people through government action. Limited government and low property taxes would well serve the interests of the state's landed elite far into the next century. Change would come to Arkansas in the last quarter of the nineteenth century, but it would often come in spite of rather than because of the efforts of the state government.[48]

The war, emancipation, and Reconstruction had been truly revolutionary experiences for the state and the region. But the return to power of the antebellum elites ensured that Reconstruction would remain, in the words of Mississippi planter James Alcorn, a "harnessed revolution." Tragically, economic prosperity would remain an elusive goal for most of the state's citizens, and African Americans in Arkansas and throughout the South would have to wait for a "second Reconstruction" in the 1950s and 1960s to attain the full civil, political, and educational rights that the first Reconstruction failed to achieve.[49]

The Ku Klux Klan was founded in Tennessee in 1866, and by 1868 had expanded its tactics to include violent, terroristic tactics to oppose Republican rule and black rights. Much of the Reconstruction violence in Arkansas stemmed from KKK activity. Courtesy of the Library of Congress Prints and Photographs Division.

Chapter 5: "It Ain't Over Till It's Over": Political Violence in Reconstruction Arkansas, 1865–1892

By Kenneth C. Barnes

The Civil War split the white population of Arkansas into two sides and highly politicized both soldiers and common folk. Lacking government in much of the state and desensitized to violence by the war, many soldiers and civilians on both sides became accustomed to the use of force to solve their problems. Yet after 1865, these former enemies had to live together in the same communities. Reconstruction became a prolonged period in which Arkansans used illegal violence to get, preserve, or increase power.[1]

In the years following the Civil War, white elites who had supported the Confederacy, and their children, battled a tenuous alliance of a few newcomers from northern states ("carpetbaggers"), larger numbers of poor whites (some who had fought for the Union), and freedmen and women. Much of this violence played out on the local level, with competing groups fighting over control of county governments. At other times, such as in 1868, the Reconstruction state governments used force to suppress localized violence. And in 1874 the local factions fed a month-long battle over control of the governor's office. In the late 1870s and 1880s, counties and congressional districts were the common staging ground of politically motivated illegal violence. Using political violence as the viewing lens, it could be argued that Reconstruction did not end in 1874 but continued until these violent tactics brought victory and total domination of one side over the other. The full deconstruction of Reconstruction did not occur until the disfranchisement of African Americans and some poor whites was achieved in the early 1890s. At that point, white elites could put away their guns, for they would no longer need them to rule on the local and state level.

***

The first three years after the Civil War were a time of tenuous peace in Arkansas. Both sides had made some gains and held out hope for more. White Unionists and freedpeople could savor victory and the end of slavery, while former Confederates plotted quietly to take back control. Arkansas began the post–Civil War period under the state government of loyal Unionist men elected in 1864, headed by Isaac Murphy, the lone delegate to vote no to secession in 1861. President Andrew Johnson's position became increasingly clear in the year that followed the end of the war. He favored a soft, non-punitive approach toward the rebellious states. In this spirit, he returned confiscated lands to planters, pardoned many former Confederate government officials and military officers, and vetoed a bill conferring civil rights and citizenship to freedpeople.

In Arkansas and throughout the South, former Confederates prepared to "recover through the ballot box what they had lost by the sword," in the words of Civil War colonel Willoughby Williams.

They called themselves Conservatives but would soon be reorganized as the Democratic Party (or Conservative-Democrats). In the August 1866 elections, this group took all the state offices except those of governor and secretary of state, which had four-year terms and did not come before voters. The former elite took over the courthouses in many areas of Arkansas and dominated the new General Assembly that convened in November. This legislature, with several former officers in the Confederate army, passed laws legitimizing Confederate debts and providing pensions to Rebel, but not Union, veterans. The assembly chose two former Confederates to represent Arkansas in the U.S. Senate.[2] These ex-Rebels seemed to think that they could take back their former dominance, simply minus slavery. To white Unionists and people of color, these events of late 1866 would most certainly have appeared to reverse the victory won at such cost in the war.

Politics on the national level overturned this situation in March 1867, when Congress passed the Military Reconstruction Act. The hard Congressional Reconstruction plan divided the South into five military districts—Arkansas was in the fourth district with Mississippi—and restricted the franchise to black men and white men who had never participated in the rebellion. These voters were to elect delegates to write a new state constitution that would guarantee freedmen the right to vote. A follow-up congressional act put Union troops in charge of voter registration. To be readmitted to the Union, these states would have to ratify the new constitutions and the proposed Fourteenth Amendment, which would grant citizenship to all persons born in the United States, voting rights to black men, and equal protection under the law to all.

Some violence ensued when white Conservatives tried to drive out some Republican organizers from several Arkansas counties.[3]

Their efforts failed, and a coalition of black men, native white Unionists, and carpetbaggers—now organized as the Republican Party—dominated the elections and the convention when it gathered in January 1868. The constitution they wrote disfranchised most Conservatives, protected the vote for black men, and provided a strong range of executive powers for the governor.[4] In a vote that followed, the constitution was ratified, and a carpetbagger—a former Union colonel from Pennsylvania, Powell Clayton—was elected governor, and the slate of Republican candidates won the other state offices. Clayton was empowered to make appointments to many offices, including judges and prosecuting attorneys in circuit courts, county officials, and local boards of registration to prepare for the fall election.[5] The new legislature ratified the Fourteenth Amendment, and Congress voted on June 22 to readmit Arkansas to the Union. Two weeks later, Powell Clayton was inaugurated as governor, completing the Republican takeover of Arkansas's government. The stage was set for a wave of political violence in 1868 and 1869 that became virtually a sequel to the Civil War.

To Conservatives, the new constitution and Republican rule from the state to local level represented the punitive defeat they had not experienced in 1865. They immediately began to organize armed resistance, as the Ku Klux Klan (KKK). The Klan had been founded in Tennessee in 1866, but by 1868 had been reworked to incorporate violent, terroristic tactics to oppose Republican rule and black rights. A former Confederate brigadier general, Robert Glenn Shaver, of Jackson County, much later claimed to have led the state KKK and boasted that he could gather on short notice fifteen thousand armed men. Shaver said he attended regular meetings in Memphis with the Grand Wizard of the organization, former Confederate general Nathan Bedford Forrest. Given that the KKK was a secret society, it is hard to say how organized it was on a state or local level. But during the intense politicking associated with the March 1868 election, Conservatives began organizing Klan dens in Little Rock and other locations around the state, including Fort Smith, Batesville, Monticello, Pine Bluff, Camden, Searcy, and El Dorado. The intensely partisan *Arkansas Gazette* practically endorsed the formation of Klans "to fight fire with fire." A KKK handbill found nailed to a tree in Pine Bluff announced: "The time has arrived. Blood must flow." Disfranchisement in 1868 eliminated political activity as an option for Conservative-Democrats, leaving illegal force as the way to pursue their interests.[6]

Robert Glenn Shaver of Jackson County, a former Confederate colonel, claimed to have led the state Ku Klux Klan and boasted that he could gather on short notice 15,000 armed men. "Robert G. Shaver," ASA_Photo_G4543_35, Arkansas State Archives, Little Rock, Arkansas.

During the spring and summer of 1868, violence broke out in several areas of the state, much of it aimed at the most vulnerable supporters of Republican rule, freedpeople. This racial violence was political violence because it aimed to change the balance of power, especially by trampling on the rights gained by people of color with the Fourteenth Amendment. In May, the Klan took a black man who was sitting in jail for vagrancy in Woodruff County and hanged him. In Bradley County, bands of men patrolled the roads at night, shooting into the homes of freedpeople. Ten black citizens were murdered in Union County in August, and Union men there took to the woods to avoid prowling bands of men. Near Lewisville, in Lafayette County, seven freedmen and a white Unionist were murdered on a single day in August. From fifty to seventy-five white and black Unionists in the area were said to be living in the woods or had been driven away. In Mississippi County a band terrorized black precincts, killing six freedmen, burning black churches, and forcing freedmen and their families to sleep in the woods. In Independence County, twenty-five disguised men terrorized black men, driving them from their homes. The Searcy Klan took a black Republican leader, Ben Humphries, from his home and shot him in the head.[7]

Conway County serves as an example of the depth of racial violence in late summer 1868. A squabble began there when a freedman friendly with local Democrats killed another black man's dog, but it percolated to the point of a potential so-called race war. Whites used the quarrel that erupted among black men at the trial in Lewisburg as a pretext for taking away their guns. When they did not return the guns as promised, black men found more weapons, began to organize, and threatened, as the *Gazette* reported it, "to exterminate the white people of Lewisburg from the cradle up." On August 24, about two hundred white men gathered under the leadership of former Confederate colonel Anderson Gordon and set up pickets on the outskirts of the town. When members of a scouting party attempted to surveil the strength of the black force, they were shot at, killing one man and the horse of another.

The standoff lasted a couple of days, with white Democrats and some black men in town and the black force, accompanied by

The Conway County river port of Lewisburg was the scene of a potential racial crisis as hundreds of armed men, both black and white, confronted each other in late August 1868. Governor Powell Clayton helped mediate the crisis with the aid of other politicians and buckets of iced champagne. Courtesy of the Permanent Collection of the Historic Arkansas Museum, Little Rock, Arkansas.

some white Republican officials, camped outside of Lewisburg. Governor Clayton tried personally to mediate the dispute, while Republican congressman James Hinds went to the plantation country southeast of Little Rock and recruited more than a hundred freedmen to go to Conway County to "fight for their race." Hinds sent the steamer *Hesper* to pick up the men and transport them to Little Rock, covered with a canvas so that citizens of the city would not see them. Then the governor apparently changed his mind. He had the black militia leave the *Hesper* while he and several other politicians (and several buckets of iced champagne) steamed on to Lewisburg. By the time Clayton arrived, the black force had surrendered its arms with the caveat that they could get them back for hunting as long as they were returned by nightfall. Nonetheless, Clayton spent two days in the town, giving speeches to mixed-race audiences at the Masonic Hall, exhorting blacks and whites to live together amicably. He scolded whites for disarming blacks, reminding them that "the colored man possesses the same rights, privileges, and immunities—civil and political—that the white man possesses." He concluded that both whites and freedmen should look to civil authorities to keep order, and not take law into their own hands.[8]

While much of the Conservatives' use of violence in 1868 targeted freedmen and freedwomen to demonstrate Conservatives' rejection of the Fourteenth Amendment, the struggle also reopened local divisions between those local whites who had fought formerly in gray and in blue. During the Conway County "race war" described above, Governor Clayton sent Adjutant General Keyes Danforth to formerly white Unionist strongholds in the northern part of the county with instructions to bring a column of armed Republican men to Lewisburg. When Clayton found the war over by the time he arrived in Lewisburg, he sent a courier north to stop the posse advancing on Lewisburg. These men, reportedly 350 strong, were reluctant to disband, for they had taken orders before leaving for "coffee and dry goods they were to bring back from the looting of Lewisburg."[9] Similarly, in the next month, the Republican sheriff of Fulton County began raising a posse of white Unionist men to combat the Klan, which had just organized in this white area in the Ozarks. The KKK ambushed and killed the posse's leader, the county's Republican registrar Simpson Mason, and the sheriff got reinforcements of around sixty Unionist men from neighboring Missouri. Klan leaders sent out a call for help, and within a few days some seven hundred armed men had converged on the county seat, Salem, ready to do battle with the smaller number of Unionist men. An all-out war between the two white groups was averted, however, through the intervention of the Republican judge newly appointed for the circuit, Elisha Baxter, who arrived from Batesville and managed to talk down both the Klan and the Unionist men.[10]

The Klan targeted Republican state and county officials and representatives of the federal government, including agents of the Freedmen's Bureau and registrars, who were local men appointed by the governor charged with administering the loyalty oaths to register voters and then overseeing elections. In August at a Democratic rally in Searcy, locals became so agitated that they burst into the registrar's hotel and demanded that he register everybody who came to him or "it would be better for him that he had a mill stone tied about his neck and thrown into the Mississippi River." According to Governor Clayton, Democrats drove away registrars in Ashley and Lafayette counties and shot the registrar in Woodruff County as he was making his rounds.[11]

Much of the KKK-related violence during Reconstruction was targeted at agents of the Freedmen's Bureau. First Lieutenant William S. McCullough served as the Freedmen's Bureau agent in DeValls Bluff from July 1865 to July 1866 and from December 1866 to December 1868. He later moved to Brinkley and ran a popular hotel there. McCullough, owner of the Brinkley Hotel, was photographed September 1899 at Brinkley. Courtesy of Jack McCullough, a great-grandson; ASA_Photo_G5744_01, Arkansas State Archives, Little Rock, Arkansas.

The Freedmen's Bureau agent in Crittenden County, Captain E. G. Barker, who was also a state senator, reported that a group of around ninety

Klansmen was trying to take over the county by assassinating leading Republicans. Soon after, they shot Barker through an open window of his office in the center of Marion at dusk. Two Freedmen's Bureau agents in Little River County, P. J. Andrews and H. F. Willis, were murdered in October by a group of seven men. The county sheriff, who was with the two agents, managed to escape. Another agent in Ashley County survived a blast of buckshot that peppered his body and resulted in the need for his arm to be amputated.[12] Dr. A. M. Johnson, a member of the legislature from Mississippi County, was murdered in August near Osceola. Stephen Wheeler, senator for White County, was on his way to speak to a political meeting when his carriage was stopped by a band of men. He was shot in the arm, but he managed to escape. For several days, he hid out in the countryside, and at one point even swam the Arkansas River, before he found safety in Little Rock. In Drew County, a band of fourteen Klansmen shot the deputy sheriff and a black man, tied their dead bodies together in a simulated embrace, and left them as a spectacle for locals to see. Other white Republican officials in the county were threatened with assassination, and freedmen with death, if they voted in the November election. The intimidation worked, for Drew County showed 1,292 votes for the Democratic candidate Horatio Seymour and only 33 for Ulysses S. Grant.[13]

The most spectacular violence aimed at Republican officials was the attack on Congressman James Hinds and state representative Joseph Brooks in late October 1868 as they were traveling in Monroe County. This county, like so much of the state, had been in turmoil through the summer and fall. Representatives from both Republicans and Democrats called for a meeting to make peace between these feuding groups, and Hinds and Brooks were on their way to speak at this reconciliation gathering. They were overtaken, however, by a local Democratic Party leader, George W. Clark, who shot both men with a double-barreled shotgun. The blast killed Congressman Hinds and wounded Brooks.[14]

Governor Powell Clayton's answer to this sort of widespread lawlessness was military force. Federal troops were already stationed at twenty-three locations in the state, but that was insufficient to keep order.[15] Clayton had called for a state militia in his inaugural address in early July, and the legislature later in the month authorized the raising of a volunteer force, placing the governor as commander in chief. The militia would be funded through a one-eighth-cent property tax. Only those who were qualified to vote under the state constitution could serve in the militia. This meant it excluded former Confederates and was open to the arming of freedmen. In a speech of August 27, Clayton used the bedlam in Conway County and other counties as his justification for organizing a Republican state militia. With the push to register more voters in September and October to prepare for the

Democratic Party leader George W. Clark shot and killed Congressman James Hinds (above) *with a shotgun as Hinds headed to a meeting to try to reconcile feuding political groups in Monroe County in late October 1868.* Courtesy of William Darrow.

November presidential and congressional election, militia companies were needed to provide security for the registrars and for the freedmen who wished to vote.[16]

During August, September, and October, Clayton's supporters recruited companies of white and black militiamen. Attempts to organize freedmen into militia companies provoked new Klan violence in a number of areas. In Woodruff and Jackson Counties, the Klan ambushed recruiters and harassed black militiamen, including raiding their homes and taking away their weapons. One of the problems for the new militiamen, especially freedmen, was inadequate weapons. Their Klan adversaries were usually better armed. Many Klansmen were ex-Confederate soldiers who kept their armaments and horses when the war ended, while Union soldiers were required to turn in their arms and equipment. Governor Clayton recognized this problem and immediately ordered four thousand rifles from New York. Once the weapons arrived at a Memphis warehouse, however, the local men there refused to transport them on to Little Rock. In early October, Clayton took matters into his own hands and dispatched the ship *Hesper*, the same one upon which he had steamed to Lewisburg six weeks before. After the guns were loaded on the *Hesper* and it made its way about twenty-five miles down the Mississippi, a group of disguised Klansmen aboard a stolen tugboat overtook the steamer, leaped aboard, held the crew at gunpoint, and stole many of the guns and ammunition while throwing the rest into the river. Clayton then appealed to the secretary of war, General John M. Schofield, asking for use of weapons at the government arsenal in Little Rock. Schofield took the request to a cabinet meeting on October 23 but was denied by opposition of the secretary of the navy and President Johnson himself.[17]

When election day arrived on Tuesday, November 3, it appears that the Klan kept many Republicans from voting. In a state where ex-Confederates had been disfranchised, Republicans won a majority by only three thousand votes of more than forty thousand cast. Republicans carried twenty-four counties to the Democrats' twenty-one. In fourteen counties where the political terror had been most acute, votes were not even counted. Clayton later claimed that threats against registrars caused them to resign in twelve counties, making elections there impossible.[18] In some counties, Governor Clayton rejected the returns as fraudulent. For example, a courier for the governor rode into Pocahontas on election day with orders that no vote be taken in Randolph County. The sheriff and clerk, however, proceeded with the election anyway, and a large Democratic majority resulted (489 to 85). Randolph was one of the fourteen counties whose votes were thrown out. However, a few other turbulent areas that returned large Democratic majorities did have their votes accepted, such as Drew, recorded as going Democratic by more than a thousand votes.[19] It is possible that Powell Clayton rejected returns from just enough counties to ensure a Republican victory for Arkansas.

On the day after the election, Governor Powell Clayton proclaimed martial law in ten Arkansas counties: Ashley, Bradley, Columbia, Lafayette, Mississippi, Woodruff, Craighead, Greene, Sevier, and Little River. The declaration suggested that authorities in these counties were incapable of carrying out their duties without military force. It was a recognition of what people throughout the state already knew: Arkansas was again in a state of war between the two sides that had fought it out earlier in the decade. But it is possible that Clayton's martial law was also an excuse to invalidate the election returns, for nine of the ten counties were among the fourteen whose returns were not counted. Clayton had summoned legislators to Little Rock for a special session for him to explain martial law, and he wrote county officials with his reasons for this drastic action. Several sheriffs from counties in addition to these ten asked Clayton to extend martial law to their counties as well. He responded that this would happen only if they were incapable of performing their duties. He encouraged sheriffs to form their own militia companies to assist them in keeping order.[20]

Immediately after the election, Clayton put the militia into action. He divided the state into four military districts, placing

PROCLAMATION

By the Governor.

WHEREAS, the counties of Ashley, Bradley, Columbia, Lafayette, Mississippi, Woodruff, Craighead, Green, Sevier, and Little River, are now in a state of insurrection, and the civil authority within them is utterly powerless to preserve order and protect the lives of the citizens; unauthorized bodies of armed men (in most cases disguised) are engaged in acts of lawlessness and violence; the county officers have either been killed or driven away from their homes or intimidated from the performance of their duties; the quiet and law-abiding citizens, in many instances, have not been allowed an expression of their sentiments, or the exercise of their duties and privileges of citizenship, and, while hundreds of them have been murdered, in no instance known to the Executive have the assassins been brought to punishment by the civil authorities; the State is being invaded by bands of outlaws from Texas and Louisiana, who are committing murders and depredations upon the citizens; the registration laws could not be fairly executed, and were necessarily set aside; and in many of these counties a perfect reign of terror now exists.

Governor Powell Clayton declared martial law the day after the 1868 elections, stating that Ashley, Bradley, Columbia, Lafayette, Mississippi, Woodruff, Craighead, Greene, Sevier, and Little River Counties "are now in a state of insurrection…and in many of these counties a perfect reign of terror now exists."
"Governor Clayton's proclamation of martial law (1868)," ASA_Photo_G2142, Arkansas State Archives, Little Rock, Arkansas.

the southwestern district under the command of Robert F. Catterson, a former brigadier general of the U.S. Army and a member of the state House of Representatives. Another representative, Daniel P. Upham, was commander for the northeastern district, and a state senator named Samuel W. Mallory was appointed to the southeastern district. The northwestern district, which contained none of the ten counties under martial law, had no one assigned. Militia units, however, were raised in this Unionist stronghold and sent to the other three districts. By November 7 the commanders received instructions to occupy the counties under martial law and raise additional militia, even through conscription if necessary. Approximately two thousand men, mostly former Union soldiers from the Ozarks and freedmen from the flatlands, served in the militia campaign. Black men probably made up the largest number of militia men. Clayton later complained that at the onset of the expedition, the militia lacked sufficient arms, ammunition, horses, mules, food, and other necessities, and had to commandeer the necessary items as they went. The ragtag troops even lacked uniforms,

Robert F. Catterson, a former brigadier general of the U.S. Army and a member of the state House of Representatives, commanded one of four military districts in Arkansas and forcefully opposed the Ku Klux Klan in the southwestern part of the state. Courtesy of the Library of Congress Prints and Photographs Division.

so they resorted to tying a strip of red cloth to their hats to designate themselves as militia. They were given vouchers to pass out to those from whom supplies were taken, but as late as 1871 some people were still waiting to be paid. The difference between commandeering and looting was indeed a thin line.[21]

By November 13, Catterson had made his way to Murfreesboro and taken command of three hundred and sixty mounted militia that had assembled there, preparatory to a march on the southwestern counties that were at the center of Klan unrest. A black militia company, about a hundred men strong, marched upon Center Point, where it seized munitions and arms, commandeered other supplies, and held a number of local people under guard in a field. Receiving word that a force upwards of four hundred men was organizing to oppose them, Catterson and the rest of the militia rushed to Center Point just in time to engage a large force of Klansmen and their supporters near town. It was rural Arkansas's equivalent of urban warfare as the two sides fought their way through buildings in Center Point, ending with the militia routing the opposition.

This flag carried by an Arkansas militia company in a heated clash with the Ku Klux Klan bears a Battle of Center Point battle honor and is in the collection of the Old State House Museum in Little Rock. Courtesy of the Old State House Museum, Little Rock, Arkansas.

Catterson took control of one structure from which snipers were firing and found it to be the headquarters of the Ku Klux Klan, with a Confederate-flag-draped altar and costumes hanging from the walls. The militia discovered several men hiding in the attic and took them and about sixty others as prisoners. From Center Point the militia marched on a route through other counties in southern Arkansas: Sevier, Little River, Lafayette, Columbia, Union, and Ashley. After the Klan's defeat in the pitched battle at Center Point, members scattered in advance of the militia march. Catterson's execution of a small number of Klan leaders apprehended along the way and arrest of other offenders neutralized the opposition.[22]

In the southeastern district, Samuel Mallory, who had no previous military experience, marched his three companies of black militiamen to Monticello, where the KKK had murdered the deputy sheriff the month before. After a few of the black troops did some indiscriminate shooting, around two hundred local whites gathered and disarmed them. The whites appealed directly to Governor Clayton, asking to be allowed to raise two companies of a home militia to keep order. He agreed, and the black militiamen were mustered out of service. In December, Catterson and his men, after their sweep through southern Arkansas, arrived in Monticello. Apparently a man of sterner stuff than Mallory, Catterson arrested several men, including a KKK leader who had killed the deputy sheriff. They tried and executed the Klansman for murder.[23]

The third militia campaign, into northeastern Arkansas, began in early December when D. P. Upham, whom historian Thomas DeBlack has called a carpetbagger's carpetbagger, brought his men to Woodruff County. When Democratic opponents gathered outside of Augusta, Upham took fifteen local people hostage and threatened to kill them and destroy the town if attacked by the Klan. He tried several men and executed some by firing squad. Eventually a public meeting brought four hundred citizens willing to pledge support for civil authorities, and order was restored. Detachments of Upham's militia went to Mississippi, Greene, and Craighead Counties and in the latter sparred with a few hundred Democrats near Jonesboro. Here, the Republicans' superior force and the threat of public executions suppressed the opposition.[24]

In December, Governor Clayton added two counties to the list for martial law. Crittenden County, just across the river from the Klan's headquarters in Memphis, was a center of terror before, during, and after the November election. A large number of mostly black militiamen arrived at Marion and made a camp around the county jail. They erected an earthen rampart eight feet thick topped with palisades and dug a ditch surrounding the enclosure. With a fort in the middle of town, they were ready to do battle with the Klan, led by Crittenden County's Major Josiah [or Joshua] F. Earle. For a week, the Klan attacked each night. Eventually, reinforcements of mounted militia from Missouri secured the county. Many Klan members, like Major Earle, fled to Memphis. Some would never return.[25]

Conway County, northwest of Little Rock, was the last county to come under martial law. In late November, the Klan began terrorizing people of color, killing one man who lived with a white woman. A locally organized black militia company responded with an attack on two Klansmen in a cane thicket, killing one, before moving on to the home of Thomas Hooper, the purported leader of the Conway County Klan. The militia carried off Hooper with his hands tied to his horse and a rope around his neck. His body was found the next day with a gunshot to the back of his head. Disguised Klansmen responded by burning down a hotel in Lewisburg co-owned by the captain of the militia company, John Matthews. The flames spread, however, and destroyed an adjacent store, two saloons, and the post office. Under martial law, three additional white militia companies arrived to occupy what was left of Lewisburg. Within a week, another fire broke out, consuming even more of the town. This one burned down a store and killed the owner. Democrats claimed that the militia shot the storeowner, looted the store, and then set it afire. Republicans countered that the militia had restrained looters and helped put out the fire.[26]

Democrats protested at the time about the harshness of martial law and would complain for years about criminal outrages by militiamen. Indeed such acts did take place, as indicated in the Conway County story. Militiamen were accused of torturing prisoners to gain confessions, in some cases hanging them by the neck. But it is clear that Republican leaders imposed a degree of military discipline. Catterson tried several black men for breaking into a house and robbing the inhabitants, with one black soldier raping a woman. The men were dishonorably discharged and the rapist shot. Four soldiers in Marion were tried, convicted, and executed by an all-black firing squad for the crime of rape. When Upham left to police other counties in northeastern Arkansas, he left Woodruff County in the hands of John H. Rosa. Captain Rosa proceeded to arrest residents and then release them on ransoms of five hundred dollars, making four thousand dollars before he himself was arrested and sent to Little Rock for trial on blackmail charges. Martial law was used only as long as was deemed necessary. It was lifted in Conway County after only two weeks. The last county to see the end of martial law was Crittenden on March 21, 1869.[27]

What is striking about the work of the militia is the efficacy of the use of state-government-sponsored force. Union troops in uniform played hardly any role in this civil war of 1868. In most cases, the Ku Klux Klan members scattered with the arrival of the militia in their area. In county after county, the troops were disbanded or withdrawn following public meetings of local people pledging to abide by the rule of law under civil authorities. There is some evidence that the KKK organizationally caved in the face of force. Authorities in Memphis arrested Crittenden County Klan leader Major Earle and found in his possession a letter indicating that the Klan was ordered disbanded throughout Arkansas on January 29, 1869.[28] The wide distribution of Klan activity throughout the state and the speed at which militia troops, both black and white, were raised testifies to the desire to use violence to accomplish political goals. Democrats, for whom the Klan served as their paramilitary organization, had underestimated the resolve of Governor Powell Clayton, if not the federal government. Historian of the Reconstruction Klan Allen Trelease has argued that Clayton did more than any other Southern governor to suppress the KKK. When Arkansas became again pacified in early 1869 it would indeed seem as if the previous year had been a sequel to the Civil War.[29]

An uneasy peace prevailed in Arkansas until the Brooks-Baxter War and the so-called end of Reconstruction in 1874. But between 1869 and 1874, on the county level, it appears that men reached for their arms at a moment's notice. In Crittenden County, the last to be pacified (in March of 1869), violence broke out again just four months later. A reported former Klansman shot a black militia captain, A. J. Haynes, in the back, and the assassination set off an angry black mob that looted and burned the Marion store where the murder had been planned. In Chicot County in 1871, a controversy between rival white and black Republican claimants to a county probate judge position motivated a black mob of around four hundred people to terrorize Lake Village, sending white residents fleeing for their lives. And in Pope County in 1872, a spate of assassinations of county officials prompted the governor to send a militia company. Instead of restoring order, the militia was accused of murdering its prisoners. Martial law was declared there, with a larger number of militia sent in to maintain the peace.[30]

Meanwhile, beginning in late 1869, the Republican Party in Arkansas was dividing into factions: Governor Clayton's "Regular" Republicans and so-called Liberal Republicans, who charged Clayton's machine with reckless spending, corruption, and abuse of power. The Liberals also called for the end of voting restrictions on former Rebels. Democrats said "Amen!" to all the Liberal Republican positions. In the 1870 congressional elections, Democrats chose not to field candidates but to support the Liberal Republican candidates and run their own candidates only for the state legislature.

Democrats and Liberal Republicans came close to a majority of the seats in both houses, but the Regular Republicans prevailed. A bigger election loomed in 1872 when county and state offices, including the position of governor, were all up for a vote. Again, the Democrats chose a fusion strategy whereby they cast their lot with the Liberal Republicans instead of fielding candidates for the state offices. They did, however, put forth candidates for county positions. Powell Clayton had resigned the year before, after a coalition of Liberal Republicans and Democrats tried to impeach him, to take the post of senator for the state of Arkansas, but he still controlled the Regular Republicans from afar. He put forward Batesville Judge Elisha Baxter as the candidate for governor against Joseph Brooks, the leader of the Liberal Republicans. The election in November 1872 ended in dispute, as fraud and intimidation were charged in many areas of the state. Returns from four counties were thrown out entirely. With Clayton's faction dominating the election system, Baxter won by a slight margin. Brooks immediately cried foul and filed a complaint in the court system. With Clayton's machine dominating the courts, the case stalled and Baxter took office.

In Baxter's inaugural address, however, he sent signals to Democrats that he was moving to their side of the political aisle. In March 1873 he supported a legislative act to vote on a constitutional amendment to end disfranchisement of former Confederates, and it passed overwhelmingly. In June he made the intensely partisan Democratic *Arkansas Gazette* the official printer of state material. Baxter went on a flurry of appointments in 1873 to fill offices in nine newly created counties (one immodestly named Baxter County), and as a result many legislators had taken full-time jobs (with full-time pay) as county officials. It necessitated a special legislative election in November in which Democrats swept the vacant positions and took control of the General Assembly. Powell Clayton recognized that Baxter was handing Arkansas back to the Democratic Party. In early 1874 he shifted his support to Joseph Brooks and convinced a Pulaski County circuit judge to rule on the case that had been sitting idle for nearly a year. In April the judge ruled that Brooks had actually won the election. Brooks and armed supporters marched to the capitol and forcibly removed Baxter, who moved down Markham Street to make his headquarters in the Anthony Hotel. Thus began the Brooks-Baxter War.[31]

Others in this volume (especially in Chapter 4) tell the story of the month-long conflict in the spring of 1874. The literature about Brooks/Baxter is surprisingly thin, and it concentrates on political machinations within the Republican Party and the military actions led by hastily appointed commanders on each side.[32] Instead of studying the Machiavellian political moves of Republican politicians, I have looked at the troops who rallied for each side. Again, it is remarkable how quickly many men—black and white, Republican and Democrat—picked up arms as an expression of their political will. My examination of the Indians rather than the chiefs, as it were, adds some pieces to our knowledge and suggests some revision of the standard view of the Brooks-Baxter War as an inter-Republican conflict.

Within a week of Brooks's coup, upwards of two thousand troops had arrived in Little Rock from various parts of the state. Brooks's men occupied the capitol building and encamped on the grounds while Baxter's men encircled his headquarters a few blocks to the east. And a couple thousand more came as reinforcements before the war ended in mid-May. A few companies of additional Baxter and Brooks men, numbering around four hundred, fought each other at New Gascony, south of Pine Bluff. Just who were these troops, and where did they come from?[33]

One piece of evidence historians have used as support for the interpretation that Brooks-Baxter was a conflict between Republicans is that African Americans served on both sides. This is indeed true, but somewhat misleading. Some of the first Baxter troops to arrive in Little Rock on April 18 were around three hundred black soldiers from Jefferson County led by a Confederate veteran, the most charismatic and flamboyant military figure of the 1874 war with a name to match, Hercules King Cannon White. White's militia included a black brass band that paraded through the streets of Little Rock to much notice in the newspapers. Arriving a few days later was another black company from Pine Bluff raised by Ferd Havis, a prominent black man who had served in the state House of

Representatives until he received Governor Baxter's appointment as tax assessor for Jefferson County. This might explain Havis's support for Baxter.[34]

However, after about a week in the capital city, both of these groups of black troops returned to Jefferson County, many back to their homes. White came with them and was reported to be raising more troops, this time only white men, according to the *Daily Republican*. A local correspondent in Pine Bluff reported that White was refusing black men and had raised more than one hundred and fifty new mounted soldiers. Some of White's former black soldiers and new white ones met a force of black Brooks men being raised in the county by Powell Clayton's brother, John M. Clayton, and White prevented them from embarking on a steamer that would take them to Little Rock. It appears that all of Baxter's black troops hailed from one county, and they left Little Rock after the first week of the conflict. Baxter's group of reinforcements, on the other hand, appears to have been entirely white. Almost all of Brooks's men were black, and they arrived in Little Rock first from the southeastern townships of Pulaski County, and then from Jefferson, Hot Spring, St. Francis, Clark, Conway, and Perry Counties. On April 19, a reporter for the *Cincinnati Commercial* described Brooks's men as "mostly colored," while Baxter's forces in Little Rock on May 10 were all white.[35]

Thus, upon closer investigation of the troops rather than the politicians, the Brooks-Baxter War appears more a conflict between white Democrats supporting Baxter and pro-Brooks Republicans, who were largely a remnant of carpetbagger officers leading black troops. Further evidence to support this argument comes from the state's regions that provided the white troops. In 1868, mountain federals had provided most of the white men in militia companies recruited to fight the Ku Klux Klan. However, in 1874, Baxter's white troops came predominately from central and southwestern Arkansas. Counties identified with a company of white Baxter troops arriving in Little Rock included Pulaski, Saline, Lonoke, White, Faulkner, Conway, Pope, Johnson, Clark, Hempstead, Howard, and Hot Spring. Jackson and Independence in the northeast also sent companies, but this is hardly surprising given that Baxter was from Batesville. Thus the counties that lent support for Baxter were areas where a Baxter victory could ensure white majorities to keep power locally over black minorities. Several of these counties saw the worst violence between the Klan and militia in 1868. Hempstead County, the scene of the worst political violence of 1868, contributed probably the most white troops for Elisha Baxter, with companies arriving on April 18, 27, and 30 and May 7 and 11. In the nearly all-white counties of the Ozarks and Ouachitas and the black-majority counties of the Delta, people largely sat out the Brooks-Baxter conflict.[36] Thus, the two sets of adversaries in the Brooks-Baxter War were essentially the sort who had battled each other in the militia/Ku Klux Klan war of 1868, which was itself reminiscent of the real war of 1861–1865. In other words, Brooks-Baxter can be seen as a continuation of the political violence born in the Civil War and renewed in 1868 and 1869.

The war ended quickly when President Ulysses Grant cabled his verdict that Baxter won and that the Brooks forces should disperse. A quick vote was held for a constitutional convention, and it brought a body dominated by Democrats. This assembly swiftly wrote a new constitution that undid many features created by the Republican convention of 1868. With voter restrictions against former Confederates now gone, the new constitution was approved overwhelmingly, and Augustus Garland, a former Confederate government official, was elected governor of Arkansas. The general understanding is that the troops just went home, and the violence ended quickly. But some Brooks men, in white-majority areas, faced retribution upon their return home from Little Rock. After John Gibbons, who had brought a company of approximately a hundred black troops from Perry County, returned home, a mob came to his house. Gibbons grabbed his guns and ran to the woods. He tried to cross the Arkansas River to get on the train to Little Rock, but the Democratic men had all the river crossings guarded all the way back to Lewisburg. He crossed on a raft, returned to Little Rock, and testified to the congressional Poland Committee in July that he would be killed if he returned to Perry County.

***

The constitutional convention election on June 30 throughout Arkansas was marred by the same sort of fraud and intimidation of which regular Republicans had been accused in 1872. The *Daily Republican* charged that militiamen intimidated voters, especially black ones, in numerous precincts and that ballots were rejected in others. In Phillips County, where black voters outnumbered whites by a two-to-one majority, all 3,296 recorded votes favored a convention with not one vote against.[37] It staggers the imagination to think that all the black men of Phillips County would have voted to write a new constitution that would drastically reduce rights for black citizens.

The standard treatment says Reconstruction thus ended in Arkansas. But so-called redemption, the reclaiming of the state government by white Democrats, may have actually happened the year before when their disfranchisement ended, allowing Democrats to take control of the General Assembly. But in some ways, the work was not yet done. The sort of political violence common throughout Reconstruction continued to erupt whenever Democratic rule on the local level was threatened by black voters, or especially by any alliance of blacks and poor whites. This violence played out on a county level, rather than statewide. Secure with a statewide Democratic majority, the Democratic governors Augustus Garland, William Miller, and Thomas Churchill occasionally took actions to protect blacks' political rights in the later 1870s where they were threatened locally.

In the lead-up to the 1878 state and local elections, for example, whites in Phillips County were determined to unseat the black men who represented the county in the General Assembly and held all county offices. In August, white Democrats formed military companies, complete with cavalry, infantry, and breech-loading rifles. They called their company, which reportedly enlisted a thousand men wearing red shirts, the Phillips County Legion. The group broke up attempts by African Americans to have political meetings. The leader of the group, W. R. Burke, was the editor of the *Helena World* and a Democratic candidate for the legislature. Burke traveled to Memphis, where he borrowed two artillery pieces owned by the state

Governor Thomas Churchill, a former Confederate general elected in 1880, made efforts to protect African American Arkansans and to uphold their political rights during his administration. "Thomas J. Churchill, Governor of Arkansas," ASA_Photo_PHC2800, Arkansas State Archives, Little Rock, Arkansas.

of Tennessee, leaving a bond and pledge to return them in thirty days, after the election. Democrats placed one cannon in a public square in Helena and pulled the other one around black settlements in rural areas of the county. They threatened the county judge with death if he appointed anyone but Democratic men as election judges throughout the county. Republicans were advised to abstain from voting or face death. Under this sort of pressure, the leader of the county's Republican organization, the black county sheriff H. B. Robinson, offered to divide local offices in a fusion arrangement, whereby Democrats would get the offices of judge, treasurer, and assessor, as well as part of the representation in the state legislature. He even agreed that Republicans would vote on the Democratic judicial and state tickets. Feeling confident that they could have it all, however, Democrats refused the fusion offer. Sheriff Robinson and another black county official traveled to Little Rock to complain to Governor William Miller, and on August 19 he telegraphed orders that the Democratic clubs of Phillips County must disband. The intimidation worked nonetheless.

The election on September 2 coincided with an outbreak of yellow fever, and Democrats reportedly corralled potential black voters under the pretext of quarantine. As a consequence, Republicans were soundly defeated in Phillips County. Even Democrats admitted the efficacy of this political violence. A white planter in Helena, James Hanks, recorded in his diary on election day: "We have had an election so-called. Any was permitted to vote the Democratic ticket—no one was permitted to vote any other….It is the first time in a long while that we have had the presence of the military overawing the civil authorities." Although Phillips County was the most spectacular case of fraud and violence, Democrats in neighboring eastern Arkansas counties successfully suppressed the black vote as well. Coming on the heels of the withdrawal of the last federal troops from the South in 1877, this erosion of black political rights motivated a mass migration from Phillips County. More than 150 African Americans left in 1879 and 1880 for the Republic of Liberia.[38]

This sort of political violence waxed and waned on the county level through the 1880s. In the state election in September 1880, just two months after the Arkansas migrants arrived in Africa, only ten Republican votes were counted in Phillips County, a county with fifteen thousand black citizens. Neighboring Lee County recorded one Republican vote, Jefferson County seven, and Crittenden none, even though these counties had large black majorities. The governor elected in 1880, Thomas Churchill, made some efforts to improve the situation by his willingness to call out militia to keep order. He sent state guards to Perry County in the summer of 1881 when some local whites identifying themselves as the Ku Klux Klan burned down the newspaper office of a former Union officer and Republican leader and then brutally murdered him. Later that summer he sent a captain to Jefferson County to organize a black militia company to keep order. In 1882 Churchill met with a black Republican delegation from Phillips County, which expressed concerns that Democrats there would prevent Republicans from voting for or even nominating a ticket. He promised he would not allow military companies to intimidate voters or interfere with the election. Democrats still carried Phillips County, but this time more than a thousand Republican votes were counted. Republicans carried black-majority counties of Crittenden, Lee, Desha, and Lincoln. Jefferson County, which had polled seven Republican votes in 1880, went for the GOP this time by three thousand votes. Republicans still charged that hundreds were prevented from voting at the courthouse in Helena. Other reports surfaced of a ballot box stolen in a black precinct in

Monroe County and that some black men of Little Rock were afraid to leave their homes to vote.[39]

Conditions generally improved in the 1880s as Republican tickets carried several black-majority counties and fusion tickets, whereby the Democrats and Republicans divided up the county offices between them, won in others. In Jefferson County, for example, Democrats usually chose the county clerk, judge, assessor, and senator while Republicans picked the sheriff, circuit clerk, and representatives. While the political situation for black citizens varied from county to county and from election to election, the black disfranchisement experienced in Delta counties in 1878 and 1880 generally reversed in the 1880s.[40]

By the last years of the decade, however, a couple of factors conspired to motivate a new round of political violence. A massive migration of African Americans from the Deep South changed the electoral dynamics in a number of counties, with the greatest growth occurring in the cotton-growing areas of the Delta and the Arkansas River Valley. The number of black-majority counties rose from twelve to fifteen between the 1880 and 1890 censuses. The second factor was the rise of a strong agrarian populist movement. Poor farmers in rural areas dissatisfied with cotton prices, mortgages, and charges for ginning and shipping began to organize. They established cooperative stores, gins, and mills to remove the capitalist middlemen from the agricultural economy. Two white farmers' organizations founded in the state merged in 1885 as the Agricultural Wheel, while a black order called itself the Sons of the Agricultural Star. In 1887 the Wheel absorbed the Star and became a biracial organization of the rural poor. By 1888 the Wheel claimed more than seventy-five thousand members in Arkansas and had spread to neighboring states, swelling to a total membership of half a million. Two hundred of the nearly two thousand local Wheels in Arkansas were black. Moreover, the organization became political, fielding candidates for local offices in some counties in 1884 and by 1886 preparing a state ticket as well.[41]

In the 1888 state and congressional elections, the Wheel cooperated with the Knights of Labor to field candidates under the Union Labor Party. Moreover, the Republicans shocked Democrats when they declined to run a candidate for governor and instead supported the Wheel candidate against Democratic candidate James P. Eagle, a planter from Lonoke County. Republicans and Wheelers entered fusion agreements to unseat Democrats in many counties and pool their votes in congressional races. This biracial alliance of the rural poor threatened to defeat Democrats on the county, state, and congressional levels, motivating the revival of the violent tactics from earlier years. Democratic leaders apparently viewed black Republican voters as the weak link in the coalition. In July 1888 in Crittenden County, which was more than four-fifths black, a group of about a hundred white men armed with Winchester rifles assembled in the county seat, Marion. They rounded up all the black officeholders and some other prominent black citizens, including a minister, a newspaper editor, and a teacher, and escorted the group of about twenty to the railway station and ordered them never to return to the county. Governor Simon Hughes sent two boxes of guns and two thousand rounds of ammunition to Conway County to arm a seventy-five-man Democratic club that was performing drills and parading in the streets two weeks before the September election. Similar shipments reportedly went to Woodruff and St. Francis Counties.

With such a buildup, election day on September 3 erupted in violence. A fight between blacks and whites at the polls in Monroe County left one black man dead and another wounded.

In a rural black precinct of St. Francis County, a row occurred while votes were counted, leaving seven men shot, one dead. In Conway County, Democrats arrested a white Republican election judge on his way to the polls in Morrilton and roughed up a party worker when he tried to distribute Republican ballots outside the polls. At Plumerville, where most of the county's black residents voted, white Democrats forcibly removed the black Republican judges. Republicans claimed fraud before, during, and after the September state election. With the local Republican/Wheel tickets counted out in many counties, their candidate for governor lost by just thirteen thousand votes.

Perhaps Democrats became overconfident, for in the congressional elections that followed in November, they used even more bold measures to ensure their victory over the Republican/Wheel alliance. In Conway County, when officials had just begun to count the votes in Plumerville, the county's largest black precinct, a group of five masked men burst in and stole the ballot box at gunpoint. The Republican/Wheel candidate for Arkansas's Second Congressional District, John M. Clayton, brother of former governor Powell Clayton, lost the election by the slimmest of margins, probably less than the number of black votes in the stolen ballot box. Similarly, in the First Congressional District, the Republican/Wheel candidate, the state Wheel president Louis Featherston, lost after several flagrant cases of fraud and intimidation in Crittenden, Lee, St. Francis, and Phillips Counties. Both candidates contested the election because of these irregularities. Clayton's contest, however, would bring about his death. When he came to Conway County to take depositions reconstructing the stolen ballots, two assassins blasted him with a load of buckshot through his hotel window in Plumerville.[42]

The election irregularities prompted congressional investigations, and in both cases the U.S. House of Representatives took the seats from the two Democrats from Arkansas, ruling that they had won illegally. The Republican representative from Massachusetts, Henry Cabot Lodge, introduced a House bill in June 1890 designed to place federal control over congressional elections to make sure fraud, as had been committed in Arkansas, would not happen again. Representative Featherston, occupying his seat only since the preceding March, took pleasure in voting for the Lodge bill, or Force bill as it was called in the South. The bill would eventually pass the House and stall in the Senate. Foreshadowing the Voting Rights Act of 1965, it was much discussed in the lead-up to the fall 1890 elections. In Arkansas these elections shaped up to be a reprise of 1888, with a farmers/Republican coalition facing off against the Democratic Party. By 1890 the Agricultural Wheel had merged with the National Farmers' Alliance, but the politics would be the same. Again, Democrats resorted to fraud and intimidation to win the election. Conway County led the way, as in 1888. In the week before the September election, a Democratic gang burst onto the train arriving at the depot in Morrilton and wrested from the hands of a Republican leader the valise that contained the printed Republican/Union Labor ballots. This time they stole the ballots *before* rather than *after* the election.

The new General Assembly elected in September met in Little Rock in January 1891. Fearing that more illegal political violence could lead to the passage of the Lodge bill and federal control of elections, the legislature chose legal restrictions of suffrage instead. Setting a tone for this legislative session, one of the House's first actions was to remove a portrait of George Washington from behind the speaker's rostrum and replace it with one of Jefferson Davis. The General Assembly also proposed and passed a Jim Crow segregation measure modeled after a Mississippi statute, and then went on to pass secret-ballot and poll-tax laws that would disfranchise poor and illiterate citizens. The poll-tax law required a referendum before voters in 1892. But the secret ballot law worked well. The number of votes in the gubernatorial elections declined by 17 percent between 1890 and 1892. The proportion of black men voting dropped from 71 percent in 1890 to 38 percent in 1892.

Using the secret ballot, Democrats carried the black-majority counties that had gone Republican for decades. Democrats took all the county offices in Desha, Lafayette, Phillips, Monroe, and St. Francis Counties. Even in Chicot County, which was 88 percent black in 1890, the local white newspaper's headline read: "After Negro Rule for Twenty-Eight Years—Democracy on Top." The poll-tax amendment passed in 1892 and would further diminish black and poor-white voting in 1894. After this election, no black man would serve in the Arkansas General Assembly until 1973.[43] The cycle of political violence that had begun with the Civil War ended with the election of 1892, for the violence brought a final victory for white Democrats. They no longer needed to use violence to gain or preserve their power.

***

The disfranchisement laws of the early 1890s were the real end of the rupture that upset the domination of power by white elites, the close of this chapter of Arkansas history that began with the Civil War. The war had unleashed a free-for-all of violence that did not end in 1865. These white elites and their opponents showed a willingness to pick up arms at a moment's notice to take or maintain power. Most often this violence played out on the local county level. One striking thing about the "long" period of Reconstruction in Arkansas was the patience and resilience of the white elites. They lost in 1865, then again in 1868. But they did not give up; they kept whittling away at Republican control of state government in 1873 and 1874, and then piece by piece extinguished black political participation. The dismantling of Reconstruction happened gradually and was only completed in 1892. Eric Foner's *Reconstruction: America's Unfinished Revolution, 1863–1877*, probably the most influential book about Reconstruction of its generation, admits in the title that it was unfinished. Yet historians have made 1877 the end of an era, and professors have used the year as the end of one survey of American history and the beginning of another. From the perspective of violence and especially from the local level, 1877—or 1874 in Arkansas—would be more the middle of a journey than the end of the road.

While I was doing research for *Who Killed John Clayton?*, a study of political violence in Conway County, several of my oral sources confused the violence of the late 1880s and 1890s with Reconstruction. I found a small book published in the 1970s by the local Daughters of the American Revolution. In it, an elderly woman, Eleanor Wood Moose, declared that Clayton's assassination ended the carpetbaggers' domination of Conway County. Even though historians would say they were wrong, that Reconstruction had ended in 1874, Moose and other locals understood that the real end to this rupture came at the end of the next decade.[44]

Another noteworthy pattern was how impotent, really invisible, was the hand of the federal government to restrain white Democrats at any of these steps. The assertive use of force against the Ku Klux Klan and restoration of order in 1868 came from Governor Clayton's use of local militia, not federal troops. Two companies of federal troops placed themselves between Brooks's and Baxter's forces in 1874 but did not send the Arkansas men home. President Grant did end the conflict, but by ultimately siding with Elisha Baxter and the Democrats. The withdrawal of the last federal troops from the South in 1877 inspired terrorism in black-majority areas of the South, such as Louisiana and South Carolina, and in Arkansas in Phillips and surrounding counties. It appears that actions of two Democratic governors, not the federal government, undid the illegal disfranchisement that took place there in 1878 and 1880. Finally, the Lodge bill of 1890 proposed the possibility of federal intervention in the fraudulent elections in Arkansas and elsewhere, but this failed bill only motivated Arkansas legislators to suppress black and poor white voting legally.

It is no surprise that the Back-to-Africa Movement again glowed white hot in Arkansas in the early 1890s, as it had in Phillips County from 1878 to 1880. By trying to immigrate to Liberia, black Arkansans were giving up not just on Arkansas but on the United States, and on any confidence that the federal government would protect them. And it is no coincidence that 1892 saw a bout of spectacle lynchings in which crowds of thousands of white people in cities such as Little Rock, Pine Bluff, and Texarkana watched black men hanged or burned alive in public squares without a trial. Political violence had become racial violence, demonstrating that African Americans in Arkansas not only lacked political rights but fundamental human rights as well. This is the sad conclusion to the deconstruction of Reconstruction: political violence worked. The bullies won and would rule Arkansas for the next seventy years until challenged by a more assertive federal government.

Chapter 6: Redeeming Arkansas: The Constitution of 1874 and Post-War Politics

By Rodney Harris

On May 15, 1874, President Ulysses S. Grant issued Proclamation 218 concerning law and order in the state of Arkansas. In what seems to have been a rather mundane matter of business, taken care of between meetings with Secretary of State Hamilton Fish and the Turkish minister, the former general-turned-president effectively cast the die that would end Reconstruction and usher in so-called Redemption in Arkansas. Grant, who must have had misgivings about Elisha Baxter, considering his movement away from the Republican establishment, ultimately acknowledged Baxter as the duly elected governor of the state and moved toward restoring the peace. Grant stated:

> I, Ulysses S. Grant, President of the United States, do hereby make proclamation and command all turbulent and disorderly persons to disperse and retire peaceably to their respective abodes within ten days from this date, and hereafter to submit themselves to the lawful authority of said executive and the other constituted authorities of said State; and I invoke the aid

> and cooperation of all good citizens thereof to uphold law and preserve public peace.[1]

Grant for his part appeared to have struggled with this decision and even attempted to negotiate some degree of middle ground, though those efforts were less than successful, in large part due to resistance from Joseph Brooks. Baxter convened the General Assembly on May 13, two days prior to the proclamation. This meeting set the final dismantlement of Reconstruction in Arkansas in motion. Shortly after being informed of the president's proclamation, Baxter addressed the legislature, telling those assembled that the president had "favored" their meeting and acknowledged him as the rightful governor. In his address before the General Assembly, Baxter issued a call that had to give Republicans great pause:

> Owing to the unsettled condition of affairs in our state, and the great want of harmony in our laws, statutory and constitutional, your earnest attention is invited to the consideration of the propriety of calling a constitutional convention, a move which I deem at this time of absolute necessity, and I hope it may be your pleasure to call a convention of the state in order that the people may have an opportunity to speak and act at once as they deem best.[2]

Republicans were in turmoil watching the candidate that many establishment or Clayton Republicans had supported swing to the conservative political decision to call a new constitutional convention that would undoubtedly wipe away the Radical Republican constitution of 1868.[3]

This unlikely turn of events was propelled by a series of blunders and missteps by Republicans. With Republicans in the General Assembly divided, the Democratic minority moved closer to Baxter during the lengthy dispute with Brooks. In fact, these Democrats offered little resistance when Republicans sought to select Stephen W. Dorsey to the U.S. Senate. Likewise, Baxter offered his support to Democratic desires to return the vote to disfranchised Southern whites. Republicans increasingly defected from Baxter, leaving the beleaguered governor to look for political allies or be isolated. In fact, Democrats were able to gain Baxter's support to hold a popular vote on a constitutional amendment to restore the franchise. The vote was held on March 3, 1873, passing overwhelmingly. This paved the way for Democrats, albeit a divided Democratic Party, to regain power at the ballot box. Due to a high number of vacancies, caused by resignations and political appointments, a special election was called for November 1873. The full extent of the Democrats' newfound electoral fortunes was on full display in this election. Democrats regained control of both houses of the legislature.[4]

President Ulysses S. Grant, despite misgivings, ultimately declared Elisha Baxter the winner of the 1872 Arkansas gubernatorial election, setting the stage for the return of former Confederates to power in the state. Courtesy of the Library of Congress Prints and Photographs Division.

With the conflict behind him and the support of his new Democratic allies in the General Assembly, Baxter felt confident—he had to recognize the political importance of his position—in calling for a new constitution. The Redeemer Democrats who won control of the legislature most likely viewed Baxter with some degree of suspicion, but they also saw a man they could work with—maybe they saw a man they could use—to achieve their own political goals. In order to achieve these goals, the constitution of 1868 would have to go. The General Assembly answered Baxter's call by setting an election for June 1874. First, this election would ask voters to call a new constitutional convention; second, voters would select delegates to serve in the convention.[5]

On June 30, 1874, the voters of Arkansas called for a constitutional convention by a vote of 80,250 to 8,607. By all accounts, most Republicans opted to sit out the election, presumably because the outcome was a foregone conclusion. Republican leaders were opposed to any effort to draft a new constitution, and many Republicans thought that their best hope lay in congressional intervention that would never materialize.[6]

When it came to the selection of delegates, the election was not as clear cut. The governor's election proposition stipulated the number of delegates each county was entitled to elect. The vast majority would elect one delegate, but seven counties were to chose two delegates; three, Phillips, Washington, and Jefferson, were allotted three; and Pulaski County was allotted four delegates.[7] Some of these counties, such as Jefferson, would reliably be Republican, leaving Democrats little hope when it came to capturing those seats. In others, Democrats held the clear edge, but Arkansas Democrats, like those elsewhere in the South, were divided.

In Arkansas these divisions appear to be along the same lines as in other states, though there is little to no existing scholarship dealing with New Departure Democrats vs. Straight-Out Democrats in the state. This divide would inform many of the internal Democratic contests that dominated the election of delegates to the 1874 convention. In many of these contests, Redeemers proved victorious. These Redeemers often represented the New Departure element of the party. This faction of the Democratic Party was willing to embrace or at least drop its opposition to some Republican policies as part of an effort to improve the party's electoral chances. Part of this effort was for Democrats to tout their loyalty to the United States. In other words, they sought to put the Civil War behind them, at least publicly, and embrace patriotism. Another element was that these white Southern Democrats now embraced civil rights to some degree. Lastly, New Departure Democrats began urging the promotion of economic development by their states. In Arkansas, as elsewhere, not all Democrats were able to accept this massive shift in policy. These "straight-out" Democrats, or Bourbons, thought that New Departure Democrats were willing to go too far in order to win and advocated staying the course. In some of these elections for seats at the convention, these divisions likely impacted the selection of delegates in some counties as well as influencing the debates and proceedings within the convention.[8]

The Constitutional Convention of 1874 becomes central to understanding the rise of Redeemers in Arkansas. Despite this centrality, little scholarship has been devoted to the study of this convention. One reason for this is the shallowness of source materials. Neither the constitution makers in Arkansas nor the political leaders who followed them ever saw the need or expended the time, effort, and expense to have the debates and proceedings of the convention published in a usable form. While the debates and proceedings of the 1868 convention were published shortly after the convention and are available in a readable format, the journal from the 1874 convention has remained handwritten. Today it is available on microfiche to anyone who has the time to slog through this handwritten treasure. This journal also fails to record all of the votes and debates of the convention. Substantial portions of the debate were conducted behind closed doors or at least off the record in committee settings or when the convention convened as a "committee of the whole." It appears that most controversial topics were discussed in the committee of the whole, thereby keeping them out of the official record.[9]

Delegates to the constitutional convention assembled on the morning of July 14, 1874, in the house chamber of the State House in downtown Little Rock. Eighty-three of the ninety-one elected delegates were present. This has been seen by both contemporary and historical accounts as a distinguished group. The delegation contained two former governors (Henry M. Rector and Harris Flanagin), three future governors (James P. Eagle, Simon P. Hughes, and William Fishback), and two future justices of the Arkansas Supreme Court (Henry G. Bunn and John A. Eakin). The body also contained many future state representatives and state senators.

This assemblage of delegates also possessed significant political, governmental, and business experience. Of the convention's seventy-nine Democrats, thirty-two held some prior political experience. Ten members of the Democratic caucus had served in the 1861 secession convention, for example. Three Democratic members had served in the 1868 constitutional convention. William Fishback, who would eventually serve as governor, earning the nickname "the great repudiator," had been appointed to the U.S. Senate by the wartime Reconstruction General Assembly, though radicals in Congress barred him from taking his seat. The two former governors who served in the convention, Rector and Flanagin, had opposed each other for the office, a campaign in which Flanagin ultimately prevailed, while two other delegates, Grandison Royston and Rufus Garland, had previously squared off on the electoral field of battle. Royston, who would be selected by his peers to lead the convention, had previously served as speaker of the house, U.S. Attorney, and a member of the Confederate Congress. He was defeated for a second term by Rufus Garland. Royston suffered from declining support for the war in Arkansas and from the fact that his son refused to enlist in the Confederate cause. Garland had taken full advantage of both of these aspects; in fact, he was known as something of a "Confederate Copperhead," and he charged Royston with being a supporter of Confederate President Jefferson Davis. Royston and Garland were not the only former members of the Confederate Congress to serve as members of the convention. Hugh F. Thomason had served one term in the Congress, as well, prior to being defeated for his lack of Confederate patriotism.[10]

Grandison D. Royston, who previously served as speaker of the house, U.S. Attorney, and a member of the Confederate Congress, was selected to serve as president of the 1874 Arkansas constitutional convention. "Grandison Royston, United States District Attorney and Member of Confederate Congress," ASA_Photo_PHC3606, Arkansas State Archives, Little Rock, Arkansas.

These Democratic constitution makers also differed when it came to occupation and nativity. Thirty-four members of the Democratic delegation were farmers. Ten of this number were members of the Grange. The delegation also contained thirty-two lawyers, seven medical doctors, two merchants, and three ministers, though not all professions are easy to establish and some of these men might fit under the heading of more than one of these professions. These Democrats came from various places and few were Arkansas natives. In fact, twenty-eight were natives of Tennessee. Virginia, Kentucky, North Carolina, Alabama, Mississippi, and South Carolina also provided natives to the convention. Two members of the Democratic delegation were Yankees, having come from New Jersey and Pennsylvania. Constitution makers wrestled with multiple issues in the convention, though the issues of centralization, retrenchment, the judicial branch, the franchise, internal improvements, and education reveal the most concerning Redemption. These issues also provide the best insight into the divisions that existed within the Democratic caucus.

The topic of centralization proved to be one of the most effective charges leveled against Republicans by Democrats. The Democrats charged that Reconstruction had given state governments too much power, thereby violating Democrats' cherished principle of local self-government. Democrats argued that both the legislative and the executive branches had seen their powers expanded, which led to political mischief. For example, Democrats charged Republicans with empowering the executive branch in the 1868 constitution with far too great a power to appoint. Democrats in general saw the outcome of the Civil War as placing too much power in the hands of a centralized government at the expense of local governments. In Arkansas, the 1868 constitution had expanded the powers of the executive branch by granting the chief executive a term of four years, giving the governor broad powers to appoint officials and creating new executive offices.[11]

Constitution makers in 1868 had granted the governor the power to appoint some local officials. This allowed a Republican governor to appoint officials in areas with few Republicans, thereby limiting local Democrats' ability to participate in government. Democrats attacked all aspects of Reconstruction governance in Arkansas just as they did elsewhere. This fight was often lodged in Democrats' commitment to local self-government. Opposition to centralization emerged as one of the main themes of Democratic opposition to Reconstruction. Arkansas Redeemers rallied around this opposition. Democrats both outside the convention and within sought means to curtail the power of government in the new constitution. They wished to limit the appointment powers of the governor by making all offices elective by the people.[12]

Not all Democrats, though, could agree on how to limit centralization. Those Democrats who hailed from counties with large African American populations or those counties where Republicans stood a good chance of continued electoral success often did not share their fellow Democrats' desire to make all offices elective. These Democrats could count on large statewide Democratic majorities; thus, a Democrat occupying the governor's chair was assured. A Democratic governor would appoint Democrats to office in Republican-leaning counties—thus these Democrats did not see this centralization in as negative a light as some. One example of this is future governor Simon Hughes of Monroe County. Hughes argued for a stronger executive at the convention. While he did not explain his position, a close examination of Monroe County's voting history provides possible answers as to why Hughes might wish to maintain a stronger executive if he had some assurances that Democrats would dominate statewide offices.[13]

Other Democrats sought to curtail the powers of the governor—be he a Democrat or a Republican. These Democrats proposed a term of two years for the governor, as well as all executive officers, and eliminated the office of superintendent of education (public instruction). These Redeemer Democrats were willing to bend at times. They provided the governor with a line-item veto or executive veto, though these Democrats saw this line-item veto as a check on legislative authority more than as an expansion of executive authority.[14]

Democratic divisions remained even after the committee on the executive presented its report to the convention. Jesse Newton Cypert, a former-Whig-turned-Democrat from White County, emerged as one of the staunchest Redeemers. Cypert had served in the 1868 convention as well as serving in the 1861 secession convention and in the Confederate army. He argued that the committee did not go far enough when it came to curtailing the powers of the executive branch. One issue that attracted special attention from Cypert and a handful of Redeemers was a proposal that would have required the state's executive officers to reside in Little Rock, the capital, during their terms of office. Cypert and others argued that this was an attempt to centralize power in Little Rock and opposed the effort. A faction of Democrats sought to limit centralization in other ways as well, as can be seen in the debate concerning the State Land Commissioner's office. Eventually the Democratic caucus was able to reach a compromise whereby the office would be continued unless the General Assembly opted to eliminate it.[15]

Arkansas Redeemers could agree in principle when it came to retrenchment. They all espoused the desire to see spending limited and government costs reduced, though they differed at times when it came to the means by which this would be accomplished. This unity, at least in theory, was understandable considering the dilemma that Redeemers faced when it came to fiscal policy. Furthermore, Democrats had made substantial use of rhetoric concerning taxation and spending in their battle against Reconstruction. Democrats had condemned Republican governments for what they charged were corrupt and wasteful spending practices. E. H. English, a former chief justice of the Arkansas Supreme Court, declared, "Our people, though upon their own soil, are like ancient Israel—Unsympathizing task masters over us, and we are oppressed with toil and burdened with unexampled taxation, to fill the pockets whom he have no voice in choosing."[16] The state's leading Democratic newspaper, the *Daily Arkansas Gazette*, said that the Republican government acted as a "pack of ravening wolves."[17]

This rhetoric would pose problems for Democrats once they came to power. In fact, Democrats' efforts to cut taxes proved problematic when trying to deal with the state's huge debt burden as well as when attempting to provide basic limited services to the state's growing population. Democratic tax cuts would increase pressure to repudiate at least a portion of the state's debt and limit public services. Historian Carl Moneyhon has suggested that Democrats "viewed taxation as potentially the greatest threat to property and sought every means to avoid increases."[18] These prevailing attitudes concerning taxation made managing the state's debt difficult if not impossible.[19]

Redeemers had promised tax reform or relief once they returned to power. These promises, though, often did not take the state's massive debt fully into consideration. During the 1874 convention Democrats had to reconcile their promises with the reality of the state's fiscal condition, a task that proved difficult. One way that Democrats would ultimately seek to balance these promises with reality was by limiting taxation. This did not mean that differences of opinion did not arise within the Democratic caucus. The committee on taxation proposed a maximum tax rate of just 1% for statewide taxation and proved to be far more grudging when it came to local tax rates. They proposed allowing cities, towns, and counties to raise only one half of one percent for their needs. This prompted some Democrats to worry about their towns and counties even being able to pay their debts, let alone being able to provide much-needed services.[20]

Redeemers ultimately placed property assessment in the hands of assessors who were to be locally elected. This served two purposes. First, it stripped the governor, even a Democratic governor, of the ability to appoint these officials. Second, it placed land and property evaluations in the hands of local interests, thereby limiting assessments. Property values throughout the state declined as a result, to the benefit of property owners. The first General Assembly to meet following the ratification of the constitution enacted just a portion of the taxes allowed under the constitution. This created a situation in which the state could not raise enough revenue to pay its debts and maintain government services. Local governments were hit harder, with more extreme measures that prevented towns, cities, and counties from raising significant revenue. A pattern emerged whereby taxes were kept low and services remained almost nonexistent.[21]

The rise of Redeemers is undoubtedly tied to the issue of debt just as it was to taxation. Arkansas entered the Civil War with a debt problem, and Reconstruction only served to worsen the situation. Democrats, however, were not unified when it came to addressing the state's growing debt crisis. This debt could be broken into two categories: first, what could be considered an undisputed portion totaling just north of six million dollars, and, second, a disputed portion that stood at more than eighteen million dollars. To fully grasp the dire nature of Arkansas's debt crisis, one must understand that the state's taxable property had an assessed value of only slightly more than one hundred million dollars. So, assuming a tax rate of one percent—and Redeemers had no intention of taxing property at that rate—this property would only produce a revenue of slightly more than one million dollars per year. By the time the state paid the interest on the debt, estimated at $848,240, there would be only $167,000 left to pay for essential state services and no revenue to pay down the principal balance on the debt.[22]

The debt question divided Redeemers within the convention as well as within the larger Democratic public. Some Democrats wished to see a three-person commission appointed to investigate the state's debt and negotiate some form of settlement. Others sought to pay the "just debts," or debts that were not in dispute, while repudiating those that were disputed. One thing remained clear during the convention: It would be almost impossible if not completely impossible for Redeemer Democrats to pay the debt or even a large portion of the debt and keep their promises to their constituents to provide tax relief. This led to some Redeemers calling for "out-and-out abandonment" of the debt. With no Redeemers calling on the state to pay the debt in totality, some Democrats such as William M. Fishback of Sebastian County and W. D. Leiper of Dallas County called for at least partial repudiation of the debt. Leiper stated, "I desire to relieve the state from the payment of all fraudulent claims and thus deliver the people all [illegible] taxation to be collected for the payment of claims they do not owe."[23] Another Democrat, J. G. Frierson of Cross County, worked to successfully steer his fellow constitution makers away from placing repudiation in the constitution. Frierson and other Democrats sought to leave it up to the court system to determine what debts were valid and what debts were fraudulent. Ultimately, Democratic constitution makers opted to leave the decision concerning just and unjust debt to the courts and future legislators, allowing the General Assembly to raise revenue to pay "just and legal" debts of the state. Arkansas would eventually repudiate much of its debt but not until William Fishback, "the great repudiator," was elected governor.[24]

When it came to Redeeming, Arkansas Democrats saw the judicial branch as an important piece of the equation. In fact, district and lower court judges exercised significant power, often more power than state officials, when it came to the daily lives of Arkansans. In part, this had to do with the number of cases that had to be decided following the Civil War—cases involving labor, debt, landholdings, and the further expansion of the market economy through the state, which found many Arkansans in complicated legal situations. When it came to the judicial system, Arkansas Redeemers addressed two issues: first, the method by which judges would be chosen, and, second, what powers and jurisdiction said judges would possess. Divisions within the Democratic ranks became evident almost immediately concerning judicial selection. Under the 1868 Constitution, Arkansas had a Supreme Court made up of five justices. The chief justice was appointed by the governor, while the associate justices were elected by the qualified voters of the state. These justices served a term of eight years. The state was also divided into circuit court districts, but the makeup of these courts was left to future legislatures. Ultimately, the state was divided into ten districts. Rather than the qualified voters electing these judges, the governor was given the power to appoint circuit court judges with the advice and consent of the Senate for a term of six years. Republicans, who were always a minority in the state despite their control of the government, preferred to appoint circuit court judges, since some districts could not be counted on to elect a reliably Republican judge. Arkansas Democrats bristled at this expanded appointment power and sought to limit future governors' powers, even if they were Democrats.[25]

Arkansas Redeemers had long been critical of the Reconstruction judiciary, though they could not agree on a system, at least initially, to replace this appointed judiciary. Some Democrats called on constitution makers to create a totally elected judiciary. Others called on some combination, while still others sought an appointed judiciary. Much of this division can be associated with fears by some of counties with black majorities electing black judges. Democrats from majority white counties who had no such fears were more willing to embrace a purely elected judiciary. For example, on May 30, 1874, the *Fort Smith Herald* called on the convention to "restore our republican institutions to their former purity…and once again let the people rule."[26] It is not surprising that such a call would appear in a newspaper from western Arkansas, as the region had no fear of blacks electing Republican or black judges.[27] In regions of the state with large black majorities or even in regions where the ratio of white to black was close to equal, Democrats were not as excited about an elected judiciary. Historian C. Vann Woodward noted that in many cases Redeemer Democrats sought to diminish the political power of African

Americans by using appointive systems. Of course, it did not hurt that this also tended to limit the power of non-elite whites.[28]

Democratic divisions existed, at least outside the convention, as to the method of judicial selection. Under the heading of "Popular Election of Judges" a letter to the *Daily Arkansas Gazette* argued that constitution makers should look to Illinois, where a judge who had just ruled against a group of farmers in a dispute with a railroad company had been defeated because of his ruling. This letter writer worried that an elected judiciary would be too susceptible to the whims of a rabble. Some offered their opinion that constitution makers should consider lifetime appointments for judges. They sought to remove the judiciary from the political process. The writer went on to say, "Voters, especially those who have controlled the state since the war, don't have or want a way to get enough information to make responsible choices."[29] Here the writer seems to be referencing black and white Republicans. In 1870, the state had eight counties with black majorities that could be expected to vote reliably for Republicans. Others urged delegates to look to South Carolina, hardly a bastion of democratic egalitarianism, claiming that the state had little crime.[30]

Some Democrats urged constitution makers to oppose the election of judges because human nature would lead to the election of men looking for personal gain. Furthermore, they claimed that if a lawyer could not make a living, he would seek such a position and they did not want such mediocre lawyers as judicial officers. One author suggested that circuit judges should be appointed by the Supreme Court and approved by the governor. As justification for this proposal, he said, "Lawyers, like women, are the proper judges of each other, and the means of knowing and forming just estimates of professional skill and weight of each other."[31] Race undeniably played a role in some opinions offered when it came to the selection of judges. On August 2, "An Appeal from Desha" appeared in the *Daily Arkansas Gazette*. Desha County had an African American population of 64% in 1870—this was a reliably Republican county. The letter writer worried about the kinds of judges that might be elected if the qualified voters were allowed to select judges. (Of course the writer meant black judges.) The letter read:

> In view of the fact that those counties bordering on the Mississippi River, and where the negro voters are largely in the majority, have no representative voice in the present state constitutional convention, on behalf of the people living in these counties. It is true these counties have individuals in that convention who draw pay and vote, but virtually represent no interest in common with the true people. We are more interested in redistricting the state for judicial purposes than any other thing.[32]

Delta Democrats were concerned about having black judges dole out justice, and this letter writer wanted constitution makers to redistrict the state in a manner that would ease this fear. He went on to say, "These river counties are rich, but with overwhelming negro ascendancy, all offices filled by them, and all officers under their control, nothing is left to our people, but to abandon their homes and property."[33] If judges were to be elected, he posited that constitution makers should draw circuit court districts in such a manner as to isolate African American voters, thereby depriving them of at least that opportunity to compete for such judgeships.[34]

Despite these attitudes, some members made it clear that their constituents expected the judiciary to be elected just as they expected other offices to be made elective. J. A. Gibson, a resident of Arkansas County, explained why he supported an elective judiciary:

> First, I vote for the resolution because I am in favor of the people electing every office from governor down to constable.

> Second, I am anxious to let the people of the state know as soon as possible how the convention stands on this important matter, and especially to let my constituents know that I will carry out the pledge I made to them on this subject as well as any other pledge made in my canvas before them.[35]

Other Democratic constitution makers declared similar sentiments, saying that their people expected an elected judiciary.[36]

Once it was established that Arkansas would have an elected judiciary, Redeemers still sought ways to limit the potential power of Republicans in some regions of the state. W. D. Leiper of Dallas County sought to make circuit judges subject to a statewide vote rather than a district vote. This would have essentially ended any possibility of Republicans, or maybe more importantly African Americans, electing judges even in regions where they held majorities. In the end, Redeemers opted to make use of gerrymandering to limit, as much as possible, African American power when it came to judges. Democrats from outside the convention sought assistance from former governor Harris Flanagin, the chair of the committee on the judiciary. Met Jones of Pine Bluff (Jefferson County contained sizable black majority) asked Flanagin to draw judicial districts in a manner that would ensure white judges. He sought to place Jefferson County in a district made up of white-majority counties to limit African American voting strength. D. H. Reynolds, who had been defeated for the convention, wrote to Flanagin wanting Chicot County placed in a white-majority judicial district. He claimed that his "people" were not represented.[37]

Constitution makers ultimately created eleven circuit court districts in a move that Mr. Reynolds of Lake Village would not have approved of. By doing so, they created a district with a large African American majority. This district encompassed Desha,

Arkansas, Lincoln, and Jefferson Counties. Redeemers had wanted these counties broken up in a manner to limit African American voting power. By packing this district so that it would undoubtedly elect a Republican and quite possibly an African American judge, constitution makers were able to ensure that the remaining districts would elect white judges. Packing would not work in other regions. In these areas, constitution makers had to rely on "cracking"—spreading African American voters among multiple districts to dilute their voting power. Here Redeemers would have been happier with the outcome. For example, Phillips County, which was 57% black, was put in a district with five white-majority counties while Crittenden County, which was 67% black, was grouped with seven white-majority counties. Chicot County saw its substantial black majority quarantined by placing the county with five white-majority counties. These moves limited the possibility of electing black judges, though black justices of the peace were still seen as a very real threat.[38]

Redeemers did not believe that every Arkansan should have the right to hold office. Redeemers, really all Democrats at this time, thought that any acceptance of African American office holding would lead to "negro rule." Even a small number of African Americans voting in the county or holding office shook white authority. Redeemers did not want to have to seek black votes because something would be expected in return. Appointing African Americans to office, soliciting their votes, or accepting their election to office weakened white supremacy. Despite these prevailing attitudes, Redeemers in Arkansas did not restrict suffrage in a manner to match their rhetoric. This restraint, however, should not be seen as the product of Redeemers' respect for black voting rights but rather as a political calculation, a calculation that arose out of fear of federal intervention if they attacked African American voting rights head on. Instead, such an attack would have to wait.[39]

Conservatives had voiced their opposition to suffrage for African Americans since 1868. Jesse N. Cypert, who had served in the 1868 convention as well, led the way in opposing the expansion of suffrage:

> The negro is not the equal of the white man. In mind and body, the differences are striking, numerous, and insurmountable. Four thousand years ago he was exactly what he is today. All history demonstrates his utter incapacity for self-government, and his utter want of appreciation of free institutions. But beyond all this, our own experiences and the teachings of history inexorably point to this dreadful result. The investing of an inferior race with social and political equality is the stepping stone to miscegenation, and the consequent utter deterioration and degeneracy of the dominant race.[40]

Despite these racist attitudes, Redeemers in Arkansas knew, as did African Americans, that Democrats simply did not embrace disfranchisement in order to win statewide elections and maintain control of the state. In the short term, Redeemers appear to have been willing to wait when it came to black voting rights. In fact, Democrats in Arkansas, as with the rest of the South, chose this path and adhered to the New Departure wing of the party. One writer put it this way in the *Gazette*:

> The new departure simply recognizes a state of facts which every citizen knows does exist. The question of colored suffrage cannot possibly form any issue in the next canvass, because the ratification of the fifteenth amendment settled that. Being settled, that's what we call a dead issue. It was now gone beyond the recall of any party. It is dead. Where would be the profit in its resurrection?[41]

Ultimately, though, Arkansas Redeemers were well aware of the state's relatively small African American population and felt safe in their ability to dominate the state politically, though this offered little comfort to Democrats in black-majority counties when it came to local office holding.[42]

Arkansas Redeemers may have accepted the fact that little could be done about African American voting for fear of federal intervention, but some Democrats sought to limit the impact of black voting by imposing stringent taxpaying requirements. The *Southern Standard*, published in Arkadelphia, expressed, "While we are in favor of the fullest and freest suffrage, yet we do not think that anyone is not interested sufficiently in government to pay at least one dollar toward its support, should have no voice in the selection of those who levy taxes for others to pay."[43] Still others made their peace with African American voting by allowing anyone over the age of twenty-one to vote. These Democrats knew well that their party would control the state even if African American suffrage continued and did not wish to raise the prospect of future federal intervention. Despite the efforts of some Redeemers, the final constitution would not contain a poll tax.[44]

Arkansas Redeemers were partaking of national trends when it came to the franchise. Across the South, Redeemers who might have sought to place limitations on African American suffrage failed to do so out of fear of federal intervention since the Fifteenth Amendment had been ratified. Redeemers delayed disfranchisement until they felt secure in the fact that the federal government would no longer intervene. For instance, Arkansas waited until the 1890s to limit black suffrage.[45]

Arkansas Redeemers also sought to promote the state's growth. Following the Civil War, Arkansas found itself in severe economic trouble. The state had no railroads to speak of (these were universally seen as a key component to economic growth and prosperity), lacked educational opportunities, and had a labor shortage. Under Radical Republican rule, the state had attempted to address these issues with programs that added substantially to the state's debt woes. Republican efforts to promote railroad construction and attract immigrants had been widely criticized by Democrats. Redeemers, though, had to balance their commitment to retrenchment and tax cuts with the state's needs. In fact, many Democrats agreed at least in principle with Republicans when it came to Arkansas's need for railroads, industrial growth, and efforts to attract immigrants to the state. Arkansas Redeemers were willing to concede that railroads, for instance, would require public support. After all, a railroad took years to return a profit.[46]

The desire to build railroads and the belief that railroads were an important element of Arkansas's future development were not new. In fact, the state had chartered railroads as early as 1844, though few miles of track were ever built. Despite this desire, railroads conjured long-held divisions among Democrats when it came to internal improvements. In fact, Elias Conway had run for governor in 1852 on a "good dirt roads" platform that demonstrates that a significant anti-development faction existed. Conway won the governorship, while Democrats who favored state-subsidized internal improvements won control of the General Assembly. The next year, legislators incorporated the Cairo and Fulton Railroad. They also granted 640 acres of public land for every mile of railroad track laid. In reality, this led to the construction of just over sixty miles of track before the Civil War. Aid to railroads would become a dominant issue in Arkansas politics following the Civil War. In 1868, Governor Isaac Murphy vetoed a bill passed by the conservative-dominated General

Assembly that would have lent the state's credit to build railroads. Conservatives in the 1866–67 General Assembly overrode his veto. In 1867, they chartered five railroad companies, an action that Redeemer Democrats would later criticize Republicans for.[47]

Beginning in 1868, Radical Republicans dominated the state politically. The General Assembly passed and Governor Powell Clayton signed legislation whereby the state would provide aid to railroad companies. Railroad companies would be given bonds ranging from ten thousand to fifteen thousand dollars per mile of track constructed. Under the provisions of the 1868 constitution, such aid schemes required approval by the registered voters of the state, which the voters overwhelmingly approved, though one must remember that former Confederates were disenfranchised and did not participate in this election. Multiple railroad companies sought money under this program. In fact, the state would approve more than nine million dollars in railroad bonds. Unfortunately, despite the state aid, few miles of track were constructed. Between 1868 and 1874, only 662 miles of track were constructed.[48]

Redeemers were quick to criticize Republicans. They claimed that such aid led to corruption and that Governor Clayton funneled aid money to his political cronies. Redeemers used the issue of state aid to attack Republicans, alleging that the only way a railroad company could obtain state aid was to bribe a state official. Redeemer Democrats made political hay out of the issue of railroad aid. On March 11, 1871, the *Daily Arkansas Gazette* said of the Republican railroad plan:

> These bonds were thrown on the New York market, as much realized from them as could be obtained, some little work done, and the enterprises brought to a standstill. This is true particularly of the Little Rock, Pine Bluff, and New Orleans, and the Mississippi, Ouachita, and Red River Railroad. Just

exactly how the affairs of these two corporations now stand are not advised.[49]

Redeemers were not bashful when it came to charging Republicans with corruption and favoritism. They were well aware that potential Democratic voters would be outraged by such behavior. Furthermore, Democratic voters were appalled by the fact that both Governor Clayton and U.S. senator Stephen W. Dorsey owned stock in railroad companies that benefited from state aid.[50]

To make matters worse, at least as far as Democrats were concerned, the bonds sold to provide aid to railroad companies were selling below face value. This led to declining revenue to fund such aid programs. Despite their earlier enthusiastic support for a railroad building program, Democrats increasingly leveled their attacks on Republicans and their aid program. These Redeemer Democrats embraced a message of retrenchment and tax cuts that, if enacted, would leave little revenue available to continue such aid programs. In fact, Redeemers sought to make sure that the new constitution prevented future railroad-subsidization plans from being implemented. Article XVI, Section 1 clarified the issue,

Stephen W. Dorsey was elected as Arkansas's junior U.S. senator in 1872, but his involvement in state railroads proved controversial. A county was named for him in 1873, but it would be changed in 1885 to honor President Grover Cleveland. Courtesy of the Library of Congress Prints and Photographs Division.

"Neither the State, nor any city, county, town, or other municipality in this state shall ever loan its credit for any purpose whatever." This provision stripped the state's ability to provide direct financial assistance to any economic activity.[51]

When it came to education, Redeemers took a decisive stand. Arkansas Redeemers were well aware that education was one of the biggest expenditures that nineteenth-century governments undertook. As such, the topic was open to much politicization when it came to the allocation of funds. From a Redeemer point of view, education raised the issue of centralization as well as that of retrenchment. Education had seen a significant rise in expenditures and power during the Republican era, and Redeemers sought to limit this trend. Many Redeemers saw education as one of the prime areas where they could limit centralization and enact retrenchment measures. According to many, education had become "extravagant" under Republican rule. Not all Redeemers could agree, however, on how to accomplish these goals in the 1874 constitutional convention. A division emerged, with some Redeemers pushing for total decentralization or the return of all elements of the education in the state to local communities. This group also sought to severely limit the funds allocated to education. Others sought to impose some degree of decentralization and retrenchment while leaving the school system intact.[52]

Arkansas developed a school system only with the emergence of Radical Republican rule. While efforts had been made previously, little had been achieved in the way of an education system. In fact, Arkansas only had 113 schools, according to the 1840 census. Prior to the Civil War, fewer than twenty-five percent of Arkansas's school-age children attended public schools. Under Republican rule, Arkansas developed a state education system with free schools maintained by taxes. These schools were to be open to both white and black students between the ages of five and twenty-one. The schools were paid for by implementing a per capita tax of one dollar on every male over the age of twenty-one. The General Assembly was granted the power to raise additional revenue if it proved necessary. Education funds were to be allocated to local districts based on the number of students enrolled in school. In order to administer this new education system, Republicans created the office of Superintendent of Public Instruction, who would be elected by the qualified voters of the state.[53]

Redeemers were quick to point to areas that they saw as ripe for corruption and malfeasance. The Republican-dominated General Assembly passed "an Act to Establish and Maintain a system of free common schools for the state." This created a state board of commissioners of common school funds made up of the governor, the secretary of state, and the state superintendent of public instruction. The act also segregated the state's schools, something Republicans had refused to do during the constitutional convention. The state was divided into school districts that would hold annual meetings where voters would select a site for their school, establish what the school term would be, and name a district trustee to conduct the district's business. While a state superintendent would be elected to a four-year term, there were also to be ten circuit superintendents appointed by the governor. This rankled Democrats, who charged Republicans with using these plum appointments to repay political supporters. Furthermore, each circuit superintendent was paid a salary of $3,000 per year. The *Daily Gazette* had this to say:

> In the administration of no department of our government has radical extravagance, profligacy and downright fraud and robbery, been more palpable and notoriously manifested, than

> in the management of the revenues of our common schools. In nothing has radicalism so much prided and valued itself in Arkansas, as in its boasted establishment of a system of public instruction for the education of the children of the poor, by means of free common schools.[54]

Redeemers charged Republicans with pilfering the state's education budget while arguing that they themselves supported education; the *Daily Gazette* went on:

> The conservative party, without exception, are in favor of a good, practical, efficient and prudently managed system of education; but as for this tub mill of radical robbery, theft and peculation—miscalled common school system, now in vogue in radical circles—we, of course, have no respect and no patience with those who have.[55]

Redeemers were divided when it came to how best to address education in the 1874 Constitution. Some wished to use the revenue from lands granted to the state by the federal government, while others charged that such a move would not sufficiently fund education. Others sought to place education on a purely local funding basis, meaning that local districts would raise revenue and all such revenue would be spent within that district. Still others sought some combination whereby the state provided the bulk of funding for local school districts but the local district could raise additional revenue when needed. Some Democrats worried that if left to local control completely, some communities would simply not attempt to provide a proper education for the children of Arkansas, while others worried that statewide taxes for education would take money from their county and give it to a county with less taxable property.[56]

Some Redeemers such as Jesse Cypert of White County and John Horner of Phillips County urged fellow constitution makers to not turn the state's education system back to local communities for fear that some communities would not be able or willing to provide their children an education. Cypert worried that Arkansas school children would once again be forced into private

Arkansas's Redeemer politicians had a difficult time reaching consensus on how public schools should be supported. This group photograph was taken at the Howard School in Fort Smith. The school was started around 1868 and likely named after Freedmen's Bureau head O. O. Howard. The building in this photo was built around 1884 to replace the original wood-frame building. "Group Photograph of Howard School, Ft. Smith, Arkansas," ASA_Photo_G5748, Arkansas State Archives, Little Rock, Arkansas.

schools or simply not attend school at all. J. G. Frierson of Cross County argued that anything less than a statewide education system funded by state taxes would create a system left to education's two enemies: "ignorance and wealth."[57]

Other Redeemers, though, were opposed to a centralized education system. Former governor Henry M. Rector of Garland County, for instance, argued that education was the job of the people of his county and not the state. He claimed that the people of Garland County would reject general free schools if it were to be put to a vote. He and other Redeemers thought that their constituents would prefer not to have schools at all if they would be placed under a statewide, centralized system. Delegate Random Gulley of Izard County opposed a statewide education system because he claimed it was just another step to centralization. These men argued that each county should keep all education taxes that had been raised in their county. This would mean that some districts were drastically better off financially than others. In fact, some districts would not have even been able to keep a school open. Still others opposed statewide school taxes being distributed based on a per pupil basis, claiming that it was redistribution of wealth. Future governor James Eagle noted that some voters were always willing to vote to increase taxes on people who owned property. J. A. Gibson of Arkansas County said, "If there are poor counties in this state they have no right to take property of other counties to apply it to their own use."[58] Redeemer attitudes concerning public schools varied considerably and eluded consensus.[59]

In the end, Redeemers accepted a statewide tax for education, set at two mills, and allowed local districts to raise an additional three mills of revenue. This decision did not please all Redeemers, but Democrats coalesced around this compromise in order to move the constitution forward.[60]

Arkansas Redeemers, like their counterparts across the South, worked to provide the state with a new constitution that would limit the problems, either real or imagined, that they had encountered with Radical Republican rule and the constitution of 1868. Arkansas Redeemers would dominate the state for decades to come. While I posited in my doctoral dissertation, "Arkansas's Divided Democracy: The Making of the Constitution of 1874," that the 1874 Constitution drafted by Redeemers was not as restrictive as some have argued, the fact remains that the Democrats who were elected following the ratification of the constitution proved to be far more restrictive than those who drafted the constitution. Ultimately, the state's landed interest emerged as the driving force in Redeemed Arkansas. The representatives who won election to the General Assembly following the ratification of the 1874 Constitution fit this pattern, as did the majority of the men who would occupy the governor's chair. As historian Carl Moneyhon has emphasized, these leaders sought to appease or represent the landed interests.

In some ways this should be seen as a lost opportunity due to the fact that the constitution was not as restrictive as it might have been. Instead, these leaders sought and did keep control of taxation in local hands—hands that also controlled the property. These propertied men in turn sought to keep taxes as low as possible. One means by which this was accomplished was by making local property assessors subject to local election, whereas they had previously been appointed. As Moneyhon suggests, property assessments declined almost overnight. While the constitution set limits on taxation, the Redeemers who followed ratification opted to not implement taxes to the limit—in other words, legislators adopted more-stringent retrenchment mechanisms than constitution makers had agreed on. In fact, the General Assembly only enacted roughly half the taxes that they had the power to implement. Without significant revenue, government services and programs were minimal, just as conservative legislators preferred. Arkansas tax rates continued to fall throughout the remainder of the century as well. While constitution makers refused to embrace re-

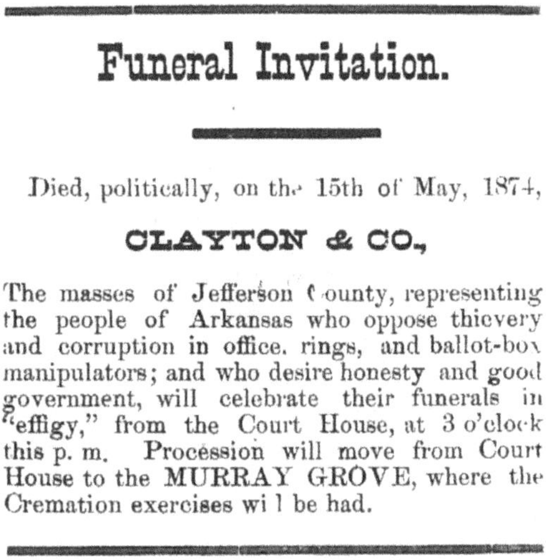

Funeral Invitation.

Died, politically, on the 15th of May, 1874,

CLAYTON & CO.,

The masses of Jefferson County, representing the people of Arkansas who oppose thievery and corruption in office, rings, and ballot-box manipulators; and who desire honesty and good government, will celebrate their funerals in "effigy," from the Court House, at 3 o'clock this p. m. Procession will move from Court House to the MURRAY GROVE, where the Cremation exercises wi l be had.

The end of Reconstruction in Arkansas resulted in a Jefferson County celebration and the burial in effigy of Powell Clayton and his supporters. Courtesy of David and Carolyn Newbern.

pudiation, the Redeemer General Assemblies that followed the constitutional convention would eventually embrace repudiation. In fact, they would have little choice due to their own suffocation of the state treasury. Legislators simply put the state on a starvation diet and little remained for basic governmental services—and nothing remained to pay the state's debt such as the Holford Bonds. Under the leadership of the Great Repudiator William Fishback, Arkansas would embrace repudiation in 1884 by a huge margin. These Redeemers would control the state well into the next century. Furthermore, they saw significant success when it came to protecting their economic and political interests, leaving behind a history of limited government, low taxation, and economic suffering for the average Arkansan.[61]

Notes

Chapter 1—The Complex Character of Post–Civil War Reconstruction, 1863–1877

1 United States, *Statutes at Large, Treaties, and Proclamations of the United States of America*, vol. 13 (Boston: Little, Brown and Company, 1866), 737–739; Peyton McCrary, *Abraham Lincoln and Reconstruction: The Louisiana Experiment* (Princeton: Princeton University Press, 1978), 3–18, 185–193; Herman Belz, *Reconstructing the Union: Theory and Policy During the Civil War* (Ithaca: Cornell University Press, 1969), 126–168; William C. Harris, *With Charity for All: Lincoln and the Restoration of the Union* (Lexington: University Press of Kentucky, 1997), 123–170.

2 Carl H. Moneyhon, *The Impact of the Civil War and Reconstruction on Arkansas: Persistence in the Midst of Ruin* (Baton Rouge: Louisiana State University Press, 1994), 159–161; Mark K. Christ, *Civil War Arkansas, 1863: The Battle for a State* (Norman: University of Oklahoma Press, 2010), 145–196; Leo E. Huff, "The Union Expedition Against Little Rock," *Arkansas Historical Quarterly* 22 (Fall 1963): 224–237.

3 C. C. Andrews to Abraham Lincoln, Jan. 10, 1864, Robert Todd Lincoln Collection, Abraham Lincoln Papers, Library of Congress; Abraham Lincoln to Frederick Steele, Jan. 30, 1864, RTLC, ALP, LC; Moneyhon, *The Impact of the Civil War and Reconstruction on Arkansas*, 161–164; Arkansas Constitution of 1864.

4 Nathan Kimball to A. Lincoln, April 11, 1864, RTLC, ALP, LC.

5 Abraham Lincoln to Frederick Steele, June 29, 1864, RTLC, ALP,

LC; Moneyhon, *The Impact of the Civil War and Reconstruction on Arkansas*, 164; McCrary, *Abraham Lincoln and Reconstruction*, 271–304.

6 "Wade-Davis Bill (1864)," https://www.ourdocuments.gov/doc.php?flash=false&doc=37 (accessed January 16, 2018); Kenneth M. Stampp, *The Era of Reconstruction, 1865–1877: A Revisionist View of One of the Most Controversial Periods in American History* (New York: Alfred Knopf, 1966), 39–40; McCrary, *Abraham Lincoln and Reconstruction*, 274–278, 282–287.

7 Andrew Johnson: "Proclamation 135—Reorganizing a Constitutional Government in North Carolina," May 29, 1865, "Proclamation 153," April 2, 1866, "Proclamation 157," August 20, 1866, *The American Presidency Project*, http://www.presidency.ucsb.edu (accessed January 16, 2018); Eric McKitrick, *Andrew Johnson and Reconstruction* (Chicago: University of Chicago Press, 1960), 6, 7 (first quotation), 8; Dan T. Carter, *When the War Was Over: The Failure of Self-Reconstruction in the South, 1865–1867* (Baton Rouge: Louisiana State University Press, 1985), 72 (second quotation).

8 Carter, *When the War Was Over*, 64–68; Eric Foner, *Reconstruction, America's Unfinished Revolution, 1863–1877* (New York: Harper & Row, Publishers, 1988), 191; Charles W. Ramsdell, *Reconstruction in Texas* (New York: Columbia University Press, 1910), 85, 86 (quotation), 87.

9 Carter, *When the War Was Over*, 70–84, 84 (first quotation); Foner, *Reconstruction*, 193–196; Ramsdell, *Reconstruction in Texas*, 100 (second quotation).

10 Foner, *Reconstruction*, 196–197; John Hope Franklin, *Reconstruction after the Civil War* (Chicago: University of Chicago Press, 1961), 43; Moneyhon, *The Impact of the Civil War and Reconstruction on Arkansas*, 193–196, 200–201.

11 Theodore Brantner Wilson, *The Black Codes of the South* (Tuscaloosa: University of Alabama Press, 1965); Carl H. Moneyhon, *Republicanism in Reconstruction Texas* (Austin: University of Texas Press, 1980), 50–51; Foner, *Reconstruction*, 196–197.

12 Isaac Murphy to E. O. C. Ord, August 1866, L. C. Gulley Collection, Arkansas History Commission; Moneyhon, *The Impact of the Civil War and Reconstruction on Arkansas*, 201–203.

13 Carter, *When the War Was Over*, 147–148 (first quotation); Roger L. Ransom and Richard Sutch, *One Kind of Freedom: The Economic Consequences of Emancipation* (Cambridge: Cambridge University Press, 1977), 21–22; Joel Williamson, *After Slavery: The Negro in South Carolina During Reconstruction, 1861–1877* (New York: W. W. Norton & Co., 1966), 97.

14 "Letter of the Secretary of War," 39th Congress, 2nd session, *Senate Executive Documents*, no. 6, 24, 33 (first quotation); "Message of President Communicating Reports of Assistant Commissioners of Freedmen's Bureau," 39th Congress, 1st session, *Senate Executive Documents*, no. 27, 28 (second quotation).

15 McKitrick, *Andrew Johnson and Reconstruction*, 11–12; United States, *Statutes at Large*, 39th Congress, 1st Session, Ch. 31.

16 McKitrick, *Andrew Johnson and Reconstruction*, 108–109, 287–289; "Veto of the Second Freedmen's Bureau Bill," 39th Congress, 1st Session (House Executive Documents), no. 25; James D. Richardson, ed., A *Compilation of the Messages and Papers of the Presidents* vol. 6, pt. 2 (New York: Bureau of National Literature, Inc.), 405.

17 Joseph B. James, *The Framing of the Fourteenth Amendment* (Urbana: University of Illinois Press, 1965), 50, 89, 97–98; Garrett Epps, *Democracy Reborn: The Fourteenth Amendment and the Fight for Equal Rights in Post–Civil War America* (New York: H. Holt, 2006).

18 James G. Hollandsworth Jr., *An Absolute Massacre: The New Orleans Race Riot of July 30, 1866* (Baton Rouge: Louisiana State University Press, 2004), 148; Stephen V. Ash, *A Massacre in Memphis: The Race Riot that Shook the Nation One Year after the Civil War* (New York: Hill and Wang, 2013); James G. Ryan, "The Memphis Riot of 1866: Terror in a Black Community during Reconstruction," *Journal of Negro History* 62, no. 3 (1977): 243–257.

19 McKitrick, *Andrew Johnson and Reconstruction*, 428–447; Hans L. Trefousse, *Andrew Johnson: A Biography* (New York: W. W. Norton & Company, 1997), 263.

20 James McPherson, *Ordeal by Fire: The Civil War and Reconstruction* (New York McGraw-Hill, Inc., 1982), 517 (quotation).

21 David Donald, *The Politics of Reconstruction, 1863–1867* (Baton Rouge: Louisiana State University Press, 1965), 65–69.

22 Donald, *The Politics of Reconstruction*, 69–82.

23 Andrew Johnson: "Veto Message," March 2, 1867, *The American Presidency Project*, http://www.presidency.ucsb.edu (accessed January 16, 2018).

24 William Gillette, *The Right to Vote: Politics and the Passage of the Fifteenth Amendment* (Baltimore: Johns Hopkins University Press, 1965), 73–76; Michael Less Benedict, *A Compromise of Principle: Congressional Republicans and Reconstruction, 1863–1869* (New York: W. W. Norton & Company, 1974), 325–338.

25 John Hope Franklin, *Reconstruction: After the Civil War* (Chicago: University of Chicago Press, 1961), 152–161; Allen W. Trelease, *White Terror: The Ku Klux Klan Conspiracy and Southern Reconstruction* (New York: Harper & Row, 1971).

26 Stampp, *The Era of Reconstruction*, 154–172; Franklin, *Reconstruction*, 85–103; Richard L. Hume, "Carpetbaggers in the Reconstruction South: A Group Portrait of Outside Whites in the 'Black and Tan' Constitutional Conventions," *Journal of American History* 64 (Sept. 1977): 313–330; Richard L. Hume, "The Arkansas Constitutional Convention of 1868: A Case Study in the Politics of Reconstruction," *Journal of Southern History* 39 (May 1973): 192–199; Joseph M. St. Hilaire, "The Negro Delegates in the Arkansas Constitutional Convention of 1868: A Group Profile," *Arkansas Historical Quarterly* 33 (Spring 1974): 38–69.

27 McPherson, *Ordeal by Fire*, 532; Franklin, *Reconstruction*, 104–119; Cal Ledbetter Jr., "The Constitution of 1868: Conqueror's Constitution or Constitutional Continuity?" *Arkansas Historical Quarterly* 44 (Spring 1985): 16–41.

28 Franklin, *Reconstruction*, 130–133; Foner, *Reconstruction*, 329–333.

29 Foner, *Reconstruction*, "Table: Major Black State Officials During Reconstruction," 353, see also 350–355; Franklin, *Reconstruction*, 130–137; Blake J. Wintory, "African-American Legislators in Arkansas General Assembly, 1868–1893," *Arkansas Historical Quarterly* 65 (Winter 2006): 385–434.

30 Foner, *Reconstruction*, 364 (quotation), 365.

31 W. E. B. DuBois, *Black Reconstruction in America* (New York: Atheneum, 1970, c. 1935), 650–663; William Preston Vaugh, *Schools for All: The Blacks and Public Education in the South, 1865–1877* (Lexington: University Press of Kentucky, 2015); James D. Anderson, *The Education of Blacks in the South, 1860–1935* (Chapel Hill: University of North Carolina Press, 1988); *Report of the Commissioner of Education. Made by the Secretary of the Interior for the Year 1872* (Washington DC: Government Printing Office, 1872), 9, 11–13.

32 Franklin, *Reconstruction*, 139–140; Foner, *Reconstruction*, 379–392; Mark W. Summers, *Railroads, Reconstruction, and the Gospel of Prosperity: Under the Radical Republicans, 1865–1877* (Princeton: Princeton University Press, 1984); Stephen E. Woods, "The Development of Arkansas Railroads, Part I," *Arkansas Historical Quarterly* 7 (Summer 1948): 103–140.

33 McPherson, *Ordeal by Fire*, 536–537 (first quotation); John Hope Franklin, "Election of 1868," in Arthur M. Schlesinger Jr. (ed.), *History of American Presidential Elections*, 4 vols. (New York, 1971), II, 1259, 1262 (second quotation), 1269.

34 McPherson, *Ordeal by Fire*, 538; Trelease, *White Terror*, xiv, 46.

35 George C. Rable, *But There Was No Peace: The Role of Violence in the Politics of Reconstruction* (Athens: University of Georgia Press, 1968), 104–106; Otis A. Singletary, "Militia Disturbances in Arkansas during Reconstruction," *Arkansas Historical Quarterly* 15 (Summer 1956): 140–150; Barry A. Crouch and Donaly E. Brice, *The Governor's Hounds: The Texas State Police, 1870–1873* (Austin: University of Texas Press, 2011), 59–69, 114–115, 83–92; Otis A. Singletary, *Negro Militia and Reconstruction* (Austin: University of Texas Press, 1957); Powell Clayton, *The Aftermath of the Civil War in Arkansas* (New York: Neale Publishing Company, 1915).

36 Foner, *Reconstruction*, 454–459, 530–531; McPherson, *Ordeal by Fire*, 559–560; William Gillette, *Retreat from Reconstruction, 1869–1879* (Baton Rouge: Louisiana State University Press, 1979), 259; *U.S. Statutes at Large*, 43rd Cong., 2nd sess., chapter 114, 335–337.

37 Stampp, *The Era of Reconstruction*, 175; Foner, *Reconstruction*, 382–384; *Report of the Commissioner of Education. Made by the Secretary of the Interior for the Year 1872* (Washington DC: Government Printing Office, 1872), 11–13, 137, 200–201.

38 *Report of the Commissioner of Education. Made by the Secretary of the Interior for the Year 1872*, 11–13; Stampp, *The Era of Reconstruction*, 175–176; Foner, *Reconstruction*, 383–384; Franklin, *Reconstruction*, 142–143; Moneyhon, *Impact of the Civil War and Reconstruction on Arkansas*, 250.

39 Franklin, *Reconstruction*, 144–151; Foner, *Reconstruction*, 415–417; Moneyhon, *Republicanism in Reconstruction Texas*, 160–163.

40 Franklin, *Reconstruction*, 197–198; Paul D. Escott, *North Carolinians in the Era of the Civil War and Reconstruction* (Chapel Hill: University of North Carolina Press, 1967); Walter L. Fleming, *Civil War and Reconstruction in Alabama* (New York: Columbia University Press, 1905); William C. Harris, *The Day of the Carpetbagger: Republican Reconstruction in Mississippi* (Baton Rouge: Louisiana State University Press, 1979).

41 Schurz quotation in Foner, *Reconstruction*, 499; Franklin, *Reconstruction*, 197; Carl H. Moneyhon, "Edmund J. Davis and the Coke-Davis Election Dispute of 1874: A Reassessment of Character," *Southwestern Historical Quarterly* 55 (Winter 1956): 383–409; Thomas A. DeBlack, *With Fire and Sword: Arkansas, 1861–1874* (Fayetteville: University of Arkansas Press, 2003), 215–223.

42 *Washington National Republican*, January 24, 1874; Nicolas Barreyre, "The Politics of Economic Crises: The Panic of 1873, the End of Reconstruction, and the Realignment of American Politics," *Journal of the Gilded Age and Progressive Era* 10 (October 2011): 403–423.

43 Gillette, *Retreat from Reconstruction*, 107; Francis Butler Simkins and Robert Hilliard Wood, *South Carolina during Reconstruction* (Chapel Hill: University of North Carolina Press, 1932); Taylor, *Louisiana Reconstructed*, 241–255; Ted Tunnell, *Crucible of Reconstruction: War, Radicalism, and Race in Louisiana, 1862–1877* (Baton Rouge: Louisiana State University Press, 1984), 196–208; Foner, *Reconstruction*, 550–552.

44 Foner, *Reconstruction*, 553–558, 580–582, 558 (quotation); Gillette, *Retreat from Reconstruction*, 259–299; Claude R. Flory, "Marcellus L. Stearns Florida's Last Reconstruction Governor," *Florida Historical Quarterly* 44 (January 1966): 181–192; Taylor, *Louisiana Reconstructed*, 241–255.

45 Gillette, *Retreat from Reconstruction*, 378; Franklin, *Reconstruction*, 227; Foner, *Reconstruction*, 612.

Chapter 2—An (Un)Exceptional Moment: The Politics of Reconstruction-Era Arkansas

1 John Hugh Reynolds, *Makers of Arkansas History* (Silver, Burdett and Company, 1918), 256.

2 Reynolds, *Makers of Arkansas History*, 257.

3 For a discussion of "friends and neighbors" voting and how it played out in Arkansas, see the chapter on Arkansas in V. O. Key's classic work *Southern Politics in State and Nation* (New York: Vintage Books, 1949).

4 "The Arkansas Election," *New York Times*, March 29, 1864.

5 For overviews of the key events in federal-state interactions during this period, see Thomas DeBlack, *With Fire and Sword: Arkansas, 1861–1874* (Fayetteville: University of Arkansas Press, 2003).

6 The *Rison et al.* precedent became important once again as the state Supreme Court shot down a modern voter identification law in *Martin, et al. v. Kohls, et al.* (2014) by the same logic.

7 On the 1868 Constitution, see Cal Ledbetter Jr., "The Constitution of 1868: Conqueror's Constitution or Constitutional Continuity?" *Arkansas Historical Quarterly* 44 (Spring 1985): 16–41.

8 See Blake Wintory's chronicling of this list of African American political leaders in the state in Chapter 3—African American Legislators in the Arkansas General Assembly, 1868–1893: Another Look.

9 1868 Democratic National Platform, available at the American Presidency Project, http://www.presidency.ucsb.edu/ws/index.php?pid=29579 (accessed January 12, 2018).

10 County-level voting data from National Historical Geographic Information System.

11 The state's Republican canvassing board had rejected votes from many Democratic-majority counties, claiming that voter intimidation had driven the results.

12 James H. Atkinson describes how these coalitions developed in detail in "The Arkansas Gubernatorial Campaign and Election of 1872," *Arkansas Historical Quarterly* 1 (1942): 307–321.

13 Michael B. Dougan, *Arkansas Odyssey: The Saga of Arkansas from Prehistoric Times to Present* (Little Rock: Rose Publishing Company, 1994), 262.

14 Key works in overviewing key tenets of APD include the following: Paul Pierson, *Politics in Time: History, Institutions, and Social Analysis* (Princeton: Princeton University Press, 2005); Paul Pierson, "Not Just What, but *When*: Timing and Sequence in Political Processes," *Studies in American Political Development* 14 (2000): 72–92; Robert Jervis, "Timing and Interaction in Politics: A Comment on Pierson"; Kathleen Thelen, "Timing and Temporality in the Analysis of Institutional Change"; and Amy Bridges, "Path Dependence, Sequence, History, Theory," *Studies in American Political Development* 14 (2000): 93–112.

15 For a discussion of the document's key elements and its longer-term impact on the state's public policy, see Chapter 7 of Diane D. Blair and Jay Barth, *Arkansas Politics and Government: Do the People Rule?* (Lincoln: University of Nebraska Press, 2005).

16 For an analysis of the Dunning School and its impact, see John David Smith and J. Vincent Lowery, eds., *The Dunning School: Historians, Race, and the Meaning of Reconstruction* (Lexington: University Press of Kentucky, 2013).

17 Eric J. Foner, "Foreword," Smith and Lowery, eds., *The Dunning School.*

18 Eric J. Foner, "Foreword," Smith and Lowery, eds., *The Dunning School.*

19 Thomas Starling Staples, *Reconstruction in Arkansas, 1862–1874* (New York: Columbia University Press, 1923), 276.

20 Staples, *Reconstruction in Arkansas*, 441.

21 "100 Years Later, What's the Legacy of 'Birth Of A Nation'?," *All Things Considered*, National Public Radio, February 8, 2015, https://www.npr.org/sections/codeswitch/2015/02/08/383279630/100-years-later-whats-the-legacy-of-birth-of-a-nation (accessed January 12, 2018).

22 Key, *Southern Politics in State and Nation*, 189.

23 Dougan, *Arkansas Odyssey*.

24 Jay Barth, "Arkansas's GOP Factions," *Arkansas Times*, May 18, 2017.

Chapter 3—African American Legislators in the Arkansas General Assembly, 1868–1893: Another Look

1 This essay and accompanying tables update Blake J. Wintory, "African-American Legislators in the Arkansas General Assembly, 1868–1893," *Arkansas Historical Quarterly* 65 (Winter 2006): 386–434. Updates include two legislators omitted in the original publication (Daniel Hunt and George E. Trower), research into black legislators who were Union Civil War veterans, citations for new scholarship, new information, and minor corrections.

2 The eight elected African American delegates to the 1868 Constitutional Convention included William H. Grey, Monroe Hawkins, Thomas P. Johnson, James W. Mason, William Murphy, Henry Rector, Richard Samuels, and James T. White. Only Thomas P. Johnson and Henry Rector would not later serve in the Arkansas General Assembly. See James Harris Fain, "Political Disfranchisement of the Negro in Arkansas," Master's Thesis, University of Arkansas, 1961, 3–4. Joseph M. St. Hilaire, "The Negro Delegates in the Arkansas Constitutional Convention of 1868: A Group Profile," *Arkansas Historical Quarterly* 33 (Spring 1974): 38–69; Carl H. Moneyhon, *The Impact of the Civil War and Reconstruction on Arkansas: Persistence in the Midst of Ruin* (Baton Rouge: Louisiana State University Press, 1994), 242–243; John William Graves, *Town and Country: Race Relations in an Urban-Rural Context, Arkansas, 1865–1905* (Fayetteville: University of Arkansas Press, 1990), 11–12; Hannah Rosen, *Terror in the Heart of Freedom: Citizenship, Sexual Violence, and the Meaning of Race in the Postemancipation South* (Chapel Hill: University of North Carolina Press, 2009), 87–175.

3 Orville Vernon Burton, *The Age of Lincoln* (New York: Hill and Wang, 2007), 288.

4 See Carl H. Moneyhon, "Black Politics in Arkansas during the Gilded Age, 1876–1900," *Arkansas Historical Quarterly* 44 (Autumn 1985): 223–226. Rosen points to an urban leadership bias in her analysis of black Republican organizing in the state in 1865; see Rosen, *Terror in the Heart of Freedom*, 99–101.

5 On the election of Rev. George E. Trower in Conway County, see Kenneth C. Barnes, *Who Killed John Clayton?: Political Violence and the Emergence of the New South, 1861–1893* (Durham: Duke University Press, 1998), 57–59; Kenneth C. Barnes, *Journey of Hope: The Back-to-Africa*

Movement in Arkansas in the Late 1800s (Chapel Hill: University of North Carolina Press, 2004), 42; Story Matkin-Rawn, "'The Great Negro State of the County': Arkansas's Reconstruction and the Other Great Migration," *Arkansas Historical Quarterly* 72 (Spring 2013): 36.

6 Census data can be inconsistent from decade to decade, but counting any Arkansas legislator who was ever classed as "mulatto" in any census totals forty-one men. Eric Foner, *Freedom's Lawmakers: A Directory of Black Officeholders during Reconstruction*, rev. ed. (Baton Rouge: Louisiana State University Press, 1996), xvi; Foner rightly notes, "These figures...should be approached with caution, since color designations generally derive from judgments of census takers and other highly subjective sources." Also see Steven Hahn, *A Nation under Our Feet: Black Political Struggles in the Rural South from Slavery to the Great Migration* (Cambridge: Belknap Press of Harvard University, 2003), 260–263; Joel Williamson, *New People: Miscegenation and Mulattoes in the United States* (Baton Rouge: Louisiana State University Press, 1980; 1995); and Thomas Holt, *Black over White: Negro Political Leadership in South Carolina during Reconstruction* (Urbana: University of Illinois Press, 1977).

7 Moneyhon, "Black Politics in Arkansas," 223–26; Hahn, *A Nation under Our Feet*, 165–198, 230–235. "Other professions" include editors, doctors, insurance and real estate agents, mechanics, photographers, blacksmiths, and bankers.

8 Benjamin F. Adair, William L. Copeland, and Richard A. Dawson claimed no property in 1870, but they were in households that claimed $3,000, $2,300, and $20,500, respectively. Since Conway Barbour appeared in the 1870 census in Illinois and Arkansas with $3,500 and $0, I used an average. Personal property tax records were unavailable for several relevant counties: St. Francis, Phillips, Monroe, Lafayette, Desha, and Mississippi. When records for more than one county tax year were found, an average was calculated.

9 Moneyhon, "Black Politics in Arkansas," 231.

10 See Walter Nunn, "The Constitutional Convention of 1874," *Arkansas Historical Quarterly* 27 (Autumn 1968): 183–186.

11 Moneyhon, "Black Politics in Arkansas," 222; Barnes, *Journey of Hope*, 20–21, 31–32; Blake Wintory, "William Hines Furbush: African-American Carpetbagger, Republican, Fusionist, and Democrat," *Arkansas Historical Quarterly* 62 (Summer 2004): 142–144.

12 Graves, *Town and Country*, 55; Moneyhon, "Black Politics in Arkansas," 222; Barnes, *Journey of Hope*, 55; Wintory, "William Hines Furbush," 107–111, 126–145.

13 W. H. Furbush was elected as a Democrat in 1879 after serving two terms as sheriff of Lee County. He previously served a term in the House as a Republican; see Wintory, "William Hines Furbush," 142–145. James Wofford is listed a Democrat in the *Arkansas Gazette* (Little Rock), November 22, 25, 1876, but as a Republican in *Rules of the House of Representatives and Joint Rules of the Senate and House of Representatives* (Little Rock: Gazette Job and Book Printing House, 1877). On Adair, see Brian K. Mitchell, "Benjamin Frank Adair (1852–1902)," *Encyclopedia of Arkansas History & Culture*, http://www.encyclopediaofarkansas.net/encyclopedia/entry-detail.aspx?entryID=12339 (accessed January 12, 2018).

14 Various primary and secondary sources helped determine the number of slaves, including place of birth. Approximately sixty-two of Arkansas's nineteenth-century black legislators hailed from Southern states (about nineteen were native to Arkansas), thirteen came from border states or the District of Columbia, and ten were born in Northern states. An 1875 dispatch from the *Fort Wayne Gazette* reported eight of Arkansas's nine black legislators had been slaves. Since William L. Copeland, born in Ohio, was known to be free, I determined the remaining legislators in the session were former slaves. See H. H. Robinson, "From the *Fort Wayne Gazette,*" in *A History of the North-Western Editorial Excursion to Arkansas* (Little Rock: T. B. Mills & Co., 1876), 207.

15 Willard B. Gatewood Jr., "John Hanks Alexander of Arkansas: Second Black Graduate of West Point," *Arkansas Historical Quarterly* (Summer 1982): 105.

16 Gatewood, "John Hanks Alexander," 105–106. The 1870 Census shows Fannie was unable to read or write; Gatewood notes Fannie was known to have some difficulty with writing.

17 Gatewood quotes Alexander's letters from the Alexander Family Papers (Huntington Library, San Marino, California); see Gatewood "John Hanks Alexander," 106–107.

18 Since Alexander's letters and other records show otherwise, Gatewood doubts later claims that Alexander purchased his family's freedom around 1850, saying that "such information is obviously incorrect." See Gatewood, "John Hanks Alexander," 107. For the early claim of freedom, see *Cleveland* (OH) *Gazette*, November 29, 1884. Much of Alexander's wealth was lost in 1867 when Helena flooded. This explains why Alexander reported no personal or real estate in the 1870 Census. See Gatewood, 109.

19 Gatewood, "John Hanks Alexander," 112.

20 *Morning Republican*, January 8, 1869; H. B. McKenzie, "Confederate

Manufactures in Southwest Arkansas," in *Publications of the Arkansas Historical Association* (Fayetteville: 1906): 2, 206.

21 Hunt replaced Rep. S. D. Belden according to 1892 *Biennial Report of the Secretary of State of the State of Arkansas*; later Secretary of State reports seem to be in error. A Daniel Hunt appears in the 1870 and 1880 Census in Hempstead County. The two men, both farmers, could be the same man, but he put his place of birth either as North Carolina or Maryland and a birth year of either 1828 or 1834. In the 1880 census, Daniel Hunt has a young son named Silas Hunt. I could find no relationship between these Hunts and Silas Hunt, also from southwestern Arkansas, who was admitted to the University of Arkansas Law School in 1948. See 1870 U.S. census, Hempstead County, Arkansas, population schedule, Ozan Township, p. 5; 1880 U.S. census, Hempstead County, Arkansas, population schedule, Saline Township, p. 17.

22 *Arkansas Democrat*, October 3, 1887.

23 The ten are William Copeland, Anderson Ebberson, William H. Furbush, John H. Johnson, Green Hill Jones, Thomas Kersh, George Washington Lowe, Americus Mayo, Carl Polk, and Anderson L. Rush. All but Copeland served in the United States Colored Troops. Copeland joined the Second Ohio Cavalry, see *General Index to Pension Files, 1861-1934*. Washington DC: National Archives and Records Administration. T288, 546 rolls (accessed on Ancestry.com).

24 On pension files, see Elizabeth A. Regosin and Donald R. Shaffer, *Voices of Emancipation: Understanding Slavery, the Civil War, and Reconstruction through the U.S. Pension Bureau Files* (New York: New York University Press, 2008).

25 1870 U.S. census, Monroe County, Arkansas, population schedule, Duncan Township, p. 30. The two children, Charley (9) and Tommy (7) Herrin, are both listed as born in Arkansas, which seems unlikely if they were Ellen's; *Morning Republican*, March 25, 1871, refers to Mayo as a minister. "Freedmen's Bureau Marriages, 1861–1872," familysearch.org (accessed December 12, 2017).

26 Depositions of Elizabeth Mayo, Feb. 7, 1898, in Pension File of Americus Mayo, 768.157, 634.399, 514.433, 460.503, 563.740, 3rd USC Cavalry, RG 15, NARA, Washington DC. Mayo's pension application was opened after his 1890 death. The interviews in the file are focused on the contested claim of the two widows for his pension.

27 Compiled Service Record of Americus Mays [Mayo], Record Group 94, NARA; Pension file of Americus Mayo. The pension office awarded Mayo's pension to his third wife, a woman also named Ellen (Horn) Mayo.

28 Hills Jones, General Affidavit, Sept. 4, 1904, in Pension File of Hill Jones [Green Hill Jones], 122.6803, 960.154, 3rd USC Heavy Artillery, RG 15, NARA, Washington DC. Many affidavits in pension files, like this one, are focused on proving the identity of the claimant.

29 Cantrell, *Kenneth and John B. Rayner*, 57–58.

30 In another document in the Pension File of Hill Jones, Jones reports, "I was a slave & come from old Col. Billy Polk's estate. But I be long [*sic*] to Kinith [*sic*] R. Rayner last." Cantrell says, "Where Rayner obtained the slaves to work his new plantation remains an unanswered question," but Jones's story fits with Rayner's claim. See Cantrell, *Kenneth and John B. Rayner and the Limits of Southern Dissent* (Urbana: University of Illinois Press, 1993), 50–51, 56.

31 Cantrell, *Kenneth and John B. Rayner*, 54–57.

32 Compiled Service Record of Hill Jones, Record Group 94, NARA; Pension File of Hill Jones. In 1876, Jones's 1869 credentials were recorded in Marriage Record Book C, 347-348, Chicot County Courthouse, Lake Village. 1870–1873 *Male Enrollment Ledger*, Hillsdale College Archives; Linda Moore, Public Service Librarian, Hillsdale College, email communication with author, July 23, 2017.

33 1880, 1900, and 1910 Census, Chicot County; Also see Chicot County Deed Book D2, p. 331; Pension File of Hill Jones.

34 "Jones, G. H. Appraisement," 116–117, Record Inventories, Appraisements and Bills Sale Book B, Chicot County Courthouse, Lake Village; G. H. Jones, Probate No. 662, Chicot County Courthouse, Lake Village.

35 Matkin-Rawn, "'The Great Negro State of the Country,'" 34.

36 Pension File of George Washington [George W. Lowe]. Also see *Indianapolis Freeman*, April 4, 1891.

37 Pension File of George Washington [George W. Lowe], 971.467, 104.9467, 1.186.653, 955.121, 5th USC Heavy Artillery, RG 15, NARA, Washington DC.

38 Barnes, *Journey of Hope*, 58–59; Omar Ali, *In the Lion's Mouth: Black Populism in the New South, 1886–1900* (Jackson: University Press of Mississippi, 2010), 32; Graves, *Town and Country*, 164–181.

39 William H. Furbush and Edward A. Fulton, both born in Kentucky, were both free men during the 1850s. The historical record is not clear if Conway Barbour, born in Kentucky, was ever a slave or if he was born free. William H. Grey, born in Washington DC, claimed he was born free. John W.

Webb's status is less clear. Born in Kentucky, he may have been enslaved in Arkansas in the 1850s since children in his Chicot County household in the 1880 census were born in Arkansas in the 1850s. Those same children are not in his Chicot County household in the 1870 census but in a nearby household. A description of Webb in the *Morning Republican*, March 25, 1871, says he, Conway Barbour, and Adam Johnson "were for many years residents of Louisville, KY." Since Barbour was known to be free, this could be interpreted that all three men were free in Louisville. An interview with a Webb descendant did not shed any light on his antebellum status. Leonard Young, phone interview with the author, November 19, 2017. On Conway Barbour, see Victoria L. Harrison, "Over the Horizon: Free Black Americans and Geographic Mobility in the Mid-Nineteenth Century, The Case of Conway Barbour," (PhD diss., St. Louis University, 2008). On Furbush, see Wintory, "William Hines Furbush," 111–112; on Fulton, see *Cleveland Gazette*, Dec. 3, 1887.

40 Benjamin F. Adair and James W. Mason were both born in Arkansas and resided in Ohio in 1860. Richard A. Dawson, born in Virginia, grew up in Illinois. Adam Johnson, born in Mississippi, lived in Kentucky prior to his arrival in Arkansas, according to *Morning Republican*, March 25, 1871. R. C. Weddington, born in Mississippi after emancipation, also never experienced slavery.

41 See Leon F. Litwack, *North of Slavery: The Negro in the Free States, 1790–1860* (Chicago: University of Chicago Press, 1961), 155–158, 178, 186–190.

42 1860 U.S. census, St. Louis County, Missouri, population schedule, p. 14; Graves, *Town and Country*, 18–19; Todd E. Lewis, "William Henry Grey," *Encyclopedia of Arkansas History & Culture*. http://www.encyclopediaofarkansas.net/encyclopedia/entry-detail.aspx?entryID=5696 (accessed January 12, 2018). Rosen, *Terror in the Heart of Freedom*, 98–99. A biographer of Grey's mentor and employer Virginia governor Henry Wise has speculated that Grey may have been Wise's son and that Wise emancipated him during childhood; Craig M. Simpson, *A Good Southerner: The Life of Henry A. Wise of Virginia* (Chapel Hill: University of North Carolina Press, 1985), 34.

43 1860 U.S. census, Marion County, Indiana, population schedule, p. 3; William J. Simmons, *Men of Mark: Eminent, Progressive and Rising* (Cleveland, OH: George M. Rewell & Co, 1887), 590–593; 1870 U.S. census, Phillips County, Arkansas, population schedule, p. 3; *Morning Republican*, January 8, 1869, March 25, 1871; *Chicago Tribune*, March 16, 1892; American Baptist Home Mission Society, *Baptist Home Missions in North America...1832-1882* (New York: George W. Wheat, 1883), 585. St.

Hilaire speculated that White may have arrived in Helena with "a detachment of Negro federal troops." While White did register for the draft in Indiana in July 1863, I can't find evidence that he actually served. See *U.S., Civil War Draft Registrations Records, 1863-1865* [database online], Provo, UT, USA: Ancestry.com. Primary sources I cite above point to his role in the church as a missionary in Helena, but Rosen repeats St. Hilaire's assertion, saying he "came with a unit of African American Union soldiers during the war." See St. Hilaire, "The Negro Delegates," 46; Rosen, *Terror in the Heart of Freedom*, 99. On missionaries and conditions in Helena, see Chandra Manning, *Troubled Refuge: Struggling for Freedom in the Civil War* (New York: Alfred A. Knopf, 2016), 106–109, 145.

44 *Morning Republican*, October 4, 1870.

45 *Arkansas Gazette*, August 26, 1886; *Chicago Tribune*, March 16, 1892.

46 1870 U.S. Census, Marion County, Indiana, population schedule, p. 50; *Memphis Daily Appeal*, Feb. 22, 1873. Stewart was said to have arrived in Helena in 1870 and taken over the city's public schools.

47 Robert L. McCaul, *The Black Struggle for Public Schooling in Nineteenth-Century Illinois* (Carbondale: Southern Illinois University Press, 1987), 82; 1870 Manuscript Census, Cook County, Illinois, population schedule, p. 79. The *Arkansas Gazette*, Feb. 1, 1873, reported Richard A. Dawson was a graduate of Oberlin, but they corrected the record a day later: "He desires us to say that he is a graduate of the law institute of the University of Chicago. He graduated in the class of 1869-1870...the first colored man who graduated at that institution," *Arkansas Gazette*, Feb. 2, 1873. This is not the same institution as today's University of Chicago Law School.

48 Willard B. Gatewood, "Sunnyside: The Evolution of an Arkansas Plantation, 1840–1945," in *Shadows over Sunnyside: An Arkansas Plantation in Transition, 1830–1945*, ed. Jeannie M. Whayne (Fayetteville: University of Arkansas Press, 1993), 5, 7; Steven Lubet, *The "Colored Hero" of Harper's Ferry: John Anthony Copeland and the War Against Slavery* (New York: Cambridge University Press. Miller, 2007), 212; Mason, Copeland, and Adair's names are found in *General catalogue of Oberlin college, 1833 [-] 1908* (Oberlin, OH: Oberlin College, 1909), www.archive.org (accessed online November 16, 2017). Darwin Payne suggests Samuel H. Scott might have attended Oberlin College, but he does not appear in Oberlin's catalog. See *Quest for Justice: Louis A. Bedford Jr. and the Struggle for Equal Rights in Texas* (Dallas, TX: Southern Methodist University, 2009), 10–11.

49 *Indianapolis Freeman*, April 4, 1891.

50 Thomas C. Kennedy, *A History of Southland College: The Society of Friends and Black Education in Arkansas* (Fayetteville: University of Arkansas Press, 2009), 292n3, 293-94n31; *Lincoln University: College and Theological Seminary* (Lincoln University, 1918), 23, www.archive.org (accessed November 7, 2017); *Lincoln University Herald* 31 (February 1917), http://www.lincoln.edu/library/specialcollections/herald/1917.pdf (accessed November 16, 2017); *Catalogue of Dartmouth College...and the Medical School...1903-1904* (Hanover, NH: Dartmouth, 1903), 263, books.google.com (accessed November 11, 2017). It's hard to know what to do with George Waltham Bell. He was likely born a slave in Mississippi or Tennessee around 1855. However, around 1917, Bell began to claim he was born in Abyssinia, the son of John Bell and Elizabeth Theodora. (His mother's name in the 1880 Census [Desha] is Betsy). According to the story, the family was exiled to Malta and later John Bell died in a coup attempt against King Menelik in 1859. Young Bell joined the British Navy and resigned when at port in the United States (no dates given). However, census data and other inconsistencies don't seem to support his claims of being born in Africa. Thomas C. Kennedy in his history of Southland College found many "discrepancies" in Bell's biography and wrote "the assertion that he had been born in Abyssinia does not [seem plausible]." In 2006, unaware of the elaborate claims, I linked Bell's assertion that he was born in Abyssinia in the 1920 census with a rise of black nationalism that emerged with Marcus Garvey's Universal Negro Improvement Association, Wintory, "African American Legislators," 389n17. Versions of the story can be found in *Lincoln University: College and Theological Seminary Biographical Catalogue* (Lincoln University, 1918), 23; *Lincoln University Herald* 21 (February 1917); Walter L. Williams, "Ethnic Relations of African Students in the United States, with Black Americans, 1870–1900," *Journal of Negro History* 65 (Summer, 1980): 228–249. Williams includes a section on students who fraudulently passed themselves off as African, but Williams calls Bell "perhaps the most interesting case of an African who made a successful career in America." Williams cites a source I have not examined: Horace Mann Bond, "God Glorified by Africa: the Story of Lincoln University and the Providence of God in the Ancestral Continent" (typewritten manuscript, Lincoln University Archives, 1955). More scholarship on Bell is needed.

51 Unlike in the rest of the South, there was no formal law forbidding educating slaves in Arkansas or Tennessee. However, Orville Taylor noted, "withholding education [from slaves] was merely accepted as a normal practice in the system of slavery." See Orville W. Taylor, *Negro Slavery in Arkansas* (1958; reprint, Fayetteville: University of Arkansas Press, 2000), 187–188. Statistics for illiteracy in 1860 are from William Preston Vaughn, *Schools for All: The Blacks and Public Education in the South, 1865–1877* (Lexington: University Press of Kentucky), 2.

52 Jerome R. Riley, *The Philosophy of Negro Suffrage* (Hartford, CT: American Publishing Co, 1895), 58–59. Riley, a physician, was born in Canada West; see Victor Ullman, *Looking to the North Star: A Life of William King* (Toronto: Umbrella Press, 1994). Robinson, "From the *Fort Wayne Gazette*," 207. Ned Hill in 1870 U.S. census, Pulaski County, Arkansas, population schedule, Big Rock Township, p. 43. Marshall M. Murray, an African American teacher in southwestern Arkansas and an 1883 veteran of the General Assembly, echoed a version of this sentiment in 1903: "this teaching [by northern carpetbaggers] so inspired the political ambition of the colored voters of that day that many of them who could neither read nor write became candidates and were elected office," *Arkansas Democrat*, March 25, 1903.

53 Eric Foner, *Reconstruction: America's Unfinished Revolution, 1863–1877* (New York: Harper-Row, 1988), 96–97; Hahn, *A Nation Under Our Feet*, 277–279.

54 Census data points to twelve men who might have been semi-literate or illiterate at one point in their lives. Several of these men were classed as illiterate in one census, but literate in the next. This change in status might be due to errors by the census taker or it could also be a reflection of the act of learning to read and write. I assumed the census was incorrect in classifying E. A. Fulton in 1870 and Samuel H. Scott in 1880 as illiterate. Fulton, a census taker in 1870 and later a newspaper editor, was classed as literate in the 1860 census and in the 1880 census. Samuel Scott, a northern-born lawyer and editor, also seems unlikely to be illiterate. Henry H. Robinson could not be found in any census, but with an occupation of teacher, he was likely literate. Kenneth C. Barnes also describes a letter Henry H. Robinson wrote to the American Colonization Society; Barnes, *Journey of Hope*, 22. There is no information regarding Richard Samuels's education or literacy.

55 Rev. A. H. Miller, *How I Succeeded in my Business* (n.p., [1911]), 6–7. Miller's book is inspired by Booker T. Washington's personal story. Miller emphasizes his achievements, including his education, as part of being a "self-made man." In regard to Miller's education, there seems to be more to the story than what he reveals in the book. In the 1880 census, Miller is a twenty-nine-year-old farmer apparently living with his father, Boyer Miller, and Henrietta Miller, his stepmother. Henrietta, born in Ohio, is listed as "mulatto" and working as a school teacher. See 1880 U.S. census, Phillips County, Arkansas, population schedule, p. 260.

56 Compiled Service Record of Anderson Rush, Record Group 94, NARA; *Morning Republican*, January 8, 1869; Pension File of Anderson Rush, 465.262, 312.767, 57th USC Infantry, RG 15, NARA, Washington, DC.

57 Compiled Service Record of Thomas Cush, Record Group 94, NARA; Sworn testimony of Thomas Kersh, Oct. 3, 1902, in Pension File of Thomas Kresh (Thomas Crush) 1.033.446, 817.095, 1.074.547, 864.063, 2nd USC Light Artillery, RG 15, NARA, Washington DC.

58 See *Morning Republican*, March 25, 1871; *Cleveland* (OH) *Gazette*, December 3, 1887; *Arkansas Gazette*, December 28, 1884.

59 Chris W. Branam, "'The Africans Have Taken Arkansas': Political Activities of African Americans in the Reconstruction Legislature," *Arkansas Historical Quarterly* 73 (Autumn 2014): 233–267.

60 Branam, "'The Africans Have Taken Arkansas,'" 233–234.

61 Branam, "'The Africans Have Taken Arkansas,'" 234, 236–238, 256–260, 266.

62 Branam, "'The Africans Have Taken Arkansas,'" 247–253, 255. James Alexander, Conway Barbour, James T. White, and James W. Mason voted consistently to restore ex-Confederate voting rights. Branam notes Mason's own father, Elisha Worthington, was among the beneficiaries.

63 Branam, "'The Africans Have Taken Arkansas,'" 265. In his 1911 autobiography, Abraham H. Miller, Phillips County representative in 1874–75, described practical legislative achievements (stock law and auction law), but he makes no mention of Reconstruction successes like civil rights or public education. See Miller, *How I Succeeded in my Business*, 8–9, 53. Ironically, the passage is accompanied by a photograph of Rev. James T. White—Reconstruction champion of civil rights and black suffrage—who was also Rev. Miller's mentor and the founder of Helena's Second Baptist Church.

64 At least one member of the black delegation in 1893, Peter H. Booth of Jefferson County, attempted to modify the 1891 election law. Booth proposed increasing the time for voters to study the ballot from five minutes to ten minutes. Booth, who was working in the State Capitol as a shoeshiner, described his attempt in an article in the *Arkansas Gazette* that mocks him, *Arkansas Gazette*, February 19, 1917.

Chapter 4—Brindletails, Minstrels, Hercules, and Lady Baxter: The Brooks-Baxter War and the End of Reconstruction in Arkansas

1 Allen W. Trelease, *White Terror: The Ku Klux Klan Conspiracy and Southern Reconstruction* (Baton Rouge: Louisiana State University Press, 1971), 174. For a detailed discussion, see Thomas A. DeBlack, *With Fire and Sword: Arkansas, 1861–1874* (Fayetteville: University of Arkansas Press, 2003), 174–200.

2 For a fuller discussion of these political machinations, see DeBlack, *With Fire and Sword*, 211–214.

3 DeBlack, *With Fire and Sword*, 213.

4 Carl Moneyhon, "Joseph Brooks," in Nancy A. Williams, ed., *Arkansas Biography: A Collection of Notable Lives* (Fayetteville: University of Arkansas Press, 2000), 41–42.

5 Moneyhon, "Joseph Brooks," 41–42.

6 Moneyhon, "Joseph Brooks," 41–42.

7 DeBlack, *With Fire and Sword*, 214; John Mortimer Harrell, *The Brooks and Baxter War: A History of the Reconstruction Period in Arkansas* (St. Louis: Slawson Printing Company, 1893), 131.

8 The entire text of Clayton's speech can be found in Harrell, 133–137.

9 The entire text of Clayton's speech can be found in Harrell, 133–137.

10 DeBlack, *With Fire and Sword*, 215.

11 Michael B. Dougan, "Elisha Baxter," in Nancy A. Williams, ed., *Arkansas Biography: A Collection of Notable Lives* (Fayetteville: University of Arkansas Press, 2000), 21–22.

12 Dougan, "Elisha Baxter," 21–22.

13 Dougan, "Elisha Baxter," 21–22; James H. Atkinson, "The Arkansas Gubernatorial Campaign and Election of 1872," *Arkansas Historical Quarterly* 1, no. 4 (December 1942): 312–313.

14 Michael B. Dougan, *Arkansas Odyssey: The Saga of Arkansas from Prehistoric Times to Present* (Little Rock: Rose Publishing Company, 1994), 258.

15 Thomas S. Staples, *Reconstruction in Arkansas: 1862–1874* (Gloucester, MA: Peter Smith, 1964), 400.

16 John I. Smith, *Forward from Rebellion: Reconstruction and Revolution in Arkansas, 1868–1874* (Little Rock: Rose Publishing Company, 1983), 105–106.

17 DeBlack, *With Fire and Sword*, 217.

18 DeBlack, *With Fire and Sword*, 218.

19 Staples, *Reconstruction in Arkansas*, 405–407.

20 DeBlack, *With Fire and Sword*, 218.

21 Staples, *Reconstruction in Arkansas*, 407–408; DeBlack, *With Fire and Sword*, 218.

22 DeBlack, *With Fire and Sword*, 218.

23 Staples, *Reconstruction in Arkansas*, 407–408; DeBlack, *With Fire and Sword*, 218.

24 Harrell, *The Brooks and Baxter War*, 202–203; DeBlack, *With Fire and Sword*, 219.

25 Staples, *Reconstruction in Arkansas*, 413–414; DeBlack, *With Fire and Sword*, 219.

26 Staples, *Reconstruction in Arkansas*, 413.

27 On White, see James W. Leslie, "Hercules King Cannon White: Hero? or Heel?" *Jefferson County Historical Quarterly* 25 (1997): 4–20. DeBlack, *With Fire and Sword*, 219–220.

28 Harrell, *The Brooks and Baxter War*, 230.

29 DeBlack, *With Fire and Sword*, 220; Harrell, *The Brooks and Baxter War*, 225–226.

30 Harrell, *The Brooks and Baxter War*, 225–227.

31 Harrell, *The Brooks and Baxter War*, 227–230.

32 Staples, *Reconstruction in Arkansas*, 411.

33 DeBlack, *With Fire and Sword*, 221.

34 J. French Hill, *The Brooks and Baxter War: First Hand Account of the Battle at New Gascony* (unpublished manuscript, 2000); Staples, *Reconstruction in Arkansas*, 414.

35 Harrell, *The Brooks and Baxter War*, 241–243; Smith, *Forward from Rebellion*, 105.

36 Kenneth C. Barnes, "The Old State House and the Brooks–Baxter War," in Mark K. Christ, ed., *Sentinels of History: Reflections on Arkansas Properties on the National Register of Historic Places* (Fayetteville: University of Arkansas Press, 2000), 52.

37 DeBlack, *With Fire and Sword*, 222–223.

38 DeBlack, *With Fire and Sword*, 223.

39 DeBlack, *With Fire and Sword*, 223.

40 Harrell, *The Brooks and Baxter War*, 256–257; Staples, *Reconstruction in Arkansas*, 414–424.

41 Staples, *Reconstruction in Arkansas*, 423–425.

42 DeBlack, *With Fire and Sword*, 224.

43 Staples, *Reconstruction in Arkansas*, 431; DeBlack, *With Fire and Sword*, 224.

44 J. Wayne Jones, "Augustus Hill Garland," in *Arkansas Biography: A Collection of Notable Lives*, 118; Beverly Watkins, "Augustus Hill Garland," *Encyclopedia of Arkansas History & Culture*, http://www.encyclopediaofarkansas.net/encyclopedia/entry-detail.aspx?entryID=106 (accessed January 17, 2018).

45 Jones, "Garland," 118; Watkins, "Garland."

46 Staples, *Reconstruction in Arkansas*, 433–441.

47 Staples, *Reconstruction in Arkansas*, 440.

48 DeBlack, *With Fire and Sword*, 232.

49 DeBlack, *With Fire and Sword*, 232–233.

Chapter 5—"It Ain't over Till It's Over": Political Violence in Reconstruction Arkansas, 1865–1892

1 For some theoretical discussion of political violence, see H. L. Nieburg, *Political Violence and the Behavioral Process* (New York: St. Martins, 1969); Peter Merkl, *Political Violence and Terror: Motifs and Motivations* (Berkeley: University of California Press, 1986); and Michael J. Boyle, *Violence after War: Explaining Instability in Post-Conflict States* (Baltimore: Johns Hopkins University Press, 2014). Boyle's study is especially useful in understanding Reconstruction violence. He examines how continuing violence often follows a war, using examples of Rwanda, Bosnia, Kosovo, Iraq, and East Timor. For an examination of the role of violence in Reconstruction, see George C. Rable, *But There Was No Peace: The Role of Violence in the Politics of Reconstruction* (Athens: University of Georgia Press, 1984).

2 Thomas A. DeBlack, *With Fire and Sword: Arkansas 1861–1874* (Fayetteville: University of Arkansas Press, 2003), 149; Carl H. Moneyhon, *The Impact of the Civil War and Reconstruction on Arkansas: Persistence in the Midst of Ruin* (Fayetteville: University of Arkansas Press, 2002), 200–202.

3 Moneyhon, *The Impact of the Civil War and Reconstruction on Arkansas*, 246.

4 For a look at the convention, see Richard L. Hume and Jerry B. Gough, *Blacks, Carpetbaggers, and Scalawags: The Constitutional Conventions of Radical Reconstruction* (Baton Rouge: Louisiana State University Press, 2008), 35–40, 44–65.

5 John M. Harrell, *The Brooks and Baxter War: A History of the Reconstruction Period in Arkansas* (St. Louis: Slawson, 1893), 52.

6 DeBlack, *With Fire and Sword*, 178–180; Allen W. Trelease, *White Terror: The Ku Klux Klan Conspiracy and Southern Reconstruction* (New York: Harper and Row, 1971), 98–99; *Daily Arkansas Gazette*, March 18, 1868; Powell Clayton, *The Aftermath of the Civil War, in Arkansas* (New York: Neal Publishing, 1915), 56–57. For a new look at the Klan, see Elaine Frantz Parsons, *Ku-Klux: The Birth of the Klan During Reconstruction* (Chapel Hill: University of North Carolina Press, 2015). Parsons's book bills itself as the first comprehensive examination of the first Klan since Trelease's work. It ignores Arkansas altogether.

7 Clayton, *Aftermath of the Civil War, in Arkansas*, 73; Trelease, *White Terror*, 101–102.

8 Kenneth C. Barnes, *Who Killed John Clayton? Political Violence and the Emergence of the New South, 1861–1893* (Durham, NC: Duke University Press, 1998), 24–27.

9 Barnes, *Who Killed John Clayton?*, 26–27.

10 Trelease, *White Terror*, 151–153; Brian Irby, "The Ku Klux Klan, Republican Militia, and Political Violence in Arkansas, 1868–1869," MA thesis, University of Central Arkansas, 1998, 45–53.

11 Irby, "The Ku Klux Klan," 19–24; Clayton, *Aftermath of the Civil War, in Arkansas*, 51, 69–70; Thomas S. Staples, *Reconstruction in Arkansas, 1862–1874* (New York: Columbia University Press, 1923), 281.

12 Trelease, *White Terror*, 102; Clayton, *Aftermath of the Civil War, in Arkansas*, 100–102, 135; Irby, "The Ku Klux Klan," 29–30.

13 Clayton, *Aftermath of the Civil War, in Arkansas*, 74; Trelease, *White Terror*, 150; Irby, "The Ku Klux Klan," 33, 75.

14 Irby, "The Ku Klux Klan," 30–32; see also William B. Darrow, "The Killing of Congressman James Hinds," *Arkansas Historical Quarterly* 74, no. 1 (Spring 2015): 18–55.

15 This number is from the Union commander of Arkansas, Gen. C. H. Smith, Trelease, *White Terror*, 102.

16 Irby, "The Ku Klux Klan, Republican Militia, and Political Violence in Arkansas, 1868–1869," 60–61; Barnes, *Who Killed John Clayton?*, 26.

17 Clayton, *Aftermath of the Civil War, in Arkansas*, 106; Irby, "The Ku Klux Klan, Republican Militia, and Political Violence in Arkansas, 1868–1869," 63–65; Trelease, *White Terror*, 153, 157–58.

18 Clayton, *Aftermath of the Civil War, in Arkansas*, 51.

19 W. Dean Burnham, *Presidential Ballots, 1836–1892* (Baltimore: Johns Hopkins University Press, 1955), 274–292; the *Daily Arkansas Gazette*,

November 11 and 17, 1868, explains the election in Randolph County. See also, Trelease, *White Terror*, 158–159.

20 Irby, "The Ku Klux Klan," 67–69.

21 Trelease, *White Terror*, 161, 164; Staples, *Reconstruction in Arkansas*, 195–197.

22 Trelease, *White Terror*, 161–163; Irby, "The Ku Klux Klan," 69–74. Democrats argued that they knew nothing about the declaration of martial law in these southwestern counties and were organizing to stop black marauders from roaming the countryside. This seems unlikely given that the governor's proclamation was published in the *Daily Arkansas Gazette* on November 4, 1874.

23 Trelease, *White Terror*, 164.

24 Trelease, *White Terror*, 165–167.

25 Trelease, *White Terror*, 167–171.

26 Barnes, *Who Killed John Clayton?*, 28–30.

27 Trelease, *White Terror*, 163, 166, 168. For a catalog of alleged militia outrage, see Harrell, *The Brooks and Baxter War*, 69–90. However, to evaluate Harrell's credibility, note that he said: "There was really no organization of the 'Ku Klux Klan' in the State of Arkansas. There were sporadic attempts to organization, but they came to naught."

28 Trelease, *White Terror*, 170–171.

29 Trelease, *White Terror*, 174.

30 Clayton, *Aftermath of the Civil War, in Arkansas*, 175–184; Nancy Snell Griffith, "The Chicot County Race War," *Encyclopedia of Arkansas History & Culture*, http://www.encyclopediaofarkansas.net/encyclopedia/entry-detail.aspx?entryID=7615 (accessed January 17, 2018); Kathleen Bell, "The Pope County Militia War," *Encyclopedia of Arkansas History & Culture*, http://www.encyclopediaofarkansas.net/encyclopedia/entry-detail.aspx?entryID=2277 (accessed January 17, 2018).

31 For the lead-up to the Brooks-Baxter War, see Earl F. Woodward, "The Brooks-Baxter War in Arkansas, 1872–1874," *Arkansas Historical Quarterly* 30, no. 4 (Winter 1971): 314–326; DeBlack, *With Fire and Sword*, 212–219; and Moneyhon, *The Impact of the Civil War and Reconstruction on Arkansas*, 257–261.

32 It is my opinion that historians have generally avoided the Brooks-Baxter War largely because it was indeed so complicated, not because of a lack of source material. In fact, the problem lies in the glut of information.

The Little Rock newspapers, the *Arkansas Gazette* and the *Daily Republican*, and some participants writing years later provided blow-by-blow accounts, but they wrote about it in such a partisan way that a historian does not know quite what to believe. A congressional committee came to Arkansas and took voluminous testimony about the 1872 election and the Brooks-Baxter conflict, published as the Poland Report, but historians have scarcely used it.

33 Michael William Kraemer, "Divisions Between Arkansans in the Brooks-Baxter War," MA thesis, University of Kentucky, 2012. Kraemer charted numbers of troops and dozens of locations from where they came, gleaned from reporting in the Little Rock newspapers, the *Arkansas Gazette* and *Daily Republican*, as well as reporting in the *Memphis Avalanche* and the *Cincinnati Commercial*. The *Commercial* had a reporter in Little Rock covering the war. Kraemer did not use, however, the detailed account of eyewitness John Harrell, which he published decades later as the *Brooks and Baxter War*, which listed several more units.

34 James W. Leslie, "Ferd Havis: Jefferson County's Black Republican Leader," *Arkansas Historical Quarterly* 37, no. 3 (Autumn 1978): 242–243.

35 *Daily Republican*, April 29, 1874; Kraemer, "Divisions Between Arkansans," 68; Harrell, *The Brooks and Baxter War*, 219. Kraemer mistakenly puts the black Perry County troops on the Baxter side, when they clearly served under John J. Gibbons for Brooks. *Daily Republican*, May 6, 1874; *Affairs in Arkansas: Report by Mr. Poland from the Select Committee to Inquire into the Conditions of Affairs in the State of Arkansas*, 43rd Congress, 2nd Session, HR Report No. 2 (Washington DC: Government Printing Office, 1874), 351.

36 Again I use Kraemer's data compiled from newspapers, supplemented by data from Harrell. Kraemer researched the 1870 census for every name identified as an officer/leader of Brooks or Baxter troops, and he found a wider geographic range represented on both sides than was the case for troops identified by place. For example, while the Ozarks contributed no troops for either side, there were Brooks officers from Madison, Izard, and Boone counties and a Baxter officer from Washington County. Kraemer, "Divisions Between Arkansans," 98–99, 106–107.

37 Staples, *Reconstruction in Arkansas*, 424–425.

38 Kenneth C. Barnes, *Journey of Hope: The Back-to-Africa Movement in Arkansas in the Late 1800s* (Chapel Hill: University of North Carolina Press, 2004), 20–32.

39 Barnes, *Journey of Hope*, 34–35; *Arkansas Gazette*, September 9, 12, 14, 1882.

40 John William Graves, *Town and Country: Race Relations in an Urban-Rural Context, Arkansas, 1865–1905* (Fayetteville: University of Arkansas Press, 1990), 54. For a discussion of black office-holding in this period see Carl Moneyhon, "Black Politics in Arkansas during the Gilded Age, 1876–1900," *Arkansas Historical Quarterly* 44, no. 3 (Autumn 1985): 222–245; and Blake J. Wintory, "African-American Legislators in the Arkansas General Assembly, 1868–1893," *Arkansas Historical Quarterly* 65, no. 4 (Winter 2006): 385–434.

41 Barnes, *Journey of Hope*, 40–41.

42 Barnes, *Journey of Hope*, 50–52; Barnes, *Who Killed John Clayton?*, 69–72.

43 The most detailed look at the impact of disfranchisement laws is J. Morgan Kousser, *The Shaping of Southern Politics: Suffrage Restriction and the Establishment of the One-Party South, 1880–1910* (New Haven, CT: Yale University Press, 1974), 127–130. See also Graves, *Town and Country*, 173–74; and Moneyhon, "Black Politics in Arkansas during the Gilded Age," 244.

44 Barnes, *Who Killed John Clayton?*, 122.

Chapter 6—Redeeming Arkansas: The Constitution of 1874 and Post-War Politics

1 "The Arkansas Conflict," *Evening Star*, Washington DC, May 15, 1874.

2 "Governor's Message," *Daily Arkansas Gazette*, May 15, 1874.

3 Michael B. Dougan, *Arkansas Odyssey: The Saga of Arkansas from Prehistoric Times to Present* (Little Rock: Rose Publishing Company, 1994), 262.

4 Carl H. Moneyhon, *The Impact of the Civil War and Reconstruction on Arkansas: Persistence in the Midst of Ruin* (Fayetteville: University of Arkansas Press, 2002), 260–261.

5 Moneyhon, *The Impact of the Civil War and Reconstruction.*

6 Dougan, *Arkansas Odyssey*, 262.

7 "Proclamation of Election," *Daily Arkansas Gazette*, June 7, 1874.

8 Michael Perman, *The Road to Redemption: Southern Politics, 1869–1879* (Chapel Hill: University of North Carolina Press, 1984), 16–17, 58–59, 108.

9 "The Journal of the Arkansas Constitution of 1874" (Manuscript, on microfilm at Mullins Library, University of Arkansas, Fayetteville.)

10 Uriah M. Rose, *The Constitution of the State of Arkansas: Framed and Adopted by the Convention Which Assembled at Little Rock, July 14, 1874, and ratified by the people of the state at the election held October 13th, 1874* (Little

Rock: Press Printing Company, 1891), 236–237; Rodney Harris, "Arkansas's Divided Democracy: The Making of the Constitution of 1874," (PhD diss., University of Arkansas, Fayetteville, 2017), 13–14; Ruth Caroline Cowen, "Reorganization of Federal Arkansas, 1862–1865," *Arkansas Historical Quarterly* 18, no. 1 (Spring 1959): 38.

11 *Debates and Proceedings of the Constitution, which assembled at Little Rock, January 7th, 1868...: To form a Constitution for the State of Arkansas* (Little Rock: J. G. Price, 1868), 873.

12 Morton Keller, *Affairs of State: Public Life in Late Nineteenth Century America* (Cambridge: Belknap Press, 1977), 31; "G," "The Convention," *Daily Arkansas Gazette*, June 17, 1874; Harris, "Arkansas's Divided Democracy," 30–31.

13 Monroe County would vote for the Republican candidate for president in 1872, 1876, and 1880. *Biennial Report of the Arkansas Secretary of State*, 1880. Special Collections, Mullins Library, University of Arkansas, Fayetteville.

14 "The New Constitution," *Daily Arkansas Gazette*, July 31, 1874; Article VI: Executive Department, 1874 Arkansas Constitution.

15 "The Journal of the Arkansas Constitution of 1874," 305–309; "The New Constitution," *Daily Arkansas Gazette*, July 31, 1874; "Article VI: Executive Department," *Debates and Proceedings...1868*, 868–873.

16 "Speech of Hon. E. H. English," *Daily Arkansas Gazette*, August 11, 1868.

17 "The State of Arkansas for Sale!" *Daily Arkansas Gazette*, June 13, 1872.

18 Carl H. Moneyhon, *The Impact of the Civil War and Reconstruction*, 84–85.

19 J. Mills Thornton, "Fiscal Policy and the Failure of Radical Reconstruction in the Lower South," in *Region, Race, and Reconstruction: Essays in Honor of C. Vann Woodward*, edited by J. Morgan Kousser and James M. McPherson (New York: Oxford University Press, 1982), 350–352, 378; Thomas A. DeBlack, *With Fire and Sword, Arkansas, 1861–1874* (Fayetteville: University of Arkansas Press, 2002), 224; Eric Foner, *Reconstruction: America's Unfinished Revolution, 1863–1877* (New York: Harper & Row, 1988), 415–416.

20 "The Convention," *Daily Arkansas Gazette*, August 11, 1874; "About Taxes," *Daily Arkansas Gazette*, February 11, 1874.

21 Carl H. Moneyhon, *Arkansas and the New South, 1874–1929* (Fayetteville: University of Arkansas Press, 1997), 19.

22 Jerry E. Hinshaw, *Call the Roll: The First One Hundred Years of the Arkansas Legislature* (Little Rock: Rose Publishing, 1986), 62–63; Harris, "Arkansas's Divided Democracy," 61.

23 "The Journal of the Arkansas Constitution of 1874," 526.

24 "Southern State Finances," *Daily Arkansas Gazette*, July 1, 1874; "The Convention," *Daily Arkansas Gazette*, July 18, 1874; "State Finances," *Daily Arkansas Gazette*, July 18, 1874; Arkansas Constitution of 1874, Article XVI, Sec. 2.

25 Patrick G. Williams, *Beyond Redemption: Texas Democrats after Reconstruction* (College Station: Texas A&M Press, 2007), 36–39; Foner, *Reconstruction*, 355–356; Keller, *Affairs of State*, 343, 354–356; Arkansas Constitution of 1868, Article VII.

26 "Regnant Populi—Our Dytym," *Fort Smith Herald*, May 30, 1874.

27 For example, Scott County was 1.6% black in 1870 and cast its votes for the Democratic candidate in a majority of the elections analyzed.

28 "Constitutional Convention," *Weekly Observer*, June 30, 1874; C. Van Woodard, *Origins of the New South, 1877–1913* (Baton Rouge: Louisiana State University Press, 1951), 54–55; also see Michael R. Hymn, *The Anti–Redeemers: Hill-Country Political Dissenters in Lower South from Redemption to Populism* (Baton Rouge: Louisiana State University Press, 1990), 87–97; Williams, *Beyond Redemption*, 50–53.

29 "The Convention: Judges for Life," *Daily Arkansas Gazette*, June 4, 1874.

30 "Popular Election of Judges," *Daily Arkansas Gazette*, June 18, 1873; Harris, "Arkansas's Divided Democracy," 75–76.

31 "The Judiciary," *Daily Arkansas Gazette*, June 23, 1874.

32 "An Appeal from Desha," *Daily Arkansas Gazette*, August 2, 1874.

33 "An Appeal from Desha."

34 "An Appeal from Desha."

35 "The Journal of the Arkansas Constitution of 1874," 82.

36 "The Journal of the Arkansas Constitution of 1874," 82; "Regnant Populi," *Daily Arkansas Gazette*, July 19, 1874.

37 "The Journal of the Arkansas Constitution of 1874," 98, 106–115; "Regnant Populi," *Daily Arkansas Gazette*, July 23, 1874; "An Appeal from Desha," *Daily Arkansas Gazette*, August 2, 1874; Letter from Met Jones to Harris Flanagin, September 3, 1874; Harris, "Arkansas's Divided Democracy," 83–85.

38 1870 Census, Population by Race and County; "The Convention," *Daily Arkansas Gazette*, September 4, 1874; "The Convention," *Daily Arkansas Gazette*, September 6, 1874.

39 Story Matkin–Rawn, "The Great Negro State of the Country: Arkansas's Reconstruction and the Other Great Migration," *Arkansas Historical Quarterly* 72, no. 1 (Spring 2013): 15–16, 21; Alexander Keyssar, *The Right to Vote: The Contested History of Democracy in the United States* (New York: Basic Books, 2000), 89, 91; Moneyhon, *The Impact of the Civil War and Reconstruction on Arkansas*, 194–195, 247, 249; DeBlack, *With Fire and Sword*, 169, 227, 232–233; Moneyhon, *Arkansas and the New South*, 89; John William Graves, *Town and Country: Race Relations in the Urban-Rural Context, Arkansas, 1865–1905* (Fayetteville: University of Arkansas Press, 1990), 48–49, 56–57; Michael Perman, *The Road to Redemption*, 10–21,58–59, 151; Woodward, *Origins of the New South*, 103–105; J. Morgan Kousser, *The Shaping of Southern Politics: Suffrage Restriction and the Establishment of the One-Party South, 1880–1910* (New Haven: Yale University Press, 1974), 17.

40 "Constitutional Convention," *Daily Arkansas Gazette*, February 8, 1868.

41 "The Way to Success," *Daily Arkansas Gazette*, July 30, 1871.

42 "Their Capacity for Self–government," *Daily Arkansas Gazette*, May 1, 1869; "The Future of the Negro," *Daily Arkansas Gazette*, December 3, 1870; "Conservative Meeting at Hot Springs," *Daily Arkansas Gazette*, September 15, 1870; Foner, *Reconstruction*, 254, 313, 330, 416; Perman, *The Road to Redemption*, 77–79.

43 "The Convention—Its Duties," *Southern Standard*, July 13, 1874.

44 "To the Voters of Scott County," *Fort Smith Herald*, June 6, 1874; "What Arkansas Is Saved From," *Weekly Observer*, June 14, 1874; Foner, *Reconstruction*, 554–555.

45 Kousser, *The Shaping of Southern Politics*, 251–253; Michael Perman, *Struggle for Mastery: Disfranchisement in the South, 1888–1908* (Chapel Hill: University of North Carolina Press, 2001), 16.

46 Moneyhon, *The Impact of the Civil War and Reconstruction on Arkansas*, 13; Michael Perman, *The Road to Redemption*, 67–76.

47 Mark W. Summer, *Railroads, Reconstruction, and the Gospel of Prosperity: Aid under the Radical Republicans, 1865–1877* (Princeton: Princeton University Press, 1984), 36; Michael B. Dougan, *Confederate Arkansas: The People and Policies of a Frontier State in War Time* (Tuscaloosa: University of Alabama Press, 1976), 7–10; DeBlack, *With Fire and Sword*, 13–14; Donald P. McNeilly, *The Old South Frontier* (Fayetteville: University of

Arkansas Press, 2002), 166–168; Cal Ledbetter Jr., "The Constitution of 1836: A New Perspective," *Arkansas Historical Quarterly* 41 (1982): 243.

48 Stephen E. Wood, "The Development of Arkansas Railroads, Part I," *Arkansas Historical Quarterly* 7, no. 3 (Autumn 1948): 126–128.

49 "Our Railroads—State Aid," *Daily Arkansas Gazette*, August 27, 1871.

50 "Rebels Opposing Railroads," *Daily Arkansas Gazette*, October 31, 1868; "State Aid to Railroads," *Daily Arkansas Gazette*, August 29, 1871.

51 "Chamber of Commerce," *Daily Arkansas Gazette*, November 5, 1871; Summers, *Railroads, Reconstruction, and the Gospel of Prosperity*, 251–252; DeBlack, *With Fire and Sword*, 209–211; Orval Truman Diggs Jr., "The Issues of the Powell Clayton Regime, 1868–1871," *Arkansas Historical Quarterly* 8, no. 1 (Spring 1949): 32–33; "Arkansas Railroads," *Daily Arkansas Gazette*, April 27, 1870; "An Extravagant Measure," *Daily Arkansas Gazette*, March 11, 1871.

52 J. Morgan Kousser, "Progressivism—For Middle Class Whites Only: North Carolina Education, 1880–1910," *Journal of Southern History* 46 (1980): 173; Perman, *The Road to Redemption*, 196; Keller, *Affairs of State*, 133–135; Robert Kelley, *The Transatlantic Persuasion: The Liberal-Democratic Mind in the Age of Gladstone* (New York: Alfred A. Knopf, 1960), 210.

53 *Acts of the General Assembly of the State of Arkansas*, "An act to establish and maintain a system of free common schools for the state of Arkansas," Approved 23 of July 1868 (Little Rock: John G. Price, 1868), 163–197, online at http://archive.org/details/acttoestablishma00arka, (accessed January 23, 2018); Constitution of 1868, Article IX; Hobby 15, 43, 36–37, 47–48; DeBlack, *With Fire and Sword: Arkansas*, 169; Graves, *Town and Country*, 30; Perman, *The Road to Redemption*, 31.

54 "Our Common School System," *Daily Arkansas Gazette*, October 26, 1870.

55 "Our Common School System."

56 "The Journal of the Arkansas Constitution of 1874," 192–193, 423; "The Convention," *Daily Arkansas Gazette*, August 21, 1874.

57 "The Convention," *Daily Arkansas Gazette*, August 21, 1874; "The Journal of the Arkansas Constitution of 1874," 420–444.

58 "The Convention," *Daily Arkansas Gazette*, August 22, 1874.

59 "The Convention," *Daily Arkansas Gazette*, August 22, 1874.

60 "The Journal of the Arkansas Constitution of 1874," 432; "The Convention," *Daily Arkansas Gazette*, August 22, 1874.

61 Moneyhon, *Arkansas and the New South*, 18–21.

For Further Reading

Books

Ali, Omar. *In the Lion's Mouth: Black Populism in the New South, 1886–1900*. Jackson: University Press of Mississippi, 2010.

Anderson, James D. *The Education of Blacks in the South, 1860–1935*. Chapel Hill: University of North Carolina Press, 1988.

Barnes, Kenneth C. *Who Killed John Clayton? Political Violence and the Emergence of the New South, 1861–1893*. Durham, NC: Duke University Press, 1998.

———. *Journey of Hope: The Back-to-Africa Movement in Arkansas in the Late 1800s*. Chapel Hill: University of North Carolina Press, 2004.

Belz, Herman. *Reconstructing the Union: Theory and Policy During the Civil War*. Ithaca, NY: Cornell University Press, 1969.

Blair, Diane D., and Jay Barth, eds. *Arkansas Politics and Government: Do the People Rule?* Lincoln: University of Nebraska Press, 2005.

Carter, Dan T. *When the War Was Over: The Failure of Self-Reconstruction in the South, 1865–1867*. Baton Rouge: Louisiana State University Press, 1985.

Christ, Mark K. *Civil War Arkansas, 1863: The Battle for a State* (Norman: University of Oklahoma Press, 2010).

Clayton, Powell. *The Aftermath of the Civil War, in Arkansas* (New York: Neal Publishing, 1915).

DeBlack, Thomas A. *With Fire and Sword: Arkansas, 1861–1874*. Fayetteville: University of Arkansas Press, 2002.

Donald, David. *The Politics of Reconstruction, 1863–1867*. Baton Rouge: Louisiana State University Press, 1965.

Dougan, Michael B. *Arkansas Odyssey: The Saga of Arkansas from Prehistoric Times to Present*. Little Rock: Rose Publishing, 1994.

———. *Confederate Arkansas: The People and Politics of a Frontier State in Wartime*. Tuscaloosa: University of Alabama Press, 1976.

DuBois, W. E. B. *Black Reconstruction in America*. New York: Atheneum, 1935.

Epps, Garrett. *Democracy Reborn: The Fourteenth Amendment and the Fight for Equal Rights in Post–Civil War America*. New York: H. Holt, 2006.

Foner, Eric. *Reconstruction: America's Unfinished Revolution, 1863–1877*. New York: Harper & Row, 1988.

———. *Freedom's Lawmakers: A Directory of Black Officeholders during Reconstruction*. Rev. ed. Baton Rouge: Louisiana State University Press, 1996.

Franklin, John Hope. *Reconstruction After the Civil War*. Chicago: University of Chicago Press, 1961.

Gillete, William. *The Right to Vote: Politics and the Passage of the Fifteenth Amendment*. Baltimore: Johns Hopkins University Press, 1965.

———. *Retreat from Reconstruction, 1869–1879*. Baton Rouge: Louisiana State University Press, 1979.

Graves, John William. *Town and Country: Race Relations in an Urban-Rural Context, Arkansas, 1865–1905*. Fayetteville: University of Arkansas Press, 1990.

Hahn, Steven. *A Nation under Our Feet: Black Political Struggles in the Rural South from Slavery to the Great Migration*. Cambridge: Belknap Press of Harvard University, 2003.

Harrell, John Mortimer. *The Brooks and Baxter War: A History of the Reconstruction Period in Arkansas*. St. Louis, MO: Slawson Printing Company, 1893.

Hinshaw, Jerry E. *Call the Roll: The First One Hundred Years of Arkansas Legislature*. Little Rock: Rose Publishing, 1986.

Hume, Richard L., and Jerry B. Gough. *Blacks, Carpetbaggers, and Scalawags: The Constitutional Conventions of Radical Reconstruction*. Baton Rouge: Louisiana State University Press, 2008.

Hymm, Michael R. *Anti-Redeemers: Hill Country Political Dissenters in the Lower South from Redemption to Populism*. Athens: University of Georgia Press, 1999.

James, Joseph B. *The Framing of the Fourteenth Amendment*. Urbana: University of Illinois Press, 1965.

Kousser, J. Morgan. *The Shaping of Southern Politics: Suffrage Restriction and the Establishment of the One-Party South, 1880–1910*. New Haven: Yale University Press, 1974.

Kousser, J. Morgan, and James M. McPherson, eds. *Region, Race, and Reconstruction: Essays in Honor of C. Vann Woodward*. New York: Oxford University Press, 1982.

Litwack, Leon F. *North of Slavery: The Negro in the Free States, 1790–1860*. University of Chicago Press, 1961.

Manning, Chandra. *Troubled Refuge: Struggling for Freedom in the Civil War*. New York: Alfred A. Knopf, 2016.

McCaul, Robert L. *The Black Struggle for Public Schooling in Nineteenth-Century Illinois*. Carbondale: Southern Illinois University Press, 1987.

McNeilly, Donald P. *The Old South Frontier*. Fayetteville: University of Arkansas Press, 2002.

McPherson, James. *Ordeal by Fire: The Civil War and Reconstruction*. New York: McGraw-Hill Inc., 1982.

Moneyhon, Carl H. *Arkansas and the New South, 1874–1929*. Fayetteville: University of Arkansas Press, 1997.

———. *The Impact of the Civil War and Reconstruction on Arkansas: Persistence in the Midst of Ruin*. Baton Rouge: Louisiana State University Press, 1994.

Parsons, Elaine Frantz. *Ku-Klux: The Birth of the Klan During Reconstruction*. Chapel Hill: University of North Carolina Press, 2015.

Perman, Michael. *Struggle for Mastery: Disfranchisement in the South, 1888–1908*. Chapel Hill: University of North Carolina Press, 2001.

———. *The Road to Redemption: Southern Politics, 1869–1879*. Chapel Hill: University of North Carolina Press, 2001.

Rable, George C. *But There Was No Peace: The Role of Violence in the Politics of Reconstruction*. Athens: University of Georgia Press, 1984.

Ransom, Roger L., and Richard Sutch. *One Kind of Freedom: The Economic Consequences of Emancipation*. Cambridge, MA: Cambridge University Press, 1977.

Regosin, Elizabeth A., and Donald R. Shaffer. *Voices of Emancipation: Understanding Slavery, the Civil War, and Reconstruction through the U.S. Pension Bureau Files*. New York: New York University Press, 2008.

Rose, Uriah M. *The Constitutional Convention of the State of Arkansas: Framed and Adopted by the Convention Which Assembled at Little Rock, July 14, 1874*. Little Rock: Press Printing, 1891.

Rosen, Hannah. *Terror in the Heart of Freedom: Citizenship, Sexual Violence, and the Meaning of Race in the Postemancipation South*. Chapel Hill: University of North Carolina Press, 2009.

Smith, John I. *Forward from Rebellion: Reconstruction and Revolution in Arkansas, 1868–1874*. Little Rock: Rose Publishing Company, 1983.

Stampp, Kenneth M. *The Era of Reconstruction, 1865–1877: A Revisionist View of One of the Most Controversial Periods in American History*. New York: Alfred A. Knopf, 1966.

Staples, Thomas Starling. *Reconstruction in Arkansas, 1862–1874*. New York: Columbia University Press, 1923.

Trelease, Allen W. *White Terror: The Ku Klux Klan Conspiracy and Southern Reconstruction*. Baton Rouge: Louisiana State University Press, 1971.

Vaugh, William Preston. *Schools for All: The Blacks and Public Education in the South, 1865–1877* Lexington: University Press of Kentucky, 2015.

Williams, Nancy A., ed., *Arkansas Biography: A Collection of Notable Lives* (Fayetteville: University of Arkansas Press, 2000).

Williams, Patrick G. *Beyond Redemption: Texas Democrats after Reconstruction*. College Station: Texas A & M Press, 2007.

Periodicals

Atkinson, James H. "The Arkansas Gubernatorial Campaign and Election of 1872." *Arkansas Historical Quarterly* 1, no. 4 (December 1942).

Branam, Chris W. "'The Africans Have Taken Arkansas': Political Activities of African Americans in the Reconstruction Legislature." *Arkansas Historical Quarterly* 73 (Autumn 2014).

Cowen, Ruth Caroline. "Reorganization of Federal Arkansas, 1862–1865." *Arkansas Historical Quarterly* 18 (Spring 1959).

Darrow, William B. "The Killing of Congressman James Hinds." *Arkansas Historical Quarterly* 74 (Spring 2015).

Diggs, Orval Truman, Jr. "The Issues of the Powell Clayton Regime, 1868–1871." *Arkansas Historical Quarterly* 8, no. 1 (Spring 1949).

Hume, Richard L. "The Arkansas Constitutional Convention of 1868: A Case Study in the Politics of Reconstruction." *Journal of Southern History* 39 (May 1973).

———. "Carpetbaggers in the Reconstruction South: A Group Portrait of Outside Whites in the 'Black and Tan' Constitutional Conventions." *Journal of American History* 64 (September 1977).

Ledbetter, Cal, Jr. "The Constitution of 1836: A New Perspective." *Arkansas Historical Quarterly* 41 (Autumn 1982).

———. "The Constitution of 1868: Conqueror's Constitution or Constitutional Continuity?" *Arkansas Historical Quarterly* 44 (Spring 1985).

Leslie, James W. "Ferd Havis: Jefferson County's Black Republican Leader." *Arkansas Historical Quarterly* 37 (Autumn 1978).

———. "Hercules King Cannon White: Hero? or Heel?" *Jefferson County Historical Quarterly* 25 (1997).

Matkin-Rawn, Story. "The Great Negro State of the Country: Arkansas's Reconstruction and the Other Great Migration." *Arkansas Historical Quarterly* 72 (Spring 2013).

Moneyhon, Carl H. "Black Politics in Arkansas During the Gilded Age, 1876–1900." *Arkansas Historical Quarterly* 44 (Autumn 1985).

———. "Edmund J. Davis and the Coke-Davis Election Dispute of 1874: A Reassessment of Character." *Southwestern Historical Quarterly* 55 (Winter 1956).

Nunn, Walter. "The Constitutional Convention of 1874." *Arkansas Historical Quarterly* 27 (Autumn 1968).

St. Hilaire, Joseph M. "The Negro Delegates in the Arkansas Constitutional Convention of 1868: A Group Profile." *Arkansas Historical Quarterly* 33 (Spring 1974).

Singletary, Otis A. "Militia Disturbances in Arkansas during Reconstruction." *Arkansas Historical* Quarterly 15 (Summer 1956).

Wintory, Blake J. "William Hines Furbush: African-American Carpetbagger, Republican, Fusionist, and Democrat." *Arkansas Historical Quarterly* 62 (Summer 2004).

Woods, Stephen E. "The Development of Arkansas Railroads, Part I." *Arkansas Historical Quarterly* 7 (Autumn 1948).

Woodward, Earl F. "The Brooks-Baxter War in Arkansas, 1872–1874." *Arkansas Historical Quarterly* 30 (Winter 1971).

Theses and Dissertations

Fain, James Harris. "Political Disfranchisement of the Negro in Arkansas," Master's thesis, University of Arkansas, Fayetteville, 1961.

Harris, Rodney W. "Arkansas's Divided Democracy: The Making of the Constitution of 1874." PhD dissertation, University of Arkansas, Fayetteville, 2017.

Hobby, Selma Ann Plowman. "The Little Rock Public Schools During Reconstruction, 1865–1874." Master's thesis, University of Arkansas, Fayetteville, 1967.

Irby, Brian. "The Ku Klux Klan, Republican Militia, and Political Violence in Arkansas, 1868–1869." Master's thesis, University of Central Arkansas, 1998.

Kraemer, Michael William. "Divisions Between Arkansans in the Brooks-Baxter War," Master's thesis, University of Kentucky, 2012.

Index

A

Adair, Benjamin F. 91, 92, 102, 122, 126, 247n, 251n

Agricultural Wheel 91, 200, 201, 202, 203

Alabama 37, 42, 52, 55, 214

Alcorn University 102

Alcorn, James 169

Alexander, Fannie Miller 92, 93

Alexander, James Milo 92, 93, 112, 126, 255n

Alexander, Lawson H. 92, 93

American Colonization Society 99

American Political Development 74

Andrews, Christopher C. 18

Andrews, P. J. 180

Anthony House 157, 158, 159, 161, 192

Arkadelphia, Arkansas 227

Arkansas Central Railroad 156

Arkansas County, Arkansas 154, 223, 225, 235

Arkansas Democrat 93

Arkansas Gazette 107, 175, 176, 192, 226

Arkansas General Assembly 12, 19, 44, 53, 84, 87–91, 99, 106, 173, 192, 196, 197, 203, 204, 208, 209, 210, 212, 216, 218, 220, 228, 229, 232, 236

Arkansas Industrial University 105

"Arkansas Mud Test" 77

Arkansas Post 103

Ashley County, Arkansas 179, 180, 183, 184, 187

Augusta, Arkansas 27, 187

B

Back-to-Africa Movement 206

Bailey, Isaac G. 119, 126

Baptist Church 101

Baptist Society 98
Barbour, Conway 112, 126, 247n, 250n, 251n, 255n
Barker, E. G. 179, 180
Barrow, Austin 112, 126
Batesville, Arkansas 152, 175, 179, 191, 195
Battle of Liberty Place 58, 59
Baxter County, Arkansas 192
Baxter, Elisha 19, 72, 73, 74, 90, 152–162, 164, 165, 179, 191–195, 206–210
Bell, George W. 102, 110, 127, 253n
Bell, John 167
Berry, James 168
Bethel Chapel 97
Biennial Report 107
Birth of a Nation 82
Black Codes 27, 28
Black Reconstruction 16
Blair, Francis P. 48
Bliss, Calvin C. 67
Booth, John Wilkes 22
Booth, Peter H. 124, 127, 255n
Boston, Levi B. 116, 127
Bradford, Joseph H. 120, 127
Bradley County, Arkansas 176, 183, 184
Branam, Chris W. 104, 105
Branch Normal School 105
"Brindletails" 72, 150, 153
Brinkley, Arkansas 179
Brooks v. Baxter 156
Brooks, Joseph 72, 73, 149, 150, 153, 156, 157, 162, 165, 180, 181, 191–195, 208
Brooks, Joseph B. 120, 127
Brooks, William 149
Brooks-Baxter War 56, 59, 64, 74, 75, 77, 85, 90, 150, 151, 157–165, 190, 192, 193, 194, 195, 260n, 261n
Brown, Charles 113, 127
Brown, Cornelius "Ned" 114, 127
Brown, Crockett 117, 127
Brown, John 102
Bunn, Henry G. 212
Bunting, Sam 97
Bureau of Refugees, Freedmen, and Abandoned Lands (see Freedmen's Bureau)
Burke, W. R. 197
Burton, Hal B. 120, 128

C

Cairo and Fulton Railroad 47, 151, 228
Camden, Arkansas 31, 175
"carpetbaggers" 42, 44, 63, 72, 79, 80, 81, 148, 153, 171, 174, 187, 194
Carr, John H. 121, 122, 124, 128
Carter, Dan 25, 28,
Catterson, Robert F. 157, 185, 186, 187, 189
Center Point, Arkansas 186, 187
Central Christian Advocate 149

Chamberlain, Daniel H. 58, 60
Chicago, Illinois 36, 104
Chicot County, Arkansas 86, 95, 96, 97, 103, 190, 204, 224, 225
Churchill, Thomas 168, 197, 199
Cincinnati Commercial 194
Cincinnati, Ohio 149
Civil Rights Act of 1866 31, 32, 41
Civil Rights Act of 1875 52, 59
Civil Rights Cases 52
Clansman, The 82
Clark County, Arkansas 194, 195
Clark, George W. 181
Clayton Republicans 208
Clayton, John M. 194, 202
Clayton, Powell 44, 50, 68, 69, 72, 80, 81, 105, 147, 148, 150, 151, 152, 155, 156, 158, 166, 167, 174, 177, 178, 179, 181, 182, 183, 184, 187, 188, 190, 191, 192, 194, 202, 205, 229, 230
Cleveland, Grover 230
Coleman, Berry 116, 117, 128
Colored Agricultural State Wheel 98
Columbia County, Arkansas 183, 184, 187
Columbia University 79
Congress, U.S. 21, 22, 23, 30, 32, 33, 36–40, 42, 44, 49, 50, 59, 72, 212, 213
Congressional Reconstruction 16, 41, 67, 88, 155, 173
Conservative Party 40, 44, 67, 71, 155, 173, 175, 178
Conservative Republicans 40, 54
Constitution of 1864 19, 66
Constitution of 1868 67, 147, 168, 174, 208, 210, 214, 215, 220, 229, 236
Constitution of 1874 74, 75, 76, 85, 166, 168, 236
Constitution, U.S. 16, 25, 33, 39, 69, 88
Constitutional Convention of 1864 18, 19
Constitutional Convention of 1868 42, 67, 88, 100, 149, 174, 195, 226
Constitutional Convention of 1874 75, 156, 165, 166, 195, 211–216, 218, 219, 221, 223, 231, 233
Constitutional Union Party 167
Conway County, Arkansas 89, 151, 176, 177, 178, 181, 188, 189,194, 195, 201, 202, 205
Conway, Elias 228
Copeland, John Anthony 102
Copeland, William L. 102, 114, 116, 128, 247n, 248n, 249n
Corbin, Joseph C. 44, 45
Coushatta Massacre 58
Craighead County, Arkansas 183, 184, 188
Crittenden County, Arkansas 179, 188, 189, 190, 199, 201, 202, 225
Cross County, Arkansas 220, 235
Cypert, Jesse Newton 216, 226, 233

D

Daily Arkansas Gazette 217, 222, 223, 229, 232, 233
Daily Republican 153, 155, 194, 196
Dallas County, Arkansas 219, 224
Danforth, Keyes 178
Dartmouth Medical College 102
Davis, Edmund J. 50, 56
Davis, Henry Winter 21, 22
Davis, Jefferson 213
Dawkins, T. N. 25
Dawson, Richard A. 102, 108, 109, 118, 128, 247, 251n, 252n
Dawson, Sebron Williams 121, 123, 128
Democrat-Conservative alliance 41, 42, 43, 50, 54, 55, 69, 79, 82, 105, 148, 149, 152, 163–167, 173, 175
Desha County, Arkansas 86, 199, 204, 223, 224
DeValls Bluff, Arkansas 179
disfranchisement (African American) 40, 64, 78, 88, 106, 172, 200, 204, 206, 226, 227
disfranchisement (white) 21, 37, 38, 42, 43, 68, 69, 73, 75, 105, 154, 155, 167, 173, 174, 175, 183, 191, 192, 196, 209, 229, 255n
Donohoo, Jacob N. 117, 120, 121, 123, 129
Dorsey, Stephen F. 155, 156, 209, 230
Dougan, Michael 153
Drew County, Arkansas 104, 180, 183
Dubuclet, Antoine 44
Dunn, Oscar J. 44
Dunning School 80
Dunning, William A. 79

E

Eagle, James P. 168, 201, 212, 235
Eakin, John A. 212
Earle, Josiah (Joshua) 188, 190
Ebberson, Anderson 117, 118, 129, 249n
Edwards, Nathan E. 124, 129
El Dorado, Arkansas 175
Election Law of 1891 91, 106
Enforcement Act 50
English, E. H. 217
Eudora, Arkansas 97
Evening Post (New York) 48
Ex Parte Garland 167

F

Fagan, James 157
Faulkner County, Arkansas 195
Fayetteville, Arkansas 105
Featherston, Louis 202, 203
Fifteenth Amendment 40, 44, 50, 57, 88, 227
Fifth U.S. Colored Heavy Artillery 97, 98
First Reconstruction Act 38, 40

Fish, Hamilton 207
Fishback, William 18, 19, 212, 219, 220, 237
Flanagin, Harris 164, 212, 213, 224
Florida 44, 53, 55, 58, 60
Foner, Eric 26, 45, 60, 80, 89, 205
Force Bill (Lodge bill of 1890) 203, 206
Forrest, Nathan Bedford 174
Fort Smith Herald 221
Fort Smith, Arkansas 18, 162, 175, 234
Fort Wayne [Indiana] *Gazette* 102
Fourteenth Amendment 33, 34, 36, 39, 41, 42, 44, 50, 57, 67, 167, 173, 175, 178
Fourth Arkansas Infantry (US) 18
Fourth Military District 38, 67, 68, 88, 173
Franklin, John Hope 26, 60
Free Will Baptists 97
Freedmen's Bureau 29, 30, 31, 32, 179, 180
Frierson, J. G. 220, 235
Fulton County, Arkansas 178
Fulton, Edward A. 104, 112, 129, 250n, 254n
Furbush, William H. 74, 114, 118, 129, 248n, 249n, 250n

G

Garland County, Arkansas 235
Garland, Augustus 78, 90, 105, 164, 166, 167, 168, 195, 197
Garland, Rufus 213
Gatewood, Willard B., Jr. 92
Georgia 40, 42, 43, 44, 49
Gibbons, John 196
Gibson, J. A. 223, 235
Gibson, Lorenzo 26
Gillam, Isaac 118, 129
Gillette, William 60
Glover, Ed 120, 130
Gordon, Anderson 176
Grand Lake, Arkansas 95, 96
Grant, Ulysses S. 39, 49, 56, 57, 59, 69, 70, 74, 78, 90, 147, 165, 180, 195, 206, 207, 208, 209
Gray, William E. "Willis" 118, 130
Greeley, Horace 71
Greenback Labor Party 91
Greene County, Arkansas 183, 184, 188
Grey, William H. 99, 100, 101, 109, 110, 130, 246n, 250n, 251n
Grissom, Toney 114, 116, 130
Gulley, Random 235

H

Hadley, Ozro 152
Hallie 162, 163
Hampton, Wade 58
Hanks, James 198
Hardeman County, Tennessee 97
Harper's Ferry 102
Harrell, John 158, 159

Haskins, Jeff 112, 130
Havis, Ferdinand "Ferd" 114, 130, 193, 194
Hawkins, Monroe E. 111, 114, 117, 130, 246n
Hayes, Rutherford B. 16, 59, 60, 78
Haynes, A. J. 190
Helena World 197
Helena, Arkansas 89, 93, 99, 100, 103, 104, 198, 199
Hempstead County, Arkansas 89, 93, 94, 195
Hendrix College 80, 81
Hesper 157, 162, 177, 182
Hill, Ned 102, 116, 130
Hillsdale College 97
Hillsdale, Michigan 95, 97
Hindman, Thomas 152
Hinds, James 150, 177, 180, 181
Historical Report 73
Hodges, James 151
Holford Bonds 237
Holland, Samuel H. 109, 131
Hollandsworth, James, Jr. 35
Holly Grove, Arkansas 99
Hooper, Thomas 188
Horner, John 233
Hot Spring County, Arkansas 194, 195
Houston, Sam 162
How I Succeeded in my Business 104, 254n
Howard County, Arkansas 195
Howard School 234
Howard, O. O. 234
Hughes, Simon 168, 201, 212, 215, 216
Humphreys, Benjamin G. 26
Humphries, Ben 176
Hunt, Daniel 93, 111, 130, 246n, 249n
Hunt, Silas 249n
Hutchinson, Asa 84

I

Illinois 222
Independence County, Arkansas 176, 195
Indiana 149
Iowa 149
Iron Clad Oath 21, 26, 66, 67, 167
Izard County, Arkansas 235

J

Jacko, William B. 120, 121, 131
Jackson County, Arkansas 174, 175, 182, 195
Jay Cooke & Company 57
Jefferson County, Arkansas 86, 89, 91, 102, 154, 193, 194, 199, 200, 210, 224, 225, 237
Jefferson, Ed 121, 122, 131
Jim Crow 204
Johnson County, Arkansas 195
Johnson, A. M. 180
Johnson, Adam R. 113, 114, 131, 251n

Johnson, Andrew 22, 25, 30, 32, 34, 35, 36, 37, 39, 167, 172, 182
Johnson, Henry A. 102, 123, 131
Johnson, James W. 105, 148, 149
Johnson, John H. 115, 131, 249n
Johnson, Robert Ward 165
Johnson, Thomas P. 246n
Joint Committee on Reconstruction 30, 33, 49
Jones, Green Hill 95, 96, 97, 103, 120, 122, 132, 249n, 250n
Jones, Met 224
Jonesboro, Arkansas 188

K

Kellogg, William P. 58, 60
Kentucky 214
Kersh, Thomas 103, 120, 121, 132, 249n
Key, V. O. 83
Kimball, Nathan 20
Knights of Labor 201
Ku Klux Klan 41, 50, 51, 55, 68, 81, 105, 147, 170, 174, 175, 176, 178, 179, 180, 182, 183, 185, 186, 187, 188, 190, 194, 195, 199, 205
Ku Klux Klan Act 51
Kyle, George H. 26

L

"Lady Baxter" 158
Lafayette County, Arkansas 86, 89, 176, 179, 183, 184, 187, 204
Lake Village, Arkansas 191
Leake-Ingham Building 31
Lee County, Arkansas 74, 90, 199, 202
Leiper, W. D. 219, 224
Lewis, Daniel W. 119, 132
Lewisburg, Arkansas 151, 176, 177, 178, 182, 189, 196
Lewisville, Arkansas 176
Liberal Republicans 57, 72, 73, 105, 148, 149, 150, 151, 155, 157, 191
Liberia 99, 199, 206
Lincoln County, Arkansas 86, 103, 154, 158, 199, 225
Lincoln University 102
Lincoln, Abraham 16, 19, 20, 21, 22, 23, 167
Little River County, Arkansas 180, 183, 184, 187
Little Rock and Fort Smith Railroad 47
Little Rock Convention of Colored Citizens 100
Little Rock, Arkansas 18, 70, 78, 89, 101, 102, 152, 156, 159, 175, 177, 180, 182, 184, 189, 193, 194, 195, 196, 198, 200, 203, 206
Little Rock, Pine Bluff and New Orleans Railroad 229
Lodge, Henry Cabot 203
Logan, William H. 110, 132
Lonoke County, Arkansas 195, 201
Louisiana 16, 20, 43, 44, 46, 49, 52, 53, 54, 55, 58, 59, 60, 206

Lowe, Ezekiel 97
Lowe, George Washington 97, 98, 99, 122, 123, 132, 249n
Lowe, Kendrick 97, 98
Lucas, John Gray 123, 133

M

Makers of Arkansas History 81
Mallory, Samuel W. 185, 187
Marion, Arkansas 180, 188, 189, 190, 201
Marshall County, Mississippi 97
Marshall, William A. 107, 115, 133
martial law 183, 185, 189, 191, 260n
Mason, James W. 91, 102, 108, 133, 246n, 251n, 255n
Mason, Simpson 178
Matthews, John 189
Maxwell, L. J. 116, 133
Mayflower, Arkansas 162
Mayo, Americus 94, 95, 113, 133, 249n
Mayo, Elizabeth Jones 94, 95
Mayo, Ellen Williams 94
McClure, John 105, 154, 157
McCullough, William S. 179
McEnery, John 58
McKay, Howard 124, 133
McKitrick, Eric 22
McPherson, James 37, 42, 56
Memphis and Little Rock Railroad 47
Memphis Daily Appeal 101
Memphis, Tennessee 35, 94, 95, 97, 174, 182, 188, 190, 197
Military Reconstruction Act 173
militias 49, 50, 58, 158, 159, 162, 177, 181, 182, 184–190, 193, 195, 196, 197, 199, 201, 205, 261n
Miller, Abraham H. 103, 104, 116, 133, 254n, 255n
Miller, William 168, 197, 198
"Minstrels" 72, 153
Mississippi 23, 25, 38, 40, 43, 44, 51, 52, 53, 55, 102, 204, 214
Mississippi County, Arkansas 86, 176, 180, 183, 184, 188
Mississippi, Ouachita and Red River Railroad 229
Missouri 104, 152, 188
Moderate Republicans 23, 30, 32, 38, 40
Monroe County, Arkansas 94, 97, 98, 99, 150, 180, 181, 200, 201, 204, 215, 216
Monticello, Arkansas 175, 187
Moose, Eleanor Wood 205
Morning Republican (Little Rock) 100, 101, 103, 104, 107
Morrilton, Arkansas 202, 203
Most Worshipful Grand Lodge (Colored) of Free and Accepted Masons of Arkansas 100
Mound City, Illinois 95, 97
Murfreesboro, Arkansas 186
Murphy, Isaac 19, 21, 67, 152, 172, 228

Murphy, J. M. 162
Murphy, William 117, 133, 246n
Murray, Marshall M. 119, 133, 254n

N

National Farmers Alliance 203
National University 102
New Departure Democrats 122, 226
New Gascony, Arkansas 162, 193
New Jersey 214
New Madrid, Missouri 95
New Orleans, Louisiana 35, 58, 59
New Orleans Massacre 35
New York City 36
Newsome, Hugh L. 121, 134
Newton, Robert C. 152, 157
Nixon, Richard 69
Norfolk, Virginia 94, 95
North Carolina 16, 22, 25, 37, 50, 51, 55, 96, 152, 214

O

oath of allegiance 17, 21, 23, 33, 66
Obama, Barack 83
Oberlin College 102
Odum, Sandy Shepard 121, 134
Ohio 99
Old State House 158, 160, 186, 212
Opelousas, Louisiana 49
Ord, Edward O. C. 67, 68, 88
Orr, James L. 26
Osceola, Arkansas 180

P

Palarm, Arkansas 162, 163
Panic of 1873 57
Payne, William C. 118, 119, 134
Pennsylvania 99, 214
Perry County, Arkansas 154, 194, 196, 199
Phelps, John S. 16
Phillips County, Arkansas 90, 92, 101, 102, 103, 104, 149, 196, 197, 198, 199, 202, 204, 206, 210, 225, 233
Phillips, Wendell 36
Pierce, M. C. 98
Pike, Albert 165
Pine Bluff, Arkansas 89, 103, 105, 158, 159, 161, 175, 193, 194, 206, 224
Plumerville, Arkansas 202
Pocahontas, Arkansas 183
Poland Committee 196
political violence 34, 35, 41, 47, 48, 49, 50, 55, 58, 59, 90, 91, 170, 171, 172, 174, 178, 183, 196, 198, 199, 201–206
Polk, Burns 117, 134
Polk, Carl R. 113, 118, 134, 249n
Polk, Susan 96
Pope County, Arkansas 159, 191, 195
Presidential Reconstruction 16, 18
Price, John G. 152
Price, Patrick T. 117, 134
Prince Hall Masons 93
Proclamation 218 207

Proclamation of Pardon and Amnesty 16, 17, 22
Proclamation Reorganizing a Constitutional Government in North Carolina 22
public schools 38, 42, 43, 45, 46, 52, 53, 54, 77, 105, 231–235
Pulaski County, Arkansas 78, 89, 102, 103, 154, 156, 192, 194, 195, 210

Q

Quakers 103

R

Rable, George 50
Radical Reconstruction 16
Radical Republicans 20, 23, 32, 35, 36, 40, 55, 67, 72, 105, 208, 228, 236
railroads 47, 52, 57, 105, 156, 228, 229, 230
Randolph County, Arkansas 183
Rayner, Kenneth R. 95, 96, 250n
Reconstruction Acts 88
Reconstruction in Arkansas 80
Reconstruction: America's Unfinished Revolution, 1863-1877 205
Rector, Henry 246n
Rector, Henry M. 212, 213, 235
Red Shirts 55
Redeemers/Redemption 60, 75, 78, 83, 88, 105, 207, 210, 215–221, 224, 226–231, 233, 235, 236, 237
Regular Republicans 72, 105, 148, 152, 153, 154, 155, 157, 163, 191
Reynolds, D. H. 224
Reynolds, John Hughes 64, 81, 82
Rice, Benjamin 149, 151
Riley, Jerome 102
Rison et al. v. Farr 66
Roane, John 158
Robinson, H. B. 198
Robinson, Henry H. 115, 134, 254n
Robinson, James A. 113, 117, 134
Rockefeller, Winthrop 62, 63
Rollins, John C. 115, 134
Rosa, John H. 189
Rose, U. M. 164
Royston, Grandison 213
Rush, Anderson L. 103, 111, 134, 249n
Ryles, Granville 119, 135

S

Salem, Arkansas 178
Saline County, Arkansas 195
Samuels, Richard R. 112, 135, 246n
Saulsbury, Tennessee 98
Sawyer, Francis "Frank" 117, 135
"scalawags" 42, 44, 79, 80, 148, 153
Schofield, John M. 182
Schurz, Carl 56
Scott, Samuel H. 120, 135, 254n
Searcy, Arkansas 175, 176, 179

Sebastian County, Arkansas 219
Second Enforcement Act 51
Second Ohio Cavalry 249n
Second U.S. Colored Light Artillery 103
Separate Coach Law 92
Sevier County, Arkansas 183, 184, 187
Seymour, Horatio 70, 180
Shaver, Robert Glenn 174, 175
Shepperson, Archie/Archer 115, 135
Sherrill, Rusty 119, 135
Shreveport, Louisiana 49
Sons of the Agricultural Star 200
South Carolina 16, 23, 25, 29, 37, 41, 43, 44, 46, 51, 53, 54, 55, 58, 103, 206, 214, 222
Southern Standard 227
Southland College 102, 103
Sprague, John W. 29, 30
Springfield, Missouri 152
St. Francis County, Arkansas 92, 103, 104, 194, 201, 202, 204
St. Landry Parish, Louisiana 49
St. Louis, Missouri 36, 99, 102, 149, 157
Stampp, Kenneth 53
Stanford, Anthony L. 110, 135
Staples, Thomas Starling 80, 81, 82, 155, 165
Steele, Frederick 18, 19, 20, 21
Stephens, Alexander 26
Stevens, Thaddeus 20, 36
Stewart, George H. W. 101, 103, 115, 135
Straight-Out Democrats (Bourbons) 211
Sumner, Charles 52
Superintendent of Public Instruction 232
"Swing Around the Circle" 36

T

Tax Resisting Association 54
Ten Percent Plan 17, 18, 20
Tennessee 16, 37, 41, 174, 198, 214
Texarkana, Arkansas 206
Texas 23, 25, 28, 40, 44, 47, 49, 50, 54, 55, 56, 59, 60
Third Arkansas Infantry (US) 18
Third U.S. Colored Cavalry 95
Third U.S. Colored Heavy Artillery 95, 96
Thirteenth Amendment 23
Thomason, Hugh F. 213
Thompson, Green W. 122, 135
Throckmorton, James W. 23
Tilden, Samuel J. 78
Trelease, Allen 190
Trower, George 121, 246n
Trumball, Lyman 30,

U

U.S. Pension Bureau 94
Union County, Arkansas 176, 187
Union Labor Party 201, 203

Union League 41
Unionists 18, 20, 26, 28, 30, 148, 172, 174, 176, 178, 179, 185
University of Arkansas 81
University of Chicago 102
Upham, Daniel P. 185, 187, 188, 189

V

Van Buren County, Arkansas 154
Vicksburg, Mississippi 95
Virginia 37, 40, 43, 214
Voting Rights Act of 1965 203

W

Wade, Benjamin 21, 22
Wade-Davis Bill 21
Wallace's Ferry 149
Washington County, Arkansas 210
Washington National Republican 56
Washington, Arkansas 93
Washington DC 20, 36, 56, 74, 99, 165
Waterhouse, Blackstone 119, 136
Watson, George W. 124, 136
Webb, John W. 113, 136, 251n
Weddington, R. C. 102, 123, 136, 251n
Wheeler, Stephen 180
Whigs 40, 71, 96, 152, 164, 167, 216
White County, Arkansas 103, 180, 195, 216, 233
White Leagues 51, 55, 58, 59
White, Francis "Frank" 119, 136
White, Hercules King Cannon 158, 159, 160, 161, 162, 193, 194
White, James T. 99, 100, 101, 108, 109, 112, 136, 246n, 252n, 255n
White, Reuben B. 101, 109, 136
White, Robert T. 67
Who Killed John Clayton? 205
Wilkins, Jack 94
Williams, George H. 74
Williams, Henry W./N. 122, 123, 136
Williams, John Willis 100, 109, 116, 137
Williams, Willoughby 168, 172
Willis, H. F. 180
Wise, Henry A. 100, 251n
Wofford, James 118, 137
Woodruff County, Arkansas 175, 179, 182, 183, 184, 187, 189, 201
Woodward, C. Vann 221
Woolfolk, Samuel L. 122, 124, 137
Worthington, Elisha 102

Y

Yazoo City, Mississippi 94
Young, William H. 113, 119, 137

CPSIA information can be obtained
at www.ICGtesting.com
Printed in the USA
FSHW01n0224250418
47276FS